VSAM

Access Method Services and application programming

Doug Lowe

Mike Murach & Associates, Inc.

4697 West Jacquelyn Avenue
Fresno, California 93722
(209) 275-3335

Development Team

Technical editor:	Steve Eckols
Production editor:	Anne Prince
Designer and production director:	Steve Ehlers
Production staff:	Carl Kisling
	Norene Foin

Related Products

MVS JCL, by Doug Lowe

DOS/VSE JCL (Second Edition), by Steve Eckols and Michele Milnes

Structured ANS COBOL, Part 1: A Course for Novices, by Mike Murach and Paul Noll

Structured ANS COBOL, Part 2: An Advanced Course, by Mike Murach and Paul Noll

VS COBOL II: A Guide for Programmers and Managers, by Anne Prince

VSAM for the COBOL Programmer (Second Edition), by Doug Lowe

CICS for the COBOL Programmer, Part 1: An Introductory Course, by Doug Lowe

CICS for the COBOL Programmer, Part 2: An Advanced Course, by Doug Lowe

DOS/VSE Assembler Language, by Kevin McQuillen and Anne Prince

MVS Assembler Language, by Kevin McQuillen and Anne Prince

Library of Congress Catalog Card Number: 86-60204

ISBN: 0-911625-33-X

Contents

Preface

If you've been involved in any type of programming activity on an IBM mainframe computer, you've almost certainly worked with files supported by VSAM, the Virtual Storage Access Method. If so, you know that VSAM provides many features and options. For example, when you issue a DEFINE CLUSTER command to create a VSAM file, you can code about 30 different parameters that select various options for the file. And you can code most of those parameters at one, two, or three levels, with varying results. Although many of those parameters have default settings, those defaults are often inappropriate for many applications. As a result, it's crucial that programmers and analysts at all levels have a solid understanding of VSAM's facilities and how they are best used in a variety of situations.

Unfortunately, that kind of understanding isn't easy to come by. Sure, it's easy to pick up an IBM manual and look up the syntax of the DEFINE CLUSTER command. But there's more to understanding VSAM than knowing the syntax of the various commands. And remember, IBM's reference manuals are just that: *reference* manuals. So although they present lots of details, they don't help you decide which VSAM features to use in a given situation.

This book is designed not only to teach you the basics of VSAM, but to help you evaluate VSAM as you learn, so you can decide for yourself how to use VSAM effectively in a wide variety of situations. So if you want to learn more than just the syntax of a few commands, this is the book for you.

Who this book is for

This book is for anyone who uses VSAM in a programming capacity. That means programmers who define and maintain VSAM files using the Access Method Services utility program as well as programmers who code COBOL, CICS, or assembler language application programs that process VSAM files.

Although you don't need any prior VSAM experience to use this book, it's a plus if you have background knowledge in two areas. First, it helps to have a basic knowledge of either the DOS or OS operating system. You don't need a detailed knowledge of how those operating systems work internally; a basic understanding of the operating system's job control language will do. You can get that background from two books available from Mike Murach & Associates: *DOS/VSE JCL* by Steve Eckols and *OS JCL* by Wayne Clary.

Second, you should have an elementary knowledge of COBOL, command-level CICS, or assembler language. You don't need a complete mastery of any of those programming languages, just the basic understanding you would get by reading the first few chapters of any good introductory COBOL, CICS, or assembler language book. You'll find books on those subjects listed near the front of this book. All are available from Mike Murach & Associates.

How to use this book

As I designed this book, I realized that two groups of people will be reading it: those who are responsible for creating and maintaining VSAM files using the Access Method Services (AMS) utility and those who are responsible for developing application programs that process VSAM files. Of course, those categories often overlap; an individual may both create a VSAM file and code a program that processes it. Nevertheless, the organization of this book reflects those two perspectives; two of the three major sections of the book are devoted to AMS and application programming.

The chapters in section 1 present the concepts and terms you need to know before you can begin to learn how to use VSAM. As a result, you should study this section whether you're more interested in AMS or application programming. Chapter 1 introduces you to the data management facilities of IBM mainframe systems. If you're an experienced programmer, feel free to skip this chapter. Chapters 2 and 3 describe how VSAM data sets and catalogs are organized and used. And chapter 4 shows you how to code MVS and DOS/VSE JCL for VSAM files, as well as how to allocate VSAM files under TSO and VM/CMS.

Once you've completed section 1, you can study section 2 or 3, depending on your interest. The chapters in section 2 show you how to use AMS and its commands. After chapter 5 briefly introduces you to AMS, chapter 6 shows you how to use the most important AMS commands. Then, chapters 7, 8, and 9 present the performance, recovery, and security considerations you should be aware of as you define a file. Once you've read chapters 5 and 6, you can study chapters 7, 8, and 9 in any order you wish.

The chapters in section 3 show you how three programming languages support VSAM file processing. In chapter 10, you'll learn how two versions of the COBOL compiler (VS COBOL, based on the 1974 COBOL standards, and VS COBOL II, based on the 1985 standards) support VSAM file processing. In chapter 11, you'll learn how command-level CICS programs can access VSAM files. And finally, in chapter 12 you'll learn how to access VSAM files from an assembler-language program. You can read the three chapters in this section in any order, but I think there's a logical progression from COBOL to command-level CICS to assembler language.

Related reference manuals

Although I think this book will be your primary VSAM reference, you'll occasionally need to refer to an IBM reference manual. The VSAM reference manuals you need depend on your operating system and the version of VSAM you're using. In addition, IBM periodically reorganizes its library of VSAM reference manuals, eliminating some manuals and creating others. So rather than give you specific order numbers, I'll just name the most useful of the VSAM reference manuals. You should then be able to find the manuals you need in your shop's reference library.

The VSAM manual you'll use most is the one that describes AMS. For MVS users, it's called *Access Method Services* (MVS/SP) or *Access Method Services Reference* (MVS/XA). For DOS/VSE users, this manual also contains information about VSAM macros used in assembler language and is called *Using VSE/VSAM Commands and Macros*. For general information about VSAM, consult the *Programmer's Guide* (MVS/SP) or *VSAM Administration Guide* and *Catalog Administration Guide* (MVS/XA). For DOS/VSE users, similar information is in *Using VSE/VSAM Commands and Macros* and *VSE/VSAM Programmer's Reference*.

Besides these manuals, you'll need manuals for the programming languages you use. And, you'll need a manual called *Messages and Codes* to help you figure out what went wrong when an error occurs.

About the AMS listings

Throughout this book, you'll find many listings of AMS job streams that invoke various AMS functions. Most of these job streams were tested using VSAM release 2 running under MVS/SP 3.8 on an IBM 3083 system. The disk devices used are either 3380s or Mass Storage System volumes staged on 3330s. Some of the jobs were tested on a small DOS/VSE system, using VSE/AF 1.3 on a 4331. For the DOS jobs, the disks are 3310 FBA devices.

Conclusion

I'm confident that this book will help you use VSAM more effectively. In fact, I guarantee it. So, if you ever decide this book wasn't worth the money, just send it back. You'll get a full refund, with no questions asked.

I'd also like to know what you think about this book. So if you have any comments, positive or negative, please use the postage-paid comment form at the back of this book. I'll read—and answer—every letter that's received, and I especially look forward to hearing from you.

Doug Lowe
Fresno, California
March, 1986

Section 1

Concepts

Before you can learn how to use VSAM, you need to understand its basic concepts. So, the four chapters in this section present those concepts. Chapter 1 presents the basic data management capabilities of IBM mainframe systems, including direct access storage device concepts and the data management facilities of the OS and DOS operating systems. In chapter 2, you'll learn how VSAM files are organized, and in chapter 3, you'll learn about catalogs. Finally, chapter 4 teaches you how to code JCL statements for VSAM files under OS and DOS.

Some of the material in this section (especially in chapter 1) may be review for you, depending on your experience. As a result, I suggest you review the objectives and terminology lists at the end of each chapter or topic to see whether you need to study it.

Chapter 1

Introduction to data management on IBM mainframe systems

This chapter's two topics present the basic device and file-processing concepts you need to understand to use VSAM. Topic 1 describes the characteristics of modern direct access devices, and topic 2 presents an overview of the data management facilities of both OS and DOS.

If you have IBM mainframe experience, you may already be familiar with the concepts this chapter presents. As a result, if you're comfortable with the terminology lists and objectives at the end of each topic, feel free to move ahead to chapter 2. Otherwise, you need to study the material in this chapter.

■ □ □ □   **Topic 1   Direct access devices**

Direct access storage devices, or *DASDs*, have been around since the mid-1960s. Because DASDs allow direct and rapid access to large quantities of data, they've become a key component of IBM mainframe systems, both OS and DOS. They're used not only to store user programs and data, but also to store operating system programs and data.

The most common type of DASD is the *disk drive*, a unit that reads and writes data on a *disk pack*, or *volume*. A disk pack, illustrated in figure 1-1, is a stack of metal platters coated with a metal oxide material. Data is recorded on both sides of the platters.

Most of IBM's older DASDs use removable disk packs, but the trend with newer IBM DASDs is for the pack to be fixed in a permanent, sealed assembly inside the drive. Nonremovable disk packs have two advantages over removable packs: they're faster and they're more reliable. Because speed and reliability are important requirements of on-line applications, DASDs with nonremovable packs are well suited for today's mainframe systems.

Tracks and cylinders

Data is recorded on the usable surfaces of a disk pack in concentric circles called *tracks*, as figure 1-2 shows. The number of tracks per surface varies with each device type. For example, the surface in figure 1-2 has 808 tracks, numbered from 0 to 807. A disk pack with 19 usable surfaces, each with 808 tracks, has a total of 15,352 tracks. Although the tracks get smaller toward the center of the surface, each track holds the same amount of data.

Figure 1-3 shows a side view of an *access mechanism*, or *actuator*, the component that reads and writes data on the tracks of a disk pack. As you can see, the actuator has one read/write head for each recording surface. When the actuator moves, all of its heads move together so that they're all positioned at the same track of each recording surface. As a result, the disk drive can access all of those tracks without moving the actuator.

The tracks that are positioned under the heads of the actuator at one time make up a *cylinder*. As a result, there are as many tracks in a cylinder as there are usable surfaces on the pack, and there are as many cylinders in a pack as there are tracks on a surface. So a pack that has 19 surfaces, each with 808 tracks, has 808 cylinders, each containing 19 tracks.

Incidentally, some DASD models provide a small amount of *fixed-head storage*. In that case, certain tracks on the disk pack have their own assemblies of read/write heads. Access to data on those tracks is faster than when a movable actuator is used because the fixed heads never move away from those tracks. However, because fixed-head storage is expensive, it's normally reserved for use by the operating system's paging files.

In addition, some newer IBM DASD units have two actuators, each of which accesses *half* of the cylinders on the device. Using two actuators like this

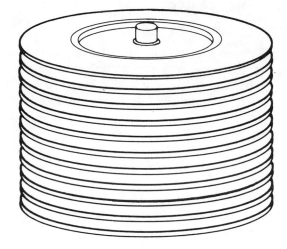

Figure 1-1   A disk pack

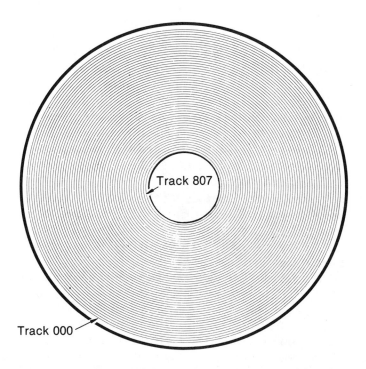

Track 807

Track 000

Figure 1-2   Tracks on a disk surface

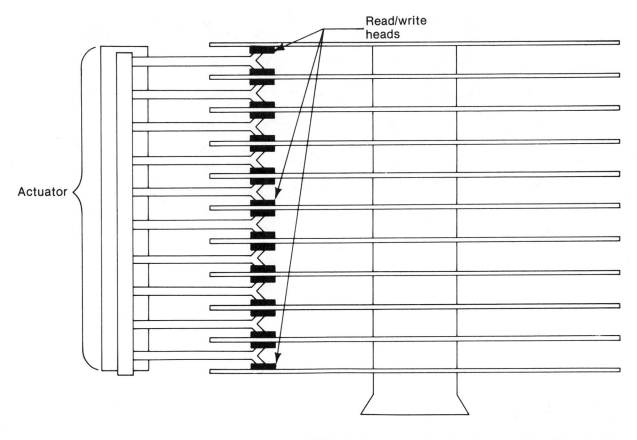

Figure 1-3   Side view of a DASD actuator

significantly improves the device's performance. But it's transparent to you as a programmer.

Characteristics of IBM DASD models

The various models of IBM DASD units can be divided into two basic categories, depending on the format in which they store data. On *count-key-data* (*CKD*) devices, data is stored in variable-length blocks. In contrast, data on *fixed-block architecture* (*FBA*) devices is always stored in 512-byte blocks. CKD devices are more common; FBA devices aren't as widely used because they're supported only by DOS/VSE on 4300-series processors.

Figure 1-4 presents some characteristics of the various IBM DASD units in use today. Frankly, many operating characteristics of DASD units, such as how fast the disk pack rotates or how fast data is transferred, aren't significant to most programmers. It's the capacity of each device that's relevant to most

Device	Type	Maximum bytes per track	Tracks per cylinder	Cylinders per drive	Total capacity per drive (MB)
3310	FBA	16,384[1]	11	358	64
3330-1	CKD	13,030	19	404	100
3330-11	CKD	13,030	19	808	200
3340-35	CKD	8,368	12	348	35
3340-70[2]	CKD	8,368	12	696	70
3350	CKD	19,069	30	555	317
3370	FBA	31,744[3]	12	1,500	571
3375	CKD	35,616	12	1,918	819
3380	CKD	47,476	15	1,770	1,260

Note 1:   The track capacity of a 3310 is 32 512-byte blocks, or 16,384 bytes.

Note 2:   The 3344, not shown, is treated as if it were four separate 3340-70 units.

Note 3:   The track capacity of a 3370 is 62 512-byte blocks, or 31,744 bytes.

Figure 1-4   Capacities of IBM DASD units

programmers: the maximum number of bytes per track, the number of tracks per cylinder, the number of cylinders per drive, and the total capacity of the drive. That's the information figure 1-4 presents.

CKD devices   Figure 1-5 shows how data is stored on a CKD device. Here, each data block is preceded by a *count area* and a *key area*. (The count area is required; the key area is optional.) Because the disk revolves counterclockwise, the read/write head encounters the count and key areas before the data area.

The count area contains the *disk address* of the data area that follows it. A disk address uniquely identifies each data area on the pack by specifying a cylinder number, a head number, and a record number. In addition to the disk address, the count area contains the length of the data area and the length of the key area, if present.

The key area, which can be from 1 to 255 bytes in length, contains a value that uniquely identifies the data in the data area. For example, in an inventory file, each key area might contain an item number. Then, you could access a

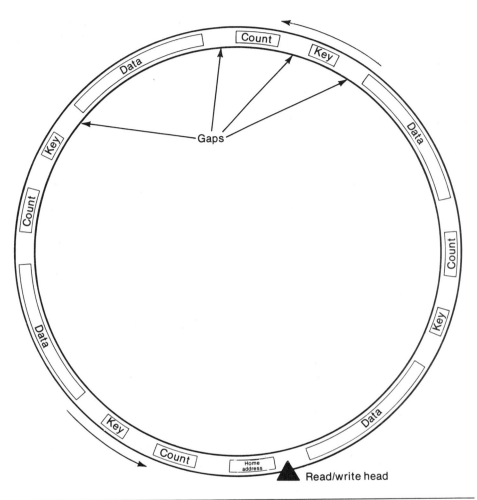

Figure 1-5   Count-key-data format

particular record by supplying the record's item number rather than its disk address. For the most part, key areas are only used for ISAM files, which I'll describe in topic 2 of this chapter.

In addition to count, key, and data areas, each track on a CKD device has a *home address*. The home address, which is immediately before the first count area on a track, uniquely identifies each track on a DASD. On a 3350 DASD, for example, there are 16,650 home addresses, one for each of the 16,650 tracks on the device.

One of the problems with CKD devices is that the data capacity of each track depends on the size of the blocks used to store the data. That's because gaps are required to separate the count, key, and data areas from one another. When smaller areas are used, more blocks of data can be stored on each track. But when more blocks are stored, more gaps are required, so the total capacity of the track is reduced.

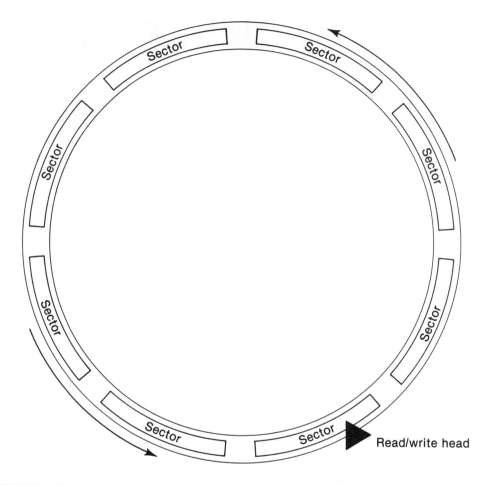

Figure 1-6   Fixed-block architecture format

The total capacity shown in figure 1-4 for each CKD device is the maximum capacity for the device. That assumes that all of the data in each track is stored in a single block; if more than one block is stored per track (and that's usually the case), the capacity is reduced because of the additional gaps required to separate the blocks.

FBA devices   Figure 1-6 shows how data is stored on an FBA device. Each track is divided into 600-byte *sectors*. Each sector contains control information and 512 bytes of user data. That doesn't mean that your files must have 512-byte records; access methods that support FBA devices automatically format your data into 512-byte blocks.

Although the sectors of an FBA device are stored in tracks and cylinders, the addressing scheme used for FBA devices is simpler than for CKD devices.

You can think of the entire range of storage available on an FBA device as a string of blocks numbered from 0 to the capacity of the unit. To refer to a particular block, you don't have to identify its cylinder and head; instead, you just supply its relative block number.

Another difference between CKD and FBA devices is that the capacity of an FBA device is always the same because the blocks are always the same length. In contrast, the capacity of a CKD device depends on the size of its data blocks.

Channels and controllers

Of course, direct access devices are of little use by themselves; they must be connected to a computer system to be useful. In a large computer system, hundreds of DASDs can be connected to one or more processor units. As you can imagine, how those connections are made is a complicated subject. Although you don't need to be familiar with all of the details of how DASDs can be connected to processors, I want you to understand two types of components that are usually a part of the connection: channels and controllers.

Channels   A *channel* is an intermediate device that connects one or more peripheral devices to a CPU. Actually, a channel is itself a small computer that executes *channel programs*. Because the channel performs relatively time-consuming I/O operations, it frees the main processor to execute other instructions. As a result, processing and I/O operations can overlap, and overall system performance is improved.

A channel on an IBM mainframe may be one of three types: (1) a selector, (2) a byte multiplexer, or (3) a block multiplexer. A *selector channel* is designed to operate with only one device at a time; it transfers data byte by byte until a complete record has been transferred. In contrast, *multiplexer channels* operate with more than one peripheral device at a time by interleaving data items. A *byte multiplexer channel* is used for low speed devices like card devices and printers. A *block multiplexer channel* is used for high-speed devices like tape drives and DASD units. It transfers data in blocks rather than one byte at a time.

Controllers   Even if a channel is connected to many DASD units, it can communicate with only one of them at a time. As a result, it would be inefficient for the channel to handle all of the details necessary to operate the disk units. Instead, several disk units are connected to a common *controller*, which is in turn connected to the channel. When a channel issues an instruction to a controller, the controller handles the necessary details. In the meantime, the channel can issue an instruction to another controller.

The group of DASD units connected to a single controller is called a *string*. All of the devices in a string must be of the same type. For most DASD types, up to four or eight units can be a part of one string.

Discussion

This topic is not a comprehensive treatment of IBM DASD technology; I've omitted many details that just aren't relevant to applications or systems programmers. Still, this topic does present the hardware details you need to know to use VSAM effectively. If you're interested in more information about IBM DASDs, I suggest you look at the manual *IBM Input/Output Device Summary*.

Terminology

direct access storage device
DASD
disk drive
disk pack
volume
track
access mechanism
actuator
cylinder
fixed-head storage
count-key-data
CKD
fixed-block architecture
FBA
count area
key area
disk address
home address
sector
channel
channel program
selector channel
multiplexer channel
byte multiplexer channel
block multiplexer channel
controller
string

Objectives

1 . Compare the techniques used to store data on CKD and FBA DASDs.

2 . Explain the functions of channels and controllers.

■ ■ ☐ ☐   # Topic 2   Data management facilities

In this topic, I'll describe the data management facilities of OS and DOS. First, I'll introduce the idea of file organizations and access methods. Then, I'll describe how labels are used to manage files and space on DASD units. Finally, I'll show you how VSAM relates to these facilities.

FILE ORGANIZATIONS AND ACCESS METHODS

File organization refers to the way data in a file is structured and processed. On storage devices other than DASDs, data is always organized and processed sequentially. For example, in a card or tape file, records follow one another in succession. To process a particular record, an application program must first process all the preceding records in the file. For some applications, that's an efficient way to organize data.

In contrast, when a file is stored on a DASD, it can be organized in more than one way. As a result, a systems designer who plans a DASD file needs to consider what the best organization for the file is. On IBM mainframe systems, there are three choices: (1) sequential organization, (2) indexed sequential organization, and (3) direct organization.

To support these three file organizations, IBM provides a variety of *access methods*. Simply put, an access method is a software interface that lets application programs maintain files in a particular format. IBM access methods come in two broad categories: *native access methods* and VSAM. Now, I'll describe sequential, indexed sequential, and direct file organizations along with the native access methods that support them. I'll describe VSAM, which is more comprehensive in scope than the native access methods, later in this topic.

Sequential organization

Just as with data on cards or tape, data on a DASD can be stored with *sequential organization*. When that's the case, records are stored one after another in consecutive order. Often, a data element within each record contains a *key* value that's used to sequence the records. For example, figure 1-7 illustrates a simple 10-record employee file in sequence by social security number. Although it's common for a sequential file to be stored in sequence based on a key value, that's not a requirement.

Sequential DASD files are most appropriate when they don't have to be accessed for random data retrieval or update. When random retrieval or update is required, either indexed sequential or direct organization is probably a better choice.

To process sequential files, you use one of the sequential access methods. On DOS systems, there's just one: *SAM*, which stands for *Sequential Access Method*. On OS systems, there are two sequential access methods. The *Basic Sequential Access Method*, or *BSAM*, provides the lowest level of support for

Disk location	Social security number	First name	Middle initial	Last name	Employee number
1	213-64-9290	Thomas	T	Bluestone	00008
2	279-00-1210	William	J	Colline	00002
3	334-96-8721	Constance	M	Harris	00007
4	498-27-6117	Ronald	W	Westbrook	00010
5	499-35-5079	Stanley	L	Abbott	00001
6	558-12-6168	Marie	A	Littlejohn	00005
7	559-35-2479	E	R	Siebart	00006
8	572-68-3100	Jean	B	Glenning	00009
9	703-47-5748	Paul	M	Collins	00004
10	899-16-9235	Alice		Crawford	00003

Figure 1-7   An employee file with sequential organization by social security number

sequential files. The *Queued Sequential Access Method*, or *QSAM*, provides more advanced processing features.

Indexed sequential organization

Indexed sequential organization makes it possible to store records sequentially but access any particular record directly. To do this, an *index* is maintained. Each index entry contains a key value and the location of the corresponding data record. Thus, to retrieve a record directly, the index is used to locate the record.

Figure 1-8 shows how the sequential file in figure 1-7 might appear with indexed sequential organization. As you can see, if a record's key value is known (employee number, in this case), it's possible to access the record directly by retrieving its disk location from the index. On the other hand, it's possible to access the records in sequence because they were stored sequentially on the DASD in the first place. Actually, indexed sequential organization is more complicated than this, but the concept is all you need to know right now.

On DOS systems, you use the *Indexed Sequential Access Method*, or *ISAM*, to process indexed sequential files. On OS systems, two access methods are used: the *Basic Indexed Sequential Access Method (BISAM)* and the *Queued Indexed Sequential Access Method (QISAM)*. In general, BISAM is used to access records randomly, while QISAM is used to process an indexed sequential file sequentially.

Direct organization

Like a record in a file with indexed sequential organization, a record in a file with *direct organization* can be accessed at random. However, unlike an

Index component   **Data component**

Employee number	Disk location	Disk location	Social security number	First name	Middle initial	Last name	Employee number
00001	5	1	213-64-9290	Thomas	T	Bluestone	00008
00002	2	2	279-00-1210	William	J	Colline	00002
00003	10	3	334-96-8721	Constance	M	Harris	00007
00004	9	4	498-27-6117	Ronald	W	Westbrook	00010
00005	6	5	499-35-5079	Stanley	L	Abbott	00001
00006	7	6	558-12-6168	Marie	A	Littlejohn	00005
00007	3	7	559-35-2479	E	R	Siebart	00006
00008	1	8	572-68-3100	Jean	B	Glenning	00009
00009	8	9	703-47-5748	Paul	M	Collins	00004
00010	4	10	899-16-9235	Alice		Crawford	00003

Figure 1-8   An employee file with indexed sequential organization

indexed sequential file, a direct file doesn't have an index. Instead, direct files depend on a direct relationship between data in each record and a DASD address, as figure 1-9 shows in simplified form. The DASD address can be an actual disk address that specifies a specific cylinder, track, and record, or it can be a relative address that specifies a record number relative to the start of the file. When direct files are used, access to particular records is rapid. But sequential processing generally isn't possible. Because of the programming complexities involved, direct files are seldom used.

In a direct file, the DASD address of a record is usually calculated based on data derived from the record. The routine that does that calculation is called a *randomizing routine*. Often, there's no apparent relationship between the data used to determine a DASD address and the actual address that the randomizing routine calculates.

Direct files are supported on DOS systems by the *Direct Access Method*, or *DAM*. On OS systems, the *Basic Direct Access Method*, or *BDAM* is used. (Contrary to what you might expect, there's no QDAM for direct files on OS systems.)

DASD LABELS AND SPACE MANAGEMENT

One of the important functions of the operating system and access methods is managing how space on a DASD volume is allocated to the files that reside on it. Not only must the system keep track of the locations of existing files, but it must also be able to add new files to the volume, allocate additional space to existing files, and remove files from a volume. The information necessary to manage all of this is stored in special DASD records called *labels*.

Disk location	Social security number	First name	Middle initial	Last name	Employee number
1	499-35-5079	Stanley	L	Abbott	00001
2	279-00-1210	William	J	Colline	00002
3	899-16-9235	Alice		Crawford	00003
4	703-47-5748	Paul	M	Collins	00004
5	558-12-6168	Marie	A	Littlejohn	00005
6	559-35-2479	E	R	Siebart	00006
7	334-96-8721	Constance	M	Harris	00007
8	213-64-9290	Thomas	T	Bluestone	00008
9	572-68-3100	Jean	B	Glenning	00009
10	498-27-6117	Ronald	W	Westbrook	00010

Figure 1-9   An employee file with direct organization

DASD labels

In general, there are two types of DASD labels you need to know about: volume labels and file labels. Figure 1-10 is a simplified example of a disk volume with labels that define several files.

Volume labels   All DASD volumes must contain a *volume label*, often called a *VOL1 label*. The VOL1 label is always in the same place on a disk volume: the third record of track 0 in cylinder 0. The VOL1 label has two important functions. First, it identifies the volume by supplying a *volume serial number*, or *vol-ser*. Every on-line DASD volume must have a unique six-character vol-ser. Second, the VOL1 label contains the disk address of the VTOC.

File labels   The *VTOC*, or *Volume Table Of Contents*, is a special file that contains the labels for the files on the volume. These *file labels*, which are also called *Data Set Control Blocks* or *DSCBs*, have several formats, called Format-1, Format-2, and so on. The first DSCB in figure 1-10 is a Format-4 DSCB; it describes the VTOC itself.

Each Format 1 DSCB in a VTOC describes a file. In figure 1-10, there are three Format-1 DSCBs, corresponding to FILE-A, FILE-B, and FILE-C. Besides the DASD location of the file, each Format-1 DSCB contains descriptive information about the file, like whether it's a sequential or indexed-sequential file, its record length, and so on.

Space is allocated to DASD files in contiguous areas called *extents*. The Format-1 DSCB has room to define three extents for a file. In other words, a file defined just by a Format-1 DSCB can reside in up to three different areas of the disk volume. As the file grows, it may require additional space. Then, a Format-3 DSCB is created; it contains room for thirteen additional extents. As a result, a file can contain up to sixteen extents: three defined in the Format-1

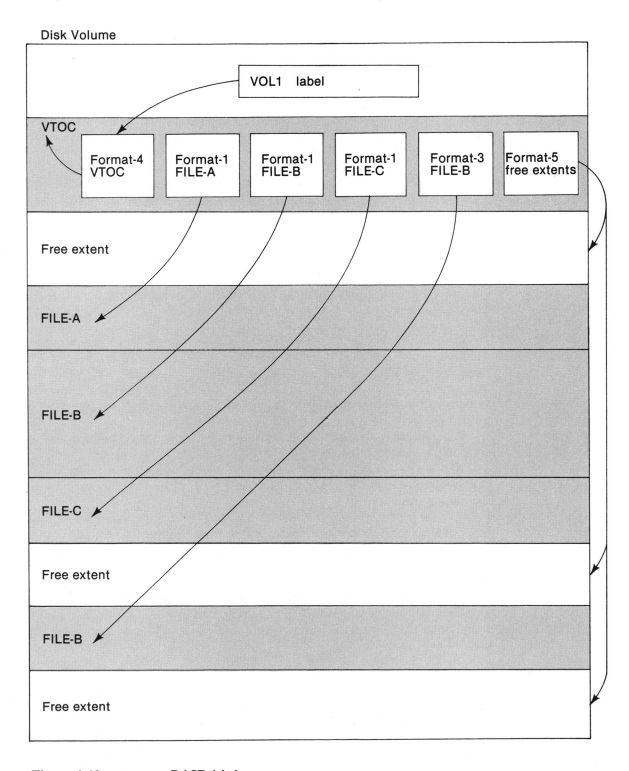

Figure 1-10   DASD labels

DSCB, and thirteen defined in the Format-3 DSCB. In figure 1-10, you can see that a Format-3 DSCB for FILE-B defines additional extents. (For simplicity, figure 1-10 doesn't show the three extents defined by the Format-1 DSCB separately.)

Format-5 DSCBs contain information about *free extents*, that is, sections of the disk volume that aren't allocated to files. Each Format-5 DSCB can define up to 26 free extents. If the volume contains more than 26 free extents, more than one Format-5 DSCB is used. The Format-5 DSCB in figure 1-10 defines three free extents on the volume.

Two DSCB formats aren't shown in figure 1-10: Format-2 and Format-6. Both are used to store special information that's unique to ISAM files.

Space management

As I mentioned earlier, an important function of an operating system is managing DASD space. On OS systems, a special operating system component called *Direct Access Device Space Management*, or *DADSM*, does that. Simply put, DADSM is responsible for keeping the VTOC in order. When a user requests space for a file, DADSM searches the Format-5 DSCBs until it finds a space large enough. Then, it allocates that space to the file using a Format-1 or Format-3 DSCB, and updates the Format-5 DSCB to indicate that the space is no longer free. In short, DADSM automates the process of allocating space to a file.

DADSM has two major drawbacks, however. The first is the limitation of sixteen file extents imposed by the structure of the Format-1 and Format-3 DSCBs. It's not uncommon for a file to grow beyond sixteen extents. When that happens, the user's program abends, and the file must be reorganized so it uses fewer extents.

The second problem has to do with how DADSM searches the VTOC for free space; it uses a technique called *first-fit*. Simply put, first-fit means that DADSM searches the Format-5 DSCBs in sequence until it finds a free extent that's large enough. Because the Format-5 DSCBs are stored in ascending track sequence, that means the first free extent large enough will be used for the file. Unfortunately, that often leads to unnecessary fragmentation of DASD space, because DADSM breaks large free extents into smaller pieces rather than searching all of the Format-5 DSCBs to find a free extent that's closer to the right size.

On DOS systems, there is no DADSM; space allocation must be done manually. In other words, when you create a file on a DOS system, you tell DOS which tracks and cylinders to use for the file. DOS stores that information in Format-1 and Format-3 DSCBs, but uses it only to retrieve the file. In fact, DOS doesn't even allow Format-5 labels in the VTOC. It's up to you to keep track of free space.

VSAM

The facilities I've described so far have evolved over a period spanning more than two decades. For example, the VTOC has had essentially the same format and function since the early 1960s. And the native access methods haven't changed much in the last 15 years.

During that time, the OS and DOS operating systems moved in different directions. As a result, the access methods and other data management facilities are different under the two operating systems. In the mid-1970's, IBM announced a new access method called the *Virtual Storage Access Method*, or *VSAM*, that would solve many problems associated with the age and incompatibilities of the OS and DOS operating systems and their native access methods.

VSAM is available under all of IBM's major operating systems: OS (OS/VS1, MVS/SP, and MVS/XA), DOS (DOS/VS and DOS/VSE), and VM. The MVS implementation of VSAM is the most comprehensive; VS1/VSAM (under OS/VS1) and VSE/VSAM (under DOS/VSE) are compatible subsets of full MVS/VSAM. Under VM, CMS/VSAM is based on VSE/VSAM. So anything this book says about VSE/VSAM applies to CMS/VSAM as well.

Now, I'll briefly describe the major facilities of VSAM: data sets (or files), catalogs, space management, Access Method Services, and facilities for application programming. Of course, this is just an overview. You'll find more detailed information about each of these subjects in the chapters that follow.

VSAM data sets

VSAM provides three types of file organizations that correspond to the three types of file organizations provided by the native access methods. An *entry-sequenced data set*, or *ESDS*, is like a standard sequential (SAM or QSAM) data set. Its records are processed one at a time in the order in which they were loaded. A *relative-record data set*, or *RRDS*, is like a direct file (DAM or BDAM). Its records can be accessed based on their relative positions in the file. A *key-sequenced data set*, or *KSDS*, is like an ISAM file. Its records may be processed sequentially or randomly based on a key value.

VSAM provides an additional feature that has no equivalent in the native access methods: alternate indexes. An *alternate index* lets you access the records in a key-sequenced data set based on a key other than the file's primary key. For example, an employee master file might be indexed by employee number. An alternate index would let you access records in this file by department number. You can also use an alternate index to access the records of an ESDS.

In VSAM terms, a file is often called a *cluster*. Simply put, a cluster is a set of catalog entries that represent a file. (I'll introduce catalogs in a moment.) A cluster consists of one or two *components*: a *data component*, which represents

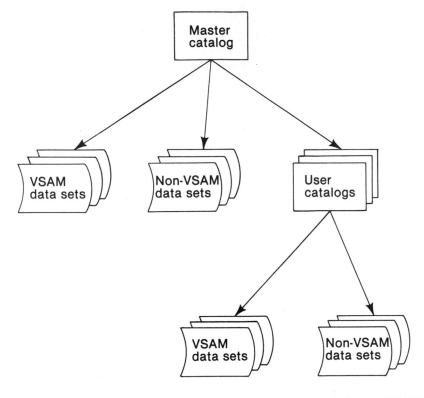

Figure 1-11   The relationship among the master catalog, user catalogs, and data sets

the actual records of a file (ESDS, RRDS, or KSDS), and an *index component*, which represents the indexes for a KSDS.

In chapter 2, I'll describe the details of how VSAM files are organized. For now, just remember that VSAM has three types of files—ESDS, RRDS, and KSDS—that correspond to the file organizations provided by the native access methods.

VSAM catalogs

VSAM provides a comprehensive catalog facility that stores information about VSAM data sets and other files. There are two types of VSAM catalogs: *master catalogs* and *user catalogs*. Although each OS or DOS system has just one master catalog, it can have an unlimited number of user catalogs. All VSAM data sets must be cataloged in the master catalog or in a user catalog. All user catalogs must be cataloged in the master catalog.

Figure 1-11 shows the relationships among the master catalog, user catalogs, and data sets. The master catalog can contain entries that define VSAM data sets, non-VSAM data sets, and user catalogs. The user catalogs can contain entries that define VSAM and non-VSAM data sets.

Some MVS installations use a facility called the *Integrated Catalog Facility*, or *ICF*, instead of standard VSAM catalogs. ICF catalogs are similar to VSAM catalogs in operation; the only differences are how the catalogs are structured internally and how you define them. All of the basic catalog manipulation functions you'll learn about in this book apply to both VSAM catalogs and ICF catalogs.

Incidentally, OS provided a limited catalog facility before VSAM was developed. The entries in an OS catalog, called a *CVOL*, identified which volume a particular file resided on. Although CVOLs can still be used, they don't affect VSAM or ICF catalogs.

In chapter 3, you'll learn more about both VSAM and ICF catalogs. For now, the only important point to remember is this: all VSAM data sets *must* be cataloged in the master catalog or a user catalog.

VSAM space management

VSAM was designed to replace the space management functions provided by the VTOC and DADSM. To do that, VSAM maintains detailed information in its catalogs about DASD space allocated to VSAM files. The allocation information stored in the catalog is more comprehensive and flexible than the equivalent information stored for a non-VSAM file in a VTOC.

Out of necessity, VSAM was designed to coexist with standard space management. To do that, the concept of data space was introduced. Simply put, a *data space*, or just *space*, is an area of a disk volume that's under the control of VSAM. To indicate that control, VSAM invokes DADSM to make an entry in the volume's VTOC for the space. (Under DOS/VSE, a limited subset of DADSM is incorporated into VSE/VSAM to manage allocation for data spaces.) Thus, to the operating system, a space is just another file. In fact, to allocate or extend a space, DADSM must be used. However, once a space has been allocated, VSAM has complete control over subsequent allocations *within* that space.

Within a space, VSAM can create *suballocated files*. Whenever a suballocated file needs to be created, extended, or deleted, VSAM uses its own space management facilities. Alternatively, an entire space can be allocated to a single VSAM file. In that case, allocation for the file, called a *unique file*, is managed by DADSM rather than by VSAM. Allocation information for unique files is maintained in two places: the VSAM catalog entry for the file and the VTOC entry for the space that contains the unique file.

To illustrate the difference between suballocated data sets and unique data sets, figure 1-12 shows two DASD volumes. The first volume has a VSAM data space that contains two suballocated files. Notice that there's unused space within the data space too. However, that space is not available to non-VSAM files because it's already under VSAM's control. The second DASD volume contains two unique VSAM data sets. All of the unused space on the volume is available to both VSAM and non-VSAM data sets.

Under VSE/VSAM and OS/VS VSAM, most VSAM data sets are

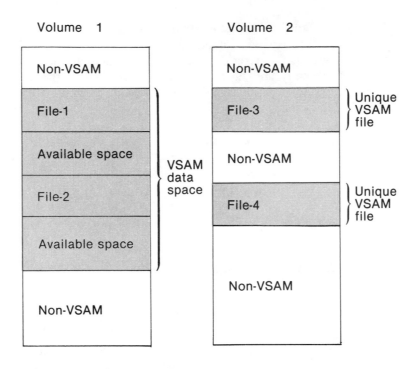

Figure 1-12   Suballocated and unique data sets

suballocated. That's because VSAM space management is typically more efficient than the operating system's standard space management. Under MVS with ICF, however, VSAM space management has been incorporated into DADSM, and the distinction between unique and suballocated files has been dropped. Under ICF, there is no VSAM space; all VSAM files are unique.

Access method services

Access Method Services, or *AMS*, is a general-purpose utility program that provides a variety of services for VSAM files. (AMS is also called *IDCAMS*; IDC is IBM's prefix for VSAM.) As a programmer, you'll use AMS frequently to define VSAM *objects* such as catalogs, spaces, and data sets, to list information about VSAM objects, or to perform basic file-maintenance functions like copying, printing, renaming, or deleting data sets.

Learning Access Method Services is an essential part of your VSAM education. That's why an entire section of this book—chapters 5 through 9—is devoted to AMS. In short, you cannot exist in a VSAM environment without knowing how to use AMS.

Application programming facilities

Like other access methods, VSAM provides extensive support for application programming. So, section 3 of this book—chapters 10 through 12—is devoted to VSAM's application programming facilities. You'll learn how to program for VSAM files in three environments: assembler language, COBOL, and command-level CICS.

As you might expect, assembler-language provides the most complete support for VSAM programming. With VSAM macros, you can use all of VSAM's processing capabilities. Some of the macros provide routine processing functions like reading or writing data set records. Others provide specialized functions like examining the contents of a catalog record or collecting statistics about VSAM's performance. Whether or not you intend to write assembler-language programs for VSAM, I think it helps to have an understanding of VSAM's assembler-language capabilities.

VS COBOL—the most widely used programming language on IBM mainframes—provides support for VSAM file processing according to the 1974 ANS COBOL standards. Although there are a few VSAM processing features that aren't available under COBOL, that's not usually a problem. COBOL provides all of the routine capabilities needed to process VSAM files.

CICS is an on-line terminal monitor that can support many concurrent users. Applications are written for CICS using a variation of COBOL called *command-level COBOL*, which supports VSAM in a way slightly different from standard batch COBOL.

Two other IBM languages support VSAM processing: PL/I and VS FORTRAN. However, I don't cover them in this book because they don't differ much from standard COBOL in the way they support VSAM file processing.

DISCUSSION

By now you should realize that the data management facilities of both OS and DOS involve complicated interrelationships among a large number of system components. Don't worry if you're confused about the relationship between VSAM and the other data management facilities of OS and DOS. That relationship will start to make more sense as you begin to use VSAM.

Terminology

file organization
access method
native access method
sequential organization

key
SAM
Sequential Access Method
Basic Sequential Access Method
BSAM
Queued Sequential Access Method
QSAM
indexed sequential organization
index
Indexed Sequential Access Method
ISAM
Basic Indexed Sequential Access Method
BISAM
Queued Indexed Sequential Access Method
QISAM
direct organization
randomizing routine
Direct Access Method
DAM
Basic Direct Access Method
BDAM
label
volume label
VOL1 label
volume serial number
vol-ser
VTOC
Volume Table Of Contents
file labels
Data Set Control Block
DSCB
extent
free extent
Direct Access Device Space Management
DADSM
first-fit
Virtual Storage Access Method
VSAM
entry-sequenced data set
ESDS
relative-record data set
RRDS
key-sequenced data set
KSDS
alternate index
cluster

component
data component
index component
master catalog
user catalog
Integrated Catalog Facility
ICF
CVOL
data space
space
suballocated file
unique file
Access Method Services
AMS
IDCAMS
object
command-level COBOL

Objectives

1. Describe the three types of file organizations and list the native access methods that can be used to support them.

2. Describe how DASD space is managed under OS and DOS.

3. List the three types of VSAM data sets along with their analogous non-VSAM file organizations.

4. Describe how VSAM space management differs from non-VSAM space management.

5. Identify the function of AMS in a VSAM environment.

6. List the programming languages that support VSAM.

Chapter 2

VSAM data sets

As you know, VSAM provides three types of data sets. An entry-sequenced data set, or ESDS, is like a standard sequential file. A key-sequenced data set, or KSDS, is like an indexed sequential file (ISAM). And a relative-record data set, or RRDS, is like a direct file.

In this chapter, you'll learn how all three types of VSAM data sets are structured internally and how you can process them. In addition, you'll learn about alternate indexes and a special type of VSAM file called a reusable data set.

A major component of VSAM, called *record management*, is responsible for maintaining the logical records of a VSAM file. (A *logical record* is a record as it's processed by an application program.) Record management is used to store records for all three types of VSAM data sets (and for alternate indexes and catalogs). Because record management concepts apply to all three types of VSAM data sets, I'll describe them before I describe the details of each kind of VSAM data set.

RECORD MANAGEMENT

Record management groups logical records into blocks called *control intervals*. Control intervals, in turn, are grouped together into *control areas*. Figure 2-1 illustrates this structure. Here, logical record 29 is stored in control interval 10, which is part of control area 2.

Control intervals

The control interval is the unit of data VSAM transfers between virtual and disk storage. The control interval concept is similar to the concept of blocking for non-VSAM files; a control interval usually contains more than one logical record. And just as block size for a non-VSAM file affects performance, the size of a control interval affects performance for a VSAM file.

The size of a control interval must be between 512 and 32,768 bytes (32K). Up to 8192 bytes (8K), the control interval size must be a multiple of 512; beyond that, it must be a multiple of 2048 (2K). For your reference, figure 2-2 lists the valid control interval sizes.

When you define a file, VSAM automatically determines a control interval size based on the record size you specify and the characteristics of the device on which the file will reside. However, in many cases, you'll want to override VSAM's selection and specify your own control interval size. I'll explain how and why you should do that in chapter 7.

Control interval structure   A control interval consists of three parts, as figure 2-3 shows: one or more logical records, control information, and (optionally) unused space. As you can see, the logical records are grouped together at the beginning of the control interval, and the control information is at the end of the control interval. That leaves the free space in the middle. If one or more of the records in the control interval is expanded or if another record is added, the unused space in the middle of the control interval is adjusted as needed.

Figure 2-4 shows three examples of how control information is stored in a control interval. As you can see, the rightmost four bytes of each control interval contain a *CIDF*, or *Control Interval Descriptor Field*. The CIDF has two main functions: (1) it keeps track of free space within the control interval and (2) it contains a flag that's set when the control interval is in the process of being updated.

To the left of the CIDF are one or more *RDFs*, or *Record Descriptor Fields*. As you might guess, these fields describe the logical records in the control interval. In the simplest case, there's one RDF for each record in the control interval. The RDFs are stored from right to left, so in figure 2-4, RDF 1 of control interval 1 describes logical record 1; RDF 2 describes logical record 2, and so on. Each of these RDFs contains just the length of its corresponding record. VSAM can determine the offset of each record in the control interval because the RDFs are stored in sequence.

Control area 1

Control interval 1	Logical record 1	Logical record 2	Logical record 3
Control interval 2	Logical record 4	Logical record 5	Logical record 6
Control interval 3	Logical record 7	Logical record 8	Logical record 9
Control interval 4	Logical record 10	Logical record 11	Logical record 12
Control interval 5	Logical record 13	Logical record 14	Logical record 15
Control interval 6	Logical record 16	Logical record 17	Logical record 18

Control area 2

Control interval 7	Logical record 19	Logical record 20	Logical record 21
Control interval 8	Logical record 22	Logical record 23	Logical record 24
Control interval 9	Logical record 25	Logical record 26	Logical record 27
Control interval 10	Logical record 28	Logical record 29	Logical record 30
Control interval 11	Logical record 31	Logical record 32	Logical record 33
Control interval 12	Logical record 34	Logical record 35	Logical record 36

Control area 3

Control interval 13	Logical record 37	Logical record 38	Logical record 39
Control interval 14	Logical record 40	Logical record 41	Logical record 42
Control interval 15	Logical record 43	Logical record 44	Logical record 45
Control interval 16	Logical record 46	Logical record 47	Logical record 48
Control interval 17	Logical record 49	Logical record 50	Logical record 51
Control interval 18	Logical record 52	Logical record 53	Logical record 54

Figure 2-1   How records are grouped together in control intervals, and control intervals are grouped together in control areas

Increments of 512 (Up to 8192 bytes)		Increments of 2048 (Over 8192 bytes)	
512	4608	10240	26624
1024	5120	12288	28672
1536	5632	14336	30720
2048	6144	16384	32768
2560	6656	18432	
3072	7168	20480	
3584	7680	22528	
4096	8192	24576	

Figure 2-2   Valid sizes for control intervals

Control interval

Logical record 1	Logical record 2	Logical record 3	Logical record 4	Unused space	Control information

Figure 2-3   The structure of a control interval

Control interval 2 in figure 2-4 shows what happens when all of the records in a control interval have the same length. In this case, it would be wasteful to store one RDF for each record. So VSAM uses just two RDFs: the first (RDF l) indicates the length of the records; the second (RDF c) indicates how many adjacent records have that length. In control interval 2, RDF l would contain 169, and RDF c would contain 6.

In control interval 3, logical records 2, 3, and 4 are 228 bytes in length, while records 1 and 5 are 64. Here, VSAM uses length and count RDFs for records 2 through 4 because those records are adjacent. Even though records 1 and 5 are the same length, they require separate RDFs because they are not adjacent.

Frankly, you don't need to know all of the details of how control information is stored within a control interval. The point I want to make is that the actual capacity of a control interval is always less than the full control interval size. If your records are all the same length, you must allow for ten bytes of control information (one 4-byte CIDF and two 3-byte RDFs). And if your record lengths vary, you must allow for more.

Control interval 1 (1024 bytes)

Logical record 1	Logical record 2	Logical record 3	Logical record 4	Free space	RDF 4	RDF 3	RDF 2	RDF 1	CIDF
185	292	128	256	147	3	3	3	3	4

Control interval 2 (1024 bytes)

Logical record 1	Logical record 2	Logical record 3	Logical record 4	Logical record 5	Logical record 6	RDF c	RDF l	CIDF
169	169	169	169	169	169	3	3	4

Control interval 3 (1024 bytes)

Logical record 1	Logical record 2	Logical record 3	Logical record 4	Logical record 5	Free space	RDF 5	RDF c	RDF l	RDF 1	CIDF
64	228	228	228	64	196	3	3	3	3	4

Figure 2-4   Three examples of how control information is stored in a control interval

Spanned records   A record that's larger than a single control interval is called a *spanned record*. Figure 2-5 shows a spanned record stored in two control intervals. Here, the first control interval contains part of the record; the second control interval contains the rest of the record. In this case, the length of the record isn't an even multiple of the available space (control interval size minus control information) in each control interval. As a result, there's unused space in the second control interval. However, because the control interval is used to store a spanned record, that extra space is *not* available for other records. It can be used only to lengthen the spanned record. Because of this restriction, spanned records aren't commonly used. In most cases, it's better to specify a control interval that's large enough to accommodate the biggest record in the file.

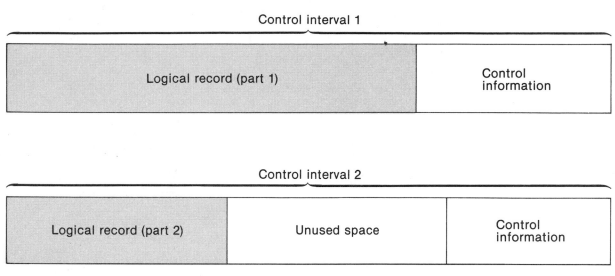

Figure 2-5   A spanned record occupies two or more control intervals

Control areas

As I said earlier, a group of adjacent control intervals is called a control area. A control area can be as small as one track or as large as one cylinder; usually, an entire cylinder is used. In VSAM literature, you'll sometimes see the terms *min-CA* and *max-CA*. These terms refer to the minimum and maximum size of a control area for a particular device. Therefore, min-CA is always the equivalent of one track and max-CA is the equivalent of one cylinder.

VSAM determines the size of a control area based on the amount of space you allocate to the file and the characteristics of the device on which the file will be stored. As additional extents are allocated to your file, they're added in units of adjacent control areas, if possible.

Just as a control interval may contain unused space, so may a control area. The available space in a control area is used to add additional control intervals as they're needed. You'll learn more about how free space within control areas is managed for the various data set types in just a moment.

CHARACTERISTICS OF VSAM DATA SETS

Now that you know how VSAM stores logical records on disk, you're ready to learn the characteristics of VSAM entry-sequenced, key-sequenced, and relative-record data sets, as well as alternate indexes and reusable data sets.

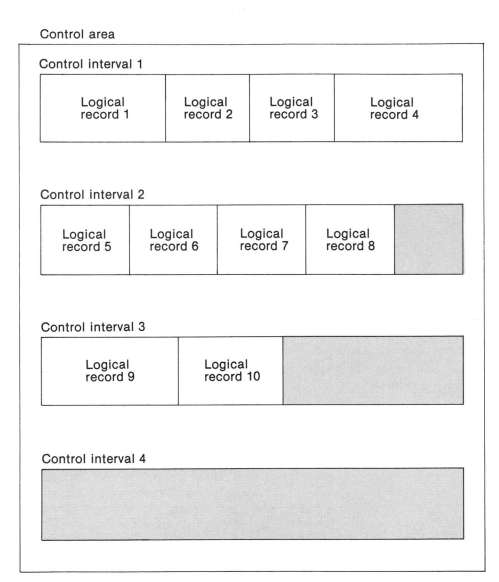

Control area

Control interval 1

| Logical record 1 | Logical record 2 | Logical record 3 | Logical record 4 |

Control interval 2

| Logical record 5 | Logical record 6 | Logical record 7 | Logical record 8 | |

Control interval 3

| Logical record 9 | Logical record 10 | |

Control interval 4

Figure 2-6   Record organization in an ESDS

Entry-sequenced data sets

An entry-sequenced data set is a sequential file, much like a standard sequential (SAM, BSAM, or QSAM) file. Records are typically retrieved in the order in which they were written to the data set. And additions are always made at the end of the file.

Figure 2-6 shows how the records of an ESDS are stored in control intervals. For clarity, I've omitted the control information that would be stored in each CI. As you can see, the records are stored in order within the control intervals. There's available free space in control interval 3, after record 10 (the last record in the file). And all of control interval 4 is available, since no records have been written to it. Notice the small amount of free space in control interval 2. That space—left over because the records of that control interval don't completely fill it—cannot be used. You can't write a new record to it, nor can you expand one of the records in control interval 2 to use it.

Although it's uncommon, you can process the records of an ESDS directly rather than sequentially. That's because each record can be identified by a *relative byte address*, or *RBA*. The RBA is an indication of how far, in bytes, each record is displaced from the beginning of the file. For example, if all of the records in an ESDS are 256 bytes in length, the RBA of the first record is 0, the second is 256, the third is 512, and so on, to the end of the control interval. Beyond the first control interval, however, records do *not* have RBAs that are multiples of 256. That's because the control information at the end of each control interval is included as part of the RBA value.

Key-sequenced data sets

A key-sequenced data set is similar in many ways to an ISAM file. In fact, one of the reasons IBM developed VSAM was to replace ISAM. Because VSAM has a better index structure and improved overflow handling, most ISAM users have converted their applications to VSAM. As a result, the VSAM KSDS is one of the most common file organizations in use today.

Like an ISAM file, you can process a KSDS sequentially or randomly. When you use sequential processing, records are processed one at a time in the order of the key values stored in the file's index. When you use random processing, you supply the value of the key in the record you want to access.

As I mentioned in chapter 1, a KSDS consists of two components: a data component and an index component. The data component contains the records and the index component contains the indexes necessary to access them. Figure 2-7 shows these two KSDS components.

The index component   As you can see in figure 2-7, the index component of a KSDS has two parts: a *sequence set* and an *index set*. The sequence set is the lowest level of the index. It's searched to determine which control interval in the data component contains a particular record. The index set is used to locate sequence set records.

Index set records are arranged in one or more levels. The index set in figure 2-7 has two levels. In an index set with more than one level, each higher level index set record contains pointers to records at the next level down; the records of the lowest level of the index set contain pointers to sequence set records. The highest level of an index set always has just one record.

To understand how the KSDS index structure works, consider the simple file in figure 2-8. In this example, the KSDS data component consists of three control areas, each with four control intervals. The numbers in the control intervals are the key values for the logical records. For example, the first

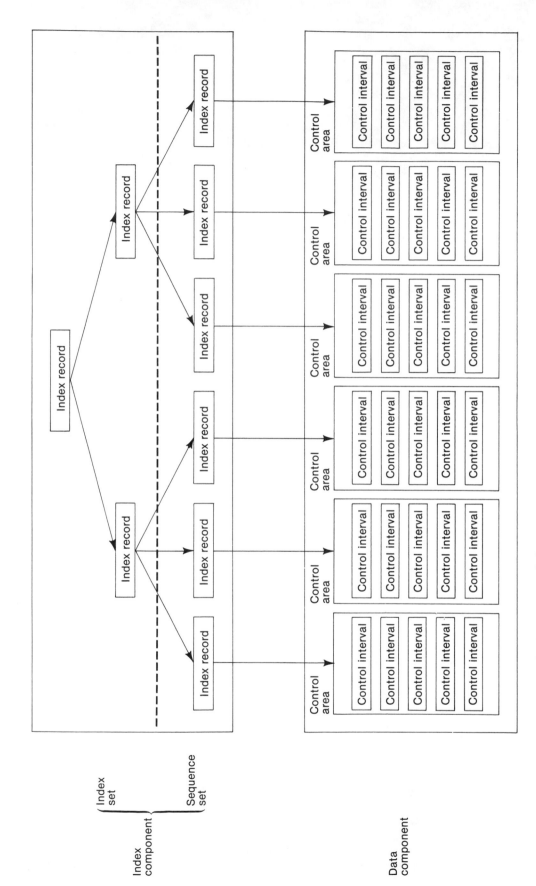

Figure 2-7   Components of a key-sequenced data set

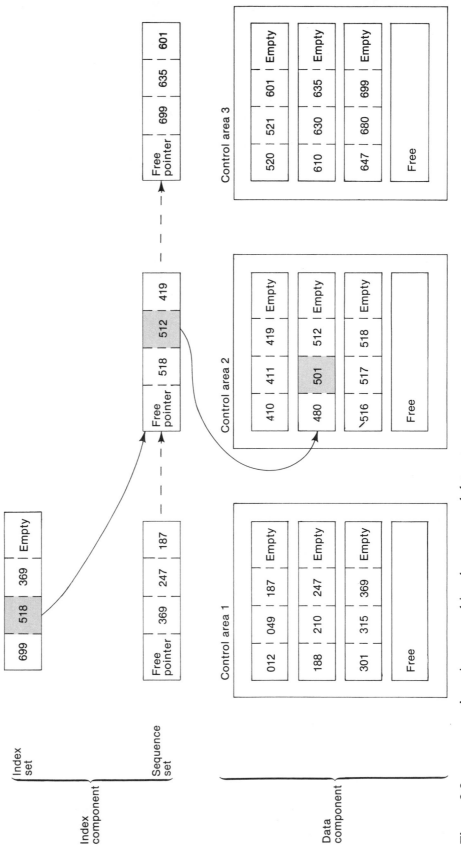

Figure 2-8 Accessing a record in a key-sequenced data set

control interval in control area 1 contains the three logical records whose key values are 012, 049, and 187.

For each control area in the data component of a KSDS, there is one record in the sequence set. As a result, the sequence set in figure 2-8 contains three records. Each sequence set record contains an *index entry* for each control interval in the corresponding control area. That index entry contains the highest key value stored in the corresponding control interval. Notice that within the sequence set records, index entries are stored in sequence from right to left. (The sequence set records also contain free pointers, which I'll explain in a moment.)

The entries in the index set record in figure 2-8 contain the highest values stored in each of the sequence set records. Many key-sequenced files use just one index set record; that's enough for 58 sequence set records, assuming an index CI-size of 512 bytes. Since each sequence set record indexes a control area, which is typically a full cylinder, a single index set record provides for up to 58 cylinders of data. On a 3350, that's about 32 million bytes. If the file is larger than that, VSAM automatically creates additional index set records as needed, arranging them in levels as figure 2-7 shows.

The solid arrows and the highlighting in figure 2-8 show the processing necessary to locate the record whose key value is 501. First, the index set record is read and searched to determine which sequence set record to use. Then, the correct sequence set record is read and searched to determine which control interval to use. Finally, the control interval is read and searched to locate the correct record. The pointers used to locate a record like this are called *vertical pointers* because they point down through the index structure to the desired record.

VSAM also provides *horizontal pointers* in the sequence set of a KSDS, indicated by the dashed arrows in figure 2-8. Each record in the sequence set contains a horizontal pointer that points to the next sequence set record in key order. Because of horizontal pointers, the records of a KSDS can be processed sequentially without accessing the index set at all.

Index performance options When you define a KSDS, you can specify several options that affect the way the index component is stored. For example, you can store the sequence set records with the data component rather than with the index set. And, you can duplicate the index records to reduce rotational delay. Because these options are used to control file performance, I'll describe them in detail in chapter 7.

In its index entries, VSAM uses a technique called *key compression* to minimize the space required to store keys. It's not uncommon for keys that are 15 bytes long to be reduced to three or four bytes by VSAM's key-compression algorithm. Like the index options I just mentioned, key compression is a performance feature. But because it's automatic, I won't describe it in detail in this book.

The data component and free space Unlike an ESDS—and unlike an ISAM file—you can reserve free space to accommodate new records within the

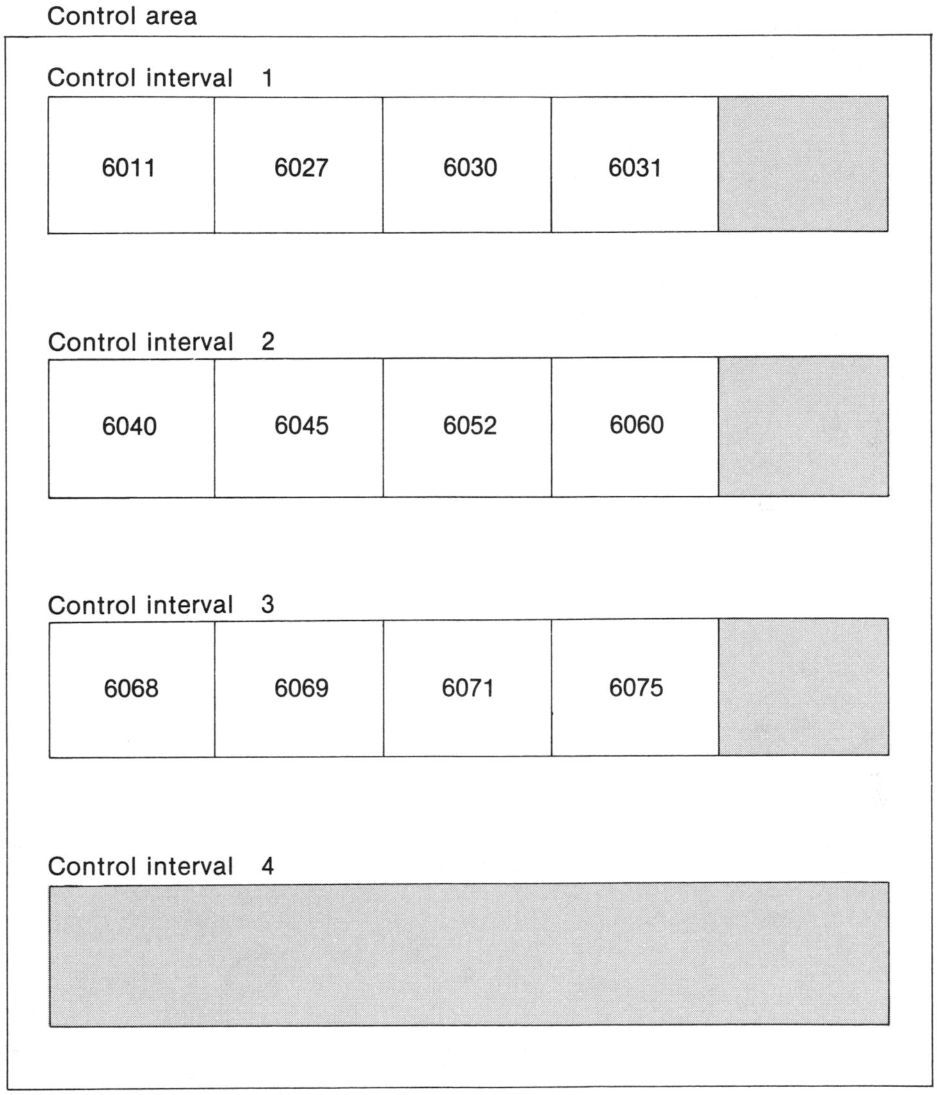

Control area

Control interval   1

| 6011 | 6027 | 6030 | 6031 | |

Control interval   2

| 6040 | 6045 | 6052 | 6060 | |

Control interval   3

| 6068 | 6069 | 6071 | 6075 | |

Control interval   4

| |

Figure 2-9   Free space distribution in the data component of a KSDS

data component of a KSDS. You can reserve this space in two ways: (1) you can leave space within each control interval and (2) you can leave entire control intervals empty. When you define a KSDS cluster using AMS, you specify both types of free space.

Figure 2-9 shows a control area that consists of four control intervals. Three of the four control intervals contain four logical records and enough space for one more. For clarity, I omitted the control information in each control interval. You should realize, though, that VSAM knows about the free space within the control intervals because of entries in each control interval's CIDF. The fourth control interval is completely empty. VSAM knows about

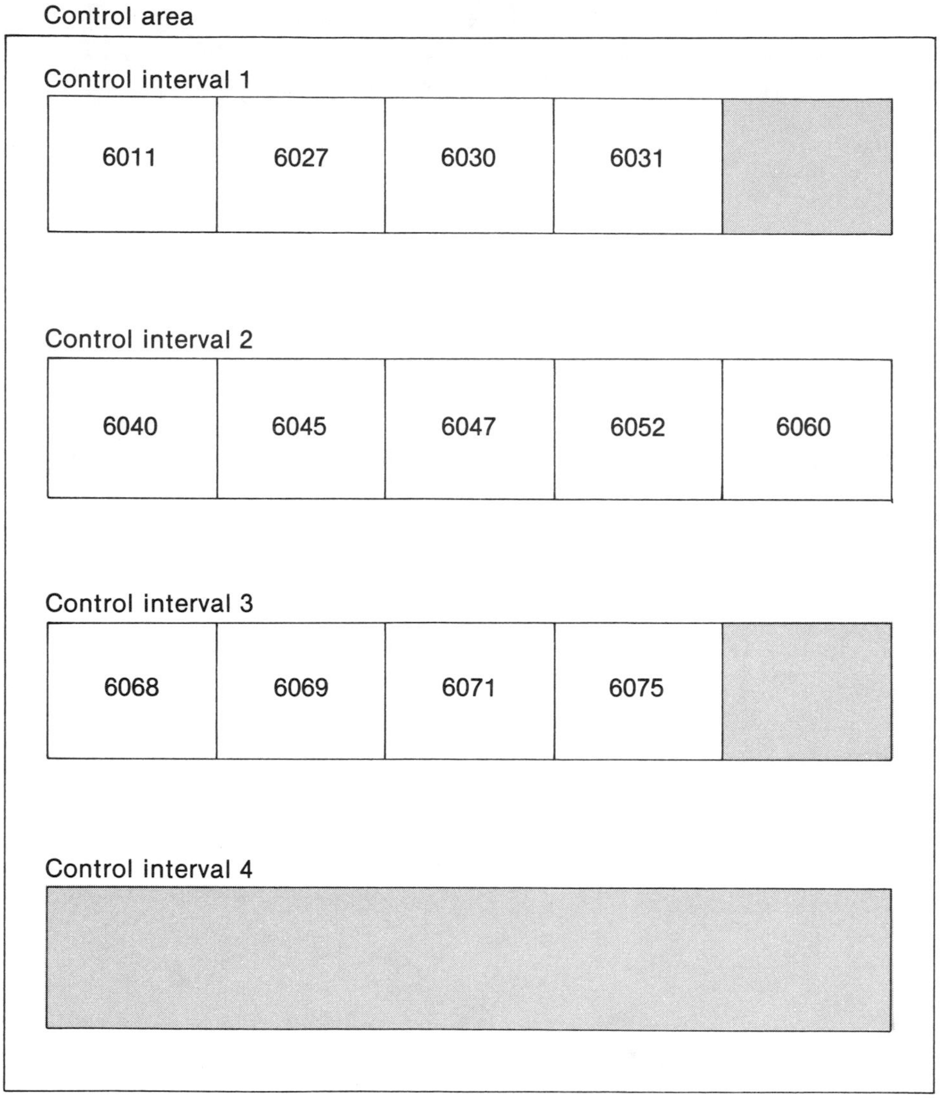

Control area

Control interval 1

| 6011 | 6027 | 6030 | 6031 | |

Control interval 2

| 6040 | 6045 | 6047 | 6052 | 6060 |

Control interval 3

| 6068 | 6069 | 6071 | 6075 | |

Control interval 4

Figure 2-10   Free space distribution in the data component of a KSDS after inserting a record

it because each sequence set record in the index component contains pointers to free control intervals in its associated control area. If you'll look back to figure 2-8, you'll see those pointers.

Notice that within the control intervals, logical records are stored in key sequence. When a record is added to a KSDS, it's inserted in its correct sequential location in the proper control interval, and the records that follow it in the control interval are shifted. That's what figure 2-10 illustrates. Here, record 6047 has been added between records 6045 and 6052.

What happens if an insertion is made into a control interval that's already full? In that case, some of the records in the full control interval are moved

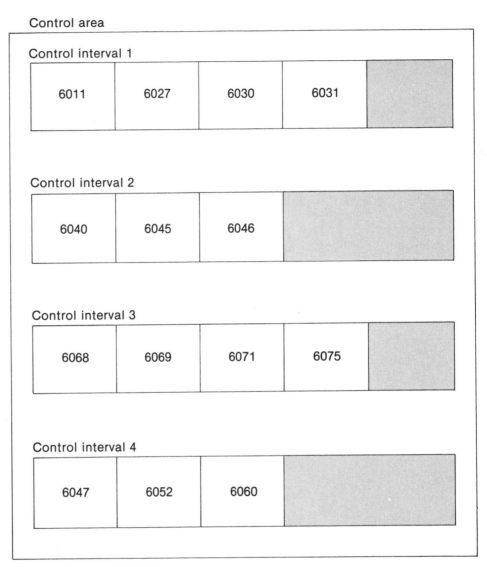

Figure 2-11   Free space distribution in the data component of a KSDS after a control interval split

into a free control interval. That's called a *control interval split*. Figure 2-11 shows the results of a control interval split; here, record 6046 was inserted between records 6045 and 6047. So records 6047, 6052, and 6060 were moved into a free control interval.

   Of course, it's possible that there may be no available free control intervals within a control area. If that happens, a *control area split* occurs before the control interval split. To do a control area split, VSAM allocates a new control area, moves about half the control intervals from the original control area to the new one, and creates a new sequence set record for the new control area. Then, the control interval split is performed. As you can imagine, a control

Control area

Control interval 1

Slot 1	Slot 2	Slot 3	Slot 4	Slot 5

Control interval 2

Slot 6	Slot 7	Slot 8 (empty)	Slot 9	Slot 10

Control interval 3

Slot 11	Slot 12 (empty)	Slot 13	Slot 14 (empty)	Slot 15

Control interval 4

Slot 16 (empty)	Slot 17	Slot 18	Slot 19	Slot 20 (empty)

Figure 2-12   Record organization in an RRDS

area split involves significant disk I/O, so it's best to allocate enough free control intervals to accommodate expected control interval splits when you define your data set.

Relative-record data sets

Figure 2-12 shows a VSAM relative-record data set. An RRDS consists of fixed-length *slots* which are numbered. It's those numbers—called *relative record numbers* (or *RRN*s)—that let you access the records of an RRDS directly. Each slot either contains a record or is empty.

Records in an RRDS can be accessed sequentially or randomly. When sequential processing is used, VSAM automatically skips over empty slots. So sequential processing for an RRDS is similar to sequential processing for an ESDS.

Random processing is based on each record's relative position in the file. Because an RRDS doesn't have an index component to search, it can be processed more efficiently than a KSDS. So if an application lends itself to the RRN addressing scheme, an RRDS can be a practical alternative to a KSDS.

Additions to an RRDS can be done in two ways. First, new records can be inserted in empty slots in the file. To do so, however, the application program must be able to identify the empty slots. And that's not always easy to do.

The second way to handle additions to an RRDS is to add them to the end of the file. For example, suppose an RRDS contains 1000 slots. If you write a record to slot 1001, VSAM allocates an additional control area if necessary, preformats the slots in it, then writes the record. You should realize that VSAM may have to allocate more than one control area to add a record. For example, suppose an RRDS has control areas large enough to store 1000 records. If your file already has 1000 slots—one control area—and you write a record to slot 5000, VSAM allocates and preformats four more control areas before it writes your record.

Alternate indexes

An *alternate index* lets you access the records of a VSAM key-sequenced data set in an order other than that of the file's *primary key* (or *base key*). The data set over which an alternate index exists is called a *base cluster*. Although you can also use an entry-sequenced data set as the base cluster for an alternate index, most alternate indexes are built over key-sequenced data sets.

To understand the concept of an alternate index, consider figure 2-13. Here, an alternate index exists for a base cluster KSDS that contains three fields: employee number, social security number, and department number. The primary key for the base cluster is employee number. As a result, you can access the base cluster sequentially or randomly based on each record's employee number.

The alternate index in figure 2-13 lets you process the base cluster in social security number sequence by relating each *alternate key* value to a primary key value. So, as the shading indicates, when you tell VSAM to retrieve the record for the employee whose social security number is 565-37-5511, VSAM searches the alternate index, retrieves the primary key (1008), and uses that value to locate the correct record in the base cluster.

In figure 2-13, each alternate key is associated with one primary key. This type of alternate key is called a *unique key*. In contrast, figure 2-14 illustrates an alternate index with *nonunique*, or *duplicate*, *keys*. Here, the alternate key is department number.

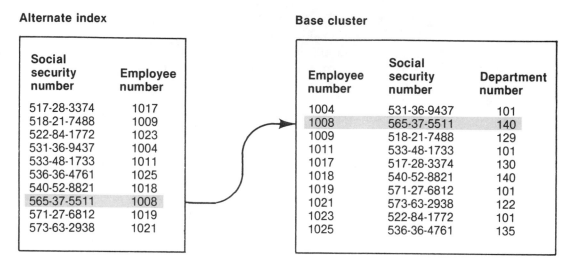

Figure 2-13   An alternate index with unique keys

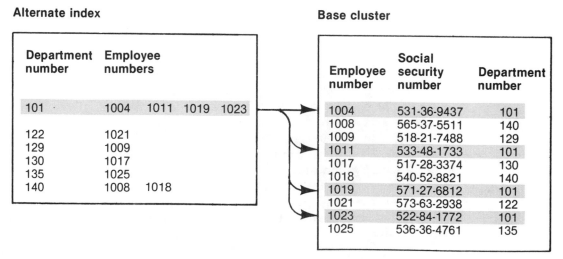

Figure 2-14   An alternate index with duplicate keys

To understand nonunique keys, consider the alternate index for department number 101. Here, four employee numbers are specified: 1004, 1011, 1019, and 1023. When you process this file sequentially, all four employee records are retrieved in turn. However, when you process an alternate index file with duplicate keys directly, only the *first* base cluster record for each alternate key value is available.

An alternate index is itself a key-sequenced data set. If the base cluster is a KSDS, each record in the alternate index's data component contains an alternate key value and one or more primary key values for the corresponding records in the base cluster. If the base cluster is an ESDS, each record in the alternate index's data component contains an alternate key value and one or more RBAs for the corresponding records in the base cluster.

The index component of an alternate index contains the alternate keys that index the records in the data component, just as in a standard KSDS. To simplify the examples in figures 2-13 and 2-14, I don't show the index and data components or the control areas and control intervals for the alternate index file or the base cluster.

You might be surprised to learn that VSAM doesn't require that an alternate index be *upgraded* each time its base cluster is changed. An alternate index is an *upgradable index* only if you specify (via AMS) that VSAM should update it automatically whenever changes are made to the base cluster. However, because upgradable indexes add considerable overhead to alternate index processing, alternate indexes are often not upgradable. Instead, the alternate indexes are commonly rebuilt nightly, and users have to realize that additions or changes to their data sets won't be reflected in the alternate indexes until the next day.

One other point I want to make has to do with the way upgradable alternate indexes are maintained. Figure 2-15 shows the employee base cluster and its two alternate indexes after the addition of a new employee record. Notice where the entry for the new employee record (primary key 1013) was made in the department-number alternate index. When you build an alternate index, entries for alternate keys with multiple prime key values are made in prime-key sequence. So the entries for department 101 were originally stored in the correct sequence: 1004, 1011, 1019, and 1023. Unfortunately, VSAM maintains upgrades in the order in which they were made, not in prime-key sequence. As a result, employee 1013 is added at the end of the entries for department 101, rather than between the entries for employees 1011 and 1019. So if you try to process the employee master file sequentially using the department number alternate index, you will *not* receive records in employee-number within department-number sequence.

To return the alternate index entries to prime-key sequence, alternate indexes are generally rebuilt during off hours, even if they are upgradable. Since making an index upgradable doesn't necessarily save additional processing, alternate indexes are generally *not* upgradable unless they absolutely must be.

Base cluster

Employee number	Social security number	Department number
1004	531-36-9437	101
1008	565-37-5511	140
1009	518-21-7488	129
1011	533-48-1733	101
1013	552-57-2735	101
1017	517-28-3374	130
1018	540-52-8821	140
1019	571-27-6812	101
1021	573-63-2938	122
1023	522-84-1772	101
1025	536-36-4761	135

Alternate index (social security number)

Social security number	Employee number
517-28-3374	1017
518-21-7488	1009
522-84-1772	1023
531-36-9437	1004
533-48-1733	1011
536-36-4761	1025
540-52-8821	1018
552-57-2735	1013
565-37-5511	1008
571-27-6812	1019
573-63-2938	1021

Alternate index (department number)

Department number	Employee numbers				
101	1004	1011	1019	1023	1013
122	1021				
129	1009				
130	1017				
135	1025				
140	1008	1018			

Figure 2-15   Base cluster and alternate indexes after insertion of employee number 1013

Reusable data sets

Some applications call for temporary data sets or work files that must be created, used, and deleted each time the application is run. To simplify those applications, VSAM lets you create *reusable files*. A reusable file is a standard VSAM ESDS, KSDS, or RRDS. The only difference is that if you open an existing reusable file for output processing, VSAM treats the file as if were empty. Any records already in the file are ignored. It's as if the file was just defined but no data has been loaded yet. So, if you use a reusable file, you don't have to define it and then delete it each time you use it. Instead, you define it just once.

To understand how a reusable data set works, you need to know about a field that's stored in the catalog entry for each VSAM file: the *high-used RBA field*. This field indicates the RBA of the last byte of the last record in the data set. When you open a reusable data set for output processing, VSAM resets the high-used RBA field to zero. The file's records aren't actually erased. But because the high-used RBA field is zero, it's as if they aren't there.

Terminology

record management
logical record
control interval
control area
CIDF
Control Interval Descriptor Field
RDF
Record Descriptor Field
spanned record
min-CA
max-CA
relative byte address
RBA
sequence set
index set
index entry
vertical pointer
horizontal pointer
key compression
control interval split
control area split
slot
relative record number
RRN
alternate index
primary key

base key
base cluster
alternate key
unique key
nonunique key
duplicate key
upgrade
upgradable index
reusable file
high-used RBA field

Objectives

1. Describe how VSAM record management stores the logical records of a VSAM data set.

2. Compare and contrast the characteristics of VSAM entry-sequenced, key-sequenced, and relative-record data sets.

3. Explain how an alternate index can be used to access the records of a base cluster.

4. Describe the factors you should consider when deciding whether or not an alternate index should be upgradable.

5. Describe the function of a reusable file.

Chapter 3

Catalog concepts

You should remember from chapter 1 that all VSAM data sets must be cataloged either in the master catalog or in a user catalog. Because of this requirement, you need to understand what catalogs are and how they're used. That's what this chapter describes.

I also mentioned in chapter 1 that there are two basic catalog environments in use today: VSAM catalogs and ICF catalogs. At the simplest level, these two environments appear to be the same; all VSAM data sets must be cataloged in a master or user catalog, and there can be just one master catalog on a system. Beyond this, however, there are major differences between VSAM and ICF catalogs. Because VSAM catalogs are older and more widely used, I'll cover them first. Then, I'll describe how ICF catalogs differ.

VSAM catalogs

Figure 3-1 shows the relationships among a VSAM master catalog, a user catalog, and several files on three disk volumes. Here, the

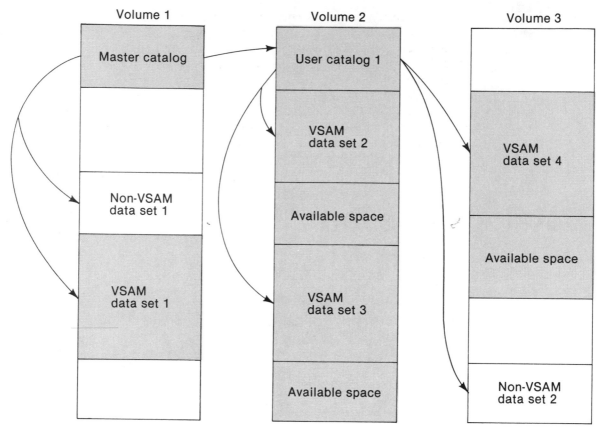

Figure 3-1   Possible VSAM catalog and file relationships

master catalog resides on disk volume 1. It contains entries for two files: a non-VSAM file and a VSAM file, both of which also reside on volume 1. In addition, the master catalog contains an entry for user catalog 1, which resides on volume 2. User catalog 1, in turn, contains entries for VSAM files on volume 2 and volume 3. Of course, this is a simple example; on a large system, dozens of user catalogs would contain entries for hundreds of files. Still, this figure illustrates the basic organization of VSAM catalogs.

VSAM data space   The shaded areas of figure 3-1 represent VSAM data spaces. VSAM space is space that's reserved for use by VSAM. In the simplest case, an entire disk volume is defined as a single VSAM space. In figure 3-1, all of volume 2 is a single VSAM space. Volume 3, on the other hand, is only partially reserved for use by VSAM. And volume 1 contains two VSAM spaces. The important point to note is this: ALL VSAM data sets on volumes 1, 2, and 3 are contained within VSAM space. You cannot define a VSAM file outside of VSAM space, nor can you create a non-VSAM file within VSAM space.

A VSAM file can be suballocated or unique. A suballocated data set shares VSAM space with other files. In contrast, a unique data set occupies its own data space. The VSAM data set on volume 1 in figure 3-1 is unique; no other VSAM files share its space. But the two VSAM files on volume 2 are suballocated out of a single space.

To indicate data spaces on a disk volume, VSAM writes labels to the volume's VTOC. To illustrate, figure 3-2 shows a VTOC listing that includes two VSAM objects: a data space and a unique file. For the data space, VSAM created a unique name that includes a timestamp. The second component of the name, VSAMDSPC, identifies the entry as a VSAM data space. As for the unique file, its name is the VSAM file name: MMA2.CRPX.DATA. For both VTOC entries, the data set organization (DSORG) is VSAM (VS).

Under OS, direct access space is allocated as VSAM data space by a system component called DADSM, which stands for Direct Access Device Space Management. DADSM is the system component that allocates space for non-VSAM data sets based on the primary and secondary extent information you supply in the data set's DD statement. As a result, data spaces on OS systems allow both primary and secondary extents. So if you try to extend a VSAM file within a data space that's full, OS/DADSM tries to extend the data space.

On DOS systems, there is no equivalent of OS/DADSM. Instead, VSE/VSAM includes a limited subset of DADSM to handle the initial allocation of data spaces on VSE systems. The subset of DADSM on VSE systems, however, does *not* provide for secondary extents. So once a data space on a VSE system is full, you must allocate more space to it. Because of this limitation, unique data sets aren't commonly used on VSE systems. That's because VSE/VSAM can handle secondary extents for suballocated files within a larger data space, but not for unique data sets that occupy their own data spaces.

Volume ownership　　One minor inconvenience you may have to contend with on OS systems is *volume ownership*. Simply put, volume ownership means that all VSAM space on a given volume—and, as a result, all VSAM files on the volume—must be cataloged in the same VSAM catalog. Once you define VSAM space on a volume, the catalog in which you define the space owns that volume; no other catalog can be used to catalog files or space on that volume. A catalog can own more than one volume, but a volume can't be owned by more than one catalog. The volume ownership concept doesn't apply to VSE systems or to MVS systems that use ICF catalogs rather than VSAM catalogs.

Interestingly, you can easily tell which volume or volumes a user catalog owns by examining the catalog. But there's no way to tell which user catalog owns a particular volume by examining the volume. An installation must keep a manual record of which user catalog owns each DASD volume, especially an installation that has dozens or hundreds of user catalogs and DASD volumes. Otherwise, it can take hours to find out what user catalog owns a particular volume.

The structure of a VSAM catalog　　A VSAM catalog is actually a special kind of key-sequenced data set that contains records describing VSAM objects

```
DATE: 85.324  TIME: 13.14.23
          CONTENTS OF VTOC ON VOL MPS800

--------DATA SET NAME-----------     ID  SER NO  SEQ NO  CREDT  EXPDT  REFDT  NO EXT  DSORG  RECFM  OPTCD  BLKSIZE
Z9999994.VSAMDSPC.T97E8DDC.T934DBCA   1  MPS800    1     25184  36599  25184    2      VS      L     00     4096

       LRECL  KEYLEN  INITIAL ALLOC  2ND ALLOC/LAST BLK PTR(T-R-L)   USED PDS BYTES   FMT 2 OR 3(C-H-R)/DSCB(C-H-R)
         0            CYLS      8         0 47968                                            295  5  5

       EXTENTS  NO  LOW(C-H)    HIGH(C-H)
                 0  300  0      319  14
               ---UNABLE TO CALCULATE EMPTY SPACE.


--------DATA SET NAME-----------     ID  SER NO  SEQ NO  CREDT  EXPDT  REFDT  NO EXT  DSORG  RECFM  OPTCD  BLKSIZE
DLOWE2.SPFLOG1.LIST                   1  MPS800    1     22485  C0000  22485    1      PS      V     CO      129

       LRECL  KEYLEN  INITIAL ALLOC  2ND ALLOC/LAST BLK PTR(T-R-L)   USED PDS BYTES   FMT 2 OR 3(C-H-R)/DSCB(C-H-R)
        125           RECS    563        0 8 43232                                          295  10  22

       EXTENTS  NO  LOW(C-H)    HIGH(C-H)
                 0  56  13      57  5
               ---ON THE ABOVE DATA SET,THERE ARE   585 EMPTY BLOCK(S).


--------DATA SET NAME-----------     ID  SER NO  SEQ NO  CREDT  EXPDT  REFDT  NO EXT  DSORG  RECFM  OPTCD  BLKSIZE
MMA2.CRPX.DATA                       1  MPS800    1     26385  36599  26385    1      VS      U     CO      2048

       LRECL  KEYLEN  INITIAL ALLOC  2ND ALLOC/LAST BLK PTR(T-R-L)   USED PDS BYTES   FMT 2 OR 3(C-H-R)/DSCB(C-H-R)
         0            CYLS      1         0 47968                                            295  10  21

       EXTENTS  NO  LOW(C-H)    HIGH(C-H)
                 0  717  0      717  14
               ---UNABLE TO CALCULATE EMPTY SPACE.
```

Figure 3-2   A VTOC listing showing a VSAM data space and a unique data set (OS)

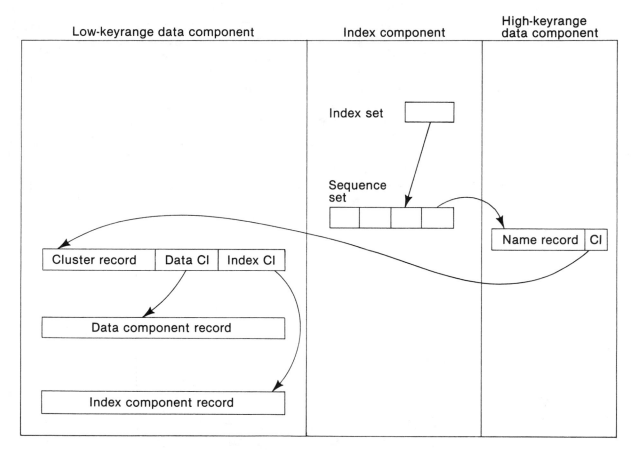

Figure 3-3   The structure of a VSAM catalog

such as spaces and files. Quite frankly, the unusual structure of VSAM catalogs is one of the major problems with VSAM catalog management. That's why, as you'll see in a moment, ICF catalogs have a completely different structure.

Figure 3-3 shows the structure of a VSAM catalog. Unlike a standard KSDS, the data component of a VSAM catalog is divided into two parts: the *low-keyrange data component* and the *high-keyrange data component*. The index component is placed physically between the low-keyrange and the high-keyrange sections of the data component.

For each cataloged object, there's a corresponding record, called the *name record*, in the high-keyrange section of the catalog's data component. The key of this record is the name of the catalog entry. So, for an ESDS named AR.TRANS.FILE, there's a high-keyrange record whose key is AR.TRANS.FILE. To locate this record, VSAM uses the catalog's index component records just as it would to locate a record in a standard KSDS.

The name record doesn't contain all the catalog information for the data set. Instead, it contains the number of a control interval in the low-keyrange section of the data component. That control interval, which is always 512 bytes long, contains the record that more fully describes the catalog entry. As you can see in figure 3-3, the name record points to a cluster record, which in turn points to other low-keyrange records for the components of the cataloged data set. Here, the cataloged data set is a KSDS, so there are two additional low-keyrange records for it. In some cases, there may be even more low-keyrange records; if there are, the cluster record points to them too. As a result, once a cluster record has been accessed, VSAM can locate all the related low-keyrange records without searching the catalog's index component again.

Although the records in the low-keyrange section are accessed by their control interval numbers, they also have keys, just as any data record in a KSDS. The key value for a low-keyrange record is its control interval number. (There's only one record per control interval in a catalog.) So, the key value for the record in control interval 5 is hexadecimal 00000005. These records are called "low-keyrange" because they all have keys that are lower than the keys of the name records in the high-keyrange section.

ICF catalogs

As more and more users began using VSAM, they realized that VSAM's catalog structure has some major weaknesses. First of all, it's often difficult to recover a VSAM catalog in the event of a system failure. That's because catalogs aren't always on the same volumes as the data sets they describe. Second, the specialized KSDS structure used for catalogs makes it difficult for an installation to improve the performance of a catalog, because many of the performance options available for a standard KSDS aren't valid for a VSAM catalog. And third, the volume ownership concept is overly restrictive in a large MVS environment that can have hundreds of DASD volumes.

To solve these problems, IBM developed a new catalog management system—available only on MVS systems—called the *Integrated Catalog Facility*, or *ICF*. ICF is actually a part of a larger system component called *Data Facility/Extended Function*, or *DF/EF*. (On MVS/XA, it's called just *Data Facility Product*, or *DFP*.) DF/EF (and DFP) consists of three elements: standard VSAM, ICF, and a few advanced record management options that aren't covered in this book. In general, whenever someone speaks of DF/EF or DFP, they're referring just to ICF.

Many MVS shops today have installed ICF but are still using a mixture of ICF and VSAM catalogs. For some, it's just a matter of time before they use ICF catalogs exclusively. Other shops, however, have chosen to maintain VSAM catalogs for certain applications.

Before I go on, I want you to realize that there are many similarities between ICF and VSAM catalogs. For example, one catalog must still be designated as the master catalog, although an unlimited number of user catalogs can be used. All VSAM files must still be cataloged in a user or master catalog. And, with few exceptions, the AMS commands you use are the same whether you're using VSAM or ICF catalogs. Although there are important conceptual differences between ICF and VSAM catalogs, those differences aren't all that important unless you're responsible for managing the catalog environment.

ICF catalog data sets   The ICF catalog environment consists of two types of catalog files: a *Basic Catalog Structure*, or *BCS*, and a *VSAM Volume Data Set*, or *VVDS*. A BCS is a standard key-sequenced data set that contains a record for each entry in the catalog; there's one BCS for each ICF master or user catalog. The BCS records contain information that doesn't typically change during normal processing, such as a file's name and attributes (like file organization, key position, and so on). Information that *does* change during normal processing (like the file extent information) is stored in the VVDS.

Every disk volume that contains VSAM files has one VVDS, and every VSAM file on that volume is defined in that VVDS, regardless of which user catalog (BCS) owns the file. The BCS that defines a VSAM file can be on a different volume, and the files defined in a VVDS can be defined in one or more BCSs. To understand how that works, look at figure 3-4. Here, a variety of possible catalog relationships are illustrated. Each volume has one VVDS that contains entries for all of the VSAM files on that volume. BCS1 and BCS2 are on volume 1, while BCS3 is on volume 2. BCS1 contains entries for files on all three volumes, while BCS2 contains entries just for files on volume 1 and BCS3 contains entries just for files on volume 2. As you can imagine, the relationships among BCSs, VVDSs, and data sets on an ICF system are typically much more complex than figure 3-4 suggests.

Figure 3-5 shows the ICF catalog structure in greater detail. Here, I show the catalog entries needed to define a VSAM file named VSAM.ESDS. In the BCS (named ICF.UCAT1), the entry for VSAM.ESDS indicates which VVDS owns the file: SYS1.VVDS.VVOL200. In the VVDS, the entry for VSAM.ESDS indicates which BCS owns the file: ICF.UCAT1. The entries in a BCS can point to any number of different VVDSs, and the entries in a VVDS can point to up to 36 different BCSs. As a result, a BCS can own files on any number of different volumes. And a volume can contain files cataloged in up to 36 different BCSs. So the ICF catalog structure eliminates the concept of volume ownership that restricts the way VSAM catalogs can be used.

Notice in figure 3-5 that the disk volume's VTOC also contains an entry for the VSAM data set and the VVDS. Under ICF, there is no concept of data space. As a result, there's no distinction between unique and suballocated files; all files have information recorded directly in the volume's VTOC. And, all data set extensions are handled by OS/DADSM rather than by VSAM.

Discussion

I mentioned at the start of this chapter that it's not essential for you to understand all of the details of VSAM and ICF catalog structure. In fact, as detailed as this chapter may seem, I've only skimmed the surface. For example, I didn't explain the format of the various types of records that are stored in a catalog. That kind of information, though interesting, just isn't vital to your day-to-day use of VSAM.

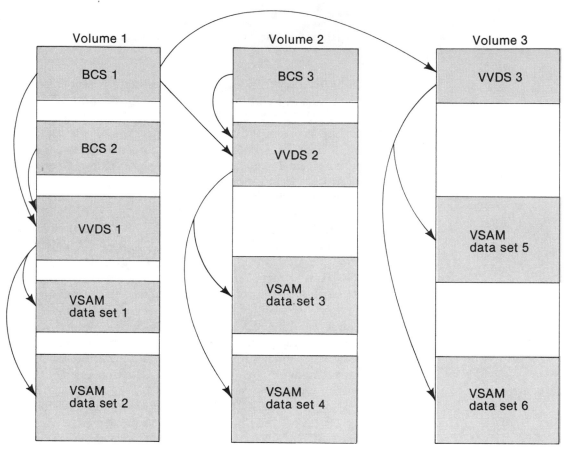

Figure 3-4   Possible ICF catalog and file relationships

Terminology

volume ownership
low-keyrange data component
high-keyrange data component
name record
Integrated Catalog Facility
ICF
Data Facility/Extended Function
DF/EF
Data Facility Product
DFP
Basic Catalog Structure
BCS
VSAM Volume Data Set
VVDS

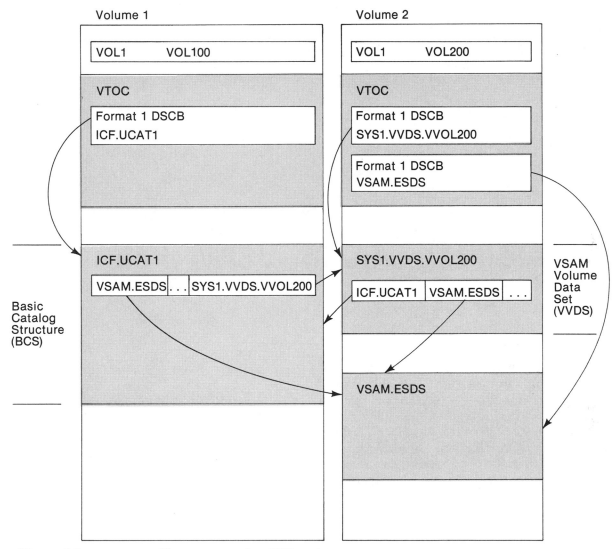

Figure 3-5   The structure of an ICF catalog

Objectives

1. Describe the concept of VSAM data space.

2. Describe the concept of volume ownership.

3. Explain the function of the three parts of a VSAM catalog.

4. List the shortcomings of VSAM catalogs that are overcome by ICF catalogs.

5. Explain the functions of the two parts of an ICF catalog.

Chapter 4

JCL requirements for VSAM files

In this chapter, you'll learn how to code JCL statements for jobs that process VSAM files. Because OS and DOS have completely different JCL requirements, this topic is divided into two main sections: the first covers OS JCL, while the second covers DOS JCL. You can read just the section that applies to your system, or you can read both if you want the additional perspective of how VSAM files are treated under both operating systems.

After I describe the JCL for OS and DOS systems, I'll describe a facility called the ISAM Interface Program that lets you easily convert existing ISAM applications to VSAM by making changes in the JCL. The ISAM Interface Program is available under both OS and DOS.

The DD statement for VSAM files

```
//ddname    DD    DSNAME=data-set-name,
                  DISP=SHR,
                  AMP=(option,option...)
```

Explanation

ddname   A one- to eight-character name used by the application program to refer to the file.

DSNAME   A one- to 44-character alphanumeric name that identifies the VSAM file in its catalog. The name you code must be the same as the one specified when the file was defined.

DISP   For VSAM files, code DISP = SHR. Then, if options specified when the file was defined allow it, the file can be shared with other jobs.

AMP   Specifies processing options for VSAM files. Valid subparameters are:
  AMORG
  BUFND
  BUFNI
  BUFSP
  CROPS
  OPTCD
  RECFM
  STRNO
  SYNAD
  TRACE

See the text for details on their effects.

Figure 4-1   The DD statement for VSAM files

OS JOB CONTROL LANGUAGE FOR VSAM

To code the JCL for jobs that process VSAM files under OS, you need to know two things: (1) how to code DD statements for VSAM files and (2) how VSAM catalogs are searched to find a file you specify. (The EXEC and JOB statements are coded the same as for non-VSAM jobs.)

The DD statement for VSAM files

Figure 4-1 gives the format of the DD statement as you code it for a VSAM file. Normally, you code the DD statement for a VSAM file like this:

```
//CUSTMAST  DD  DSNAME=MMA.CUSTMAST,DISP=SHR
```

Here, CUSTMAST is the ddname that the application program uses to refer to the data set and MMA.CUSTMAST is the VSAM file name. DISP=SHR means that the data set can be shared by other jobs, provided the options specified when the file was defined allow it. Had I specified DISP=OLD, the file would not be shared regardless of what options were specified when the file was defined.

One DD statement parameter, AMP, applies to VSAM files only. It has a variety of subparameters that can affect how the VSAM file is processed. The CROPS, OPTCD, RECFM, and TRACE subparameters aren't commonly used, so I won't cover them. The SYNAD subparameter is related to assembler-language programming, so I won't cover it here either.

The BUFND, BUFNI, BUFSP, and STRNO subparameters let you override specific options you code when you define a data set using AMS or when you open a data set in an application program. You code these sub-parameters for performance reasons. They are described in greater detail in chapter 7, where I discuss them along with other performance options for VSAM files.

You code the AMORG subparameter to tell OS that you're processing a VSAM file. There are only two cases where you need to specify AMORG. The first is when you specify the UNIT and VOL parameters on a DD statement for a VSAM file. Normally, you shouldn't do that. The second is when you specify DUMMY on the DD statement to process a dummy file.

Catalog considerations

As you know, all VSAM files must be cataloged in a user catalog or the master catalog. Under MVS, the high-level qualifier of a data set name normally indicates the user catalog that owns the file. For example, a file named MMA.CUSTOMER.MASTER.FILE is cataloged in a user catalog indicated by MMA. Since the file name indicates the user catalog, no special coding is required to identify it.

In some cases, the high-level qualifier and the user catalog name are the same. More often, though, the high-level qualifier is an *alias* of the actual name. (An alias is simply an alternate name for a user catalog.) For example, if MMA is an alias for a user catalog named VCAT.MPS800, any file whose high-level qualifier is MMA is cataloged in VCAT.MPS800. And, if DEPT5 is an alias of VCAT.MPS800, any file whose high-level qualifier is DEPT5 is cataloged in that user catalog too. By using aliases, files with different high-level qualifiers can be cataloged in the same user catalog. You'll learn how to assign catalog aliases in chapter 6.

You can override the user catalog indicated by the high-level qualifier by specifying a JOBCAT or STEPCAT DD statement. If you specify a JOBCAT DD statement before the first step in your job, MVS searches the catalog you specify before it uses the high-level qualifier. And if you specify a STEPCAT DD statement within a job step, MVS searches that catalog before it searches the JOBCAT catalog or uses the high-level qualifier. However, it's relatively uncommon to specify a job or step catalog under MVS.

Under OS/VS1, the high-level qualifier of a data-set name is *not* used to identify a user catalog. In that case, you must supply a STEPCAT or JOBCAT DD statement unless your data set is cataloged in the master catalog. For example, suppose you code this statement at the beginning of a job:

```
//JOBCAT   DD   DSN=ACCT.USER.CATALOG,DISP=SHR
```

Then, the user catalog named ACCT.USER.CATALOG is used to locate the VSAM data sets required by the job.

If your job or job step uses data sets from more than one user catalog, you must concatenate the catalogs on the JOBCAT or STEPCAT DD statement, like this:

```
//JOBCAT   DD   DSN=ACCT.USER.CATALOG,DISP=SHR
//         DD   DSN=GROUP2.USER.CATALOG,DISP=SHR
```

Here, the two user catalogs ACCT.USER.CATALOG and GROUP2.USER.CATALOG are searched in that order to locate the VSAM files used by the job.

DOS/VSE JOB CONTROL LANGUAGE FOR VSAM

To code the JCL for jobs that process VSAM files under DOS/VSE, you need to know how to do three things: (1) code a DLBL statement to identify a VSAM catalog, (2) code a DLBL statement to identify a VSAM file, and (3) code an EXEC statement to invoke a program that processes VSAM files.

The DLBL statement for the master catalog

Because the VSAM catalog structure is used to locate VSAM files, you have to include DLBL statements for the catalogs that own the files your jobs use. That's why all jobs that access VSAM files require a DLBL statement for the VSAM master catalog. The name of the master catalog is *IJSYSCT*. As a result, its DLBL statement should look something like this:

```
// DLBL   IJSYSCT,'VSAM.MASTER.CATALOG',,VSAM
```

No EXTENT statement is required.

Because it's a universal requirement for jobs that access VSAM files, this DLBL statement should be stored as a system standard label so you don't have to include it in each job. If it's not, have your systems programmer add the proper DLBL statement to the system start-up job stream that loads the label information area.

Besides the master catalog, you also have to identify the user catalogs that own the VSAM files your job processes. I'll show you how to do that in a moment.

The DLBL statement for VSAM files

```
// DLBL    file-name,'file-id',,VSAM[,BUFSP=n]
                        [,CAT=catalog-name][,DISP=disp]
```

Explanation

file-name   A one- to seven-character name used by the application program to refer to the file.

file-id   A one- to 44-character alphanumeric name that identifies the VSAM file in its catalog. The name you code must be the same as the one specified when the file was defined.

VSAM   Specifies that the file is a VSAM file.

BUFSP = n   Specifies the number of bytes available for VSAM buffers.

catalog-name   Specifies the file-name of a DLBL statement that identifies the catalog that owns the file.

disp   For a reusable file, you can code one of these values in the DISP operand:

                NEW
                (NEW,KEEP)
                (NEW,DELETE)
                (NEW,DATE)
                OLD
                (OLD,KEEP)
                (OLD,DELETE)
                (OLD,DATE)
                (,KEEP)
                (,DELETE)
                (,DATE)

                See the text for details on their effects.

Figure 4-2   The DLBL statement for VSAM files

The DLBL statement for a VSAM file

Figure 4-2 presents the format of the DLBL statement for a VSAM file. The first four operands are the same as in DLBL statements for non-VSAM files. The file-name operand specifies the name the application program uses to refer to the VSAM file. The file-id operand supplies the name (up to 44 characters) given to the cluster when it was defined. The date operand, omitted in figure 4-2, is meaningless for VSAM files, since expiration dates are specified by AMS when a VSAM file is defined. Be sure to code an extra comma, though, to indicate that you've omitted the date operand. Finally, always code VSAM to indicate that the file is a VSAM file. You don't have to indicate whether the file is an ESDS, KSDS, or RRDS.

Following the four positional operands I've just described are three keyword operands you can code in any order: BUFSP, CAT, and DISP. Unlike the first four operands, you code the BUFSP, CAT, and DISP operands only for VSAM files.

The BUFSP operand VSAM uses buffers in virtual storage to transfer data to and from disk. It determines the default buffer size for a file based on control interval size and file type. If you have a good reason to alter a file's default buffer size, you can code the BUFSP operand on its DLBL statement. Code the number of bytes of storage, up to 999999, that should be allocated. If the value you code is less than the file's default buffer size, VSAM ignores your entry and uses the larger default size. You'll learn more about how to select an appropriate buffer size in chapter 7.

The CAT operand You can use the CAT operand to specify what catalog owns the file the DLBL statement describes. The value you code for CAT is the file name of a catalog defined by a preceding DLBL statement.

The usual way to specify a user catalog is to define a *job catalog* in your job stream. A job catalog is a VSAM user catalog that owns the files your job uses (or most of them). To specify a job catalog, you code a DLBL statement with the file name *IJSYSUC*, like this:

```
// DLBL   IJSYSUC,'AR.USER.CATALOG',,VSAM,CAT=IJSYSCT
```

Then, unless you specify otherwise, the system assumes that all subsequent DLBL statements for VSAM files refer to files cataloged in the user catalog identified by the IJSYSUC DLBL statement. You can code CAT=IJSYSUC on the DLBL statements for those files, but you don't have to because DOS uses IJSYSUC by default.

To access a file that's owned by a user catalog other than the job catalog, you must code the CAT operand on its DLBL statement. For that to work, you must have already coded a DLBL statement for the other user catalog using a name other than IJSYSUC. Then, the file name from the DLBL statement for the other catalog must agree with the name you code on the file's DLBL CAT operand.

To illustrate, figure 4-3 shows a job to execute a program named AR9000 that uses four VSAM files called OPNITEM, PDBILL, BADDEBT, and CUSTMAS. Their VSAM names are AR.OPEN.ITEMS, AR.PAID.BILLS, AR.BAD.DEBTS, and CUSTOMER.MASTER.FILE. All files are owned by AR.USER.CATALOG, except CUSTMAS; it's owned by MMA.USER.CATALOG. To identify the user catalogs, I included two DLBL statements. I used AR.USER.CATALOG as the job catalog (IJSYSUC) because it owns three of the four required VSAM files. So, the CAT operand isn't required on the DLBL statements for those files. However,

```
// JOB       AR9000
// DLBL      IJSYSUC,'AR.USER.CATALCG',,VSAM,CAT=IJSYSCT
// DLBL      OPNITEM,'AR.OPEN.ITEMS',,VSAM
// DLBL      PDBILL,'AR.PAID.BILLS',,VSAM
// DLBL      BADDEBT,'AR.BAD.DEBTS',,VSAM
// DLBL      MMACAT,'MMA.USER.CATALOG',,VSAM,CAT=IJSYSCT
// DLBL      CUSTMAS,'CUSTCMER.MASTER.FILE',,VSAM,CAT=MMACAT
// EXEC      AR9000,SIZE=AR9000
/*
/&
```

Figure 4-3	A DOS job stream to run a program that uses four VSAM files from two different catalogs

the DLBL statement for the fourth file, CUSTMAS, does require CAT. The name I coded on the CAT operand is the same as the file name on the DLBL statement for the catalog that owns it (MMACAT).

The DISP operand   You can code the DISP operand of DLBL to specify what's to be done with a reusable file when it's opened and closed. Since most VSAM files aren't reusable, you won't code the DISP operand often. (Under OS, the DISP parameter has a different function; it controls how VSAM files are shared among jobs.)

Figure 4-2 shows the values you can code for the DISP operand. The NEW and OLD options affect how the file is handled when it's opened for output. If you code NEW, the file is reset; the high-used RBA field is set to zero and the previous contents of the file are lost. If you code OLD, however, the file is not reset; its contents are retained.

KEEP, DELETE, and DATE affect how the file is handled when it's closed. KEEP causes the contents of the file to be retained, while DELETE causes the file to be reset. (Note that DELETE doesn't actually delete the file; it just resets the high-used RBA field so the file appears to be empty.) DATE is conditional. If the file's expiration date (specified when the file was defined) hasn't been reached, DATE has the same effect as KEEP. But if the expiration date *has* been reached, the file is reset as if DELETE had been specified.

If you omit the DISP operand on the DLBL statement for a reusable file, DOS uses (OLD,KEEP) by default. That way, no data is lost.

The EXEC statement for programs that access VSAM files

When you invoke a program that uses VSAM, you must insure that there's enough available storage for VSAM to allocate its I/O buffers and control blocks. This storage can be significant: 40K for a catalog, 12K for a KSDS, and 10K for an RRDS or ESDS. VSAM acquires this storage from the partition's GETVIS area. (That's the area of storage within the partition that's not allocated to your program.)

Fortunately, you don't have to calculate VSAM's storage requirements for each program you write. Instead, just specify SIZE=AUTO or SIZE=*phasename* on the EXEC statement, as illustrated in figure 4-3, for each program that processes VSAM files. That way, DOS will allocate as much storage as possible to your partition's GETVIS area. Assuming your partition is large enough, then, VSAM will be able to acquire all of its storage areas.

THE ISAM INTERFACE PROGRAM

If you work in a shop that hasn't completely converted from ISAM to VSAM, it's likely that many of your application programs are still written to process ISAM files. Since reprogramming is one of the greatest expenses in an ISAM to VSAM conversion, it may take years to complete. To make the transition from ISAM to VSAM easier, IBM includes, as part of VSAM under both OS and DOS, an interface program that lets application programs written to process ISAM files access and manipulate VSAM key-sequenced data sets instead. It's called the *ISAM Interface Program*, or *IIP*.

Once you've converted your ISAM files to VSAM using AMS commands or other facilities, all you do to use the ISAM interface is change the JCL. Normally, there are no special JCL implications for the IIP. You just change your JCL streams so that they refer to VSAM data sets instead of ISAM files. When you try to open an ISAM file and the system finds a VSAM file instead, the ISAM Interface Program is automatically invoked.

Under DOS, you replace the ISAM file's DLBL, ASSGN, and EXTENT statements with a DLBL statement in the VSAM format. Under OS, you replace the ISAM DD statements with DD statements that identify the VSAM file. In addition, OS provides some additional options available through the AMP parameter. In some cases, you may need to code one or more of those options. For more information, consult the appropriate manuals for your system.

DISCUSSION

With this background, you should be able to code JCL statements for jobs that use VSAM files. You'll need to do that not only for jobs that invoke application programs that process VSAM files, but also when you code jobs that invoke Access Method Services.

Terminology

alias	IJSYSUC
IJSYSCT	ISAM Interface Program
job catalog	IIP

Objectives

1. (OS users) Code a DD statement to identify a VSAM file.

2. (DOS users) Code the EXEC statement to invoke a program that processes VSAM files and the DLBL statements to identify those files and the catalogs that own them.

Section 2

Access Method Services

In this section, you'll learn how to use AMS, the Access Method Services program. You can use AMS for practically any utility function involving VSAM files, including setting up and maintaining the VSAM environment. So you need to know how to use AMS whether you're a system or application programmer.

There are five chapters in this section. After chapter 5 introduces you to AMS, chapter 6 shows you how to code the AMS commands you're likely to use. Then, chapters 7, 8, and 9 describe performance, recovery, and security considerations that affect the way you code the commands presented in chapter 6.

Chapter 5

How to use Access Method Services

This chapter introduces you to Access Method Services. First, I'll introduce the AMS functional and modal commands this book covers. Then, I'll show you the details of coding AMS commands, including how to code parameters and subparameters, continuation lines, and comments. Next, I'll present three modal commands that affect the way AMS processes the functional commands you code. And finally, I'll show you how to invoke AMS under OS, TSO, DOS, and VM/CMS.

AMS commands

Figure 5-1 is an overview of the AMS commands this book covers. As you can see, the commands fall into two catagories: functional commands and modal commands. *Functional commands* instruct AMS to actually do something, while *modal commands* control the execution of functional commands. Study figure 5-1 for a moment to get an idea of the function each command provides. I'll describe the functional commands in detail in chapters 6 through 9. As for the modal commands, you'll learn how to use them later in this chapter.

	AMS command	Function
Functional commands	ALTER	Changes information specified for a catalog, cluster, alternate index, or path at define time.
	BLDINDEX	Builds an alternate index.
	DEFINE ALTERNATEINDEX	Defines an alternate index.
	DEFINE CLUSTER	Defines a VSAM file, whether it's key-sequenced, entry-sequenced, or relative-record.
	DEFINE MASTERCATALOG	Defines a master catalog.
	DEFINE PATH	Defines the path that relates an alternate index to its base cluster.
	DEFINE USERCATALOG	Defines a user catalog.
	DELETE	Removes a catalog entry for a catalog, cluster, alternate index, or path.
	EXPORT	Produces a transportable file.
	IMPORT	Copies a previously exported file.
	LISTCAT	Lists information about data sets.
	PRINT	Prints the contents of a VSAM or non-VSAM file.
	REPRO	Copies records from one file to another. The input and output files can be VSAM or non-VSAM.
Modal commands	IF	Controls the flow of command execution by testing condition codes returned by functional commands.
	SET	Controls the flow of command execution by altering condition codes returned by functional commands.
	PARM	Sets option values that affect the way AMS executes.

Figure 5-1   AMS commands described in this book

There are other functional commands besides those listed in figure 5-1. I don't cover them in this book, however, either because they don't relate directly to VSAM or they provide obscure functions you aren't likely to use.

How to code AMS commands

Quite frankly, AMS commands have relatively complicated formatting requirements. To begin with, you can code AMS commands anywhere in columns 2 through 72. It's easy to code your commands in column 1 so be sure to avoid that common mistake.

Each AMS command follows this general format:

```
verb  parameters...
```

where *verb* is one of the commands listed in figure 5-1 (DEFINE CLUSTER, LISTCAT, and so on). The *parameters* supply additional information that tells AMS what you want it to do. Figure 5-2 gives five examples of valid ways to code parameters on AMS commands.

Parameters and continuation lines   As you can see, most commands require more than one parameter. To make them easy to read, I coded one parameter per line in the commands in figure 5-2. I suggest you do the same. The hyphens in figure 5-2 are required to continue an AMS command from one line to the next. If you omit the hyphens, AMS will reject your command. In examples 1 and 2, the hyphens are placed after one blank following the end of the parameter. In examples 3 and 4, though, all the hyphens are aligned. How you code the hyphens on your commands is a matter of personal preference. Just be sure there's at least one blank between the end of the parameter and the hyphen.

Most AMS command parameters have one or more abbreviated forms. For example, you can abbreviate RECORDS as REC. And you can code CISZ or CNVSZ instead of CONTROLINTERVALSIZE. Frankly, most of the abbreviations are harder to remember than the full form of the parameter. So I use abbreviations only for long parameters like CONTROLINTER-VALSIZE. As I present each AMS command along with its parameters, I'll include any useful abbreviations.

Parameter values and subparameter lists   Most parameters require that you code a value enclosed in parentheses, like this:

```
RECORDS(500)
```

If a parameter requires more than one value, you code a *subparameter list*, separating each value with spaces or a comma, like this:

```
KEYS(5 0)
```

or

```
ENTRIES(FILE1,FILE2,FILE3,FILE4)
```

Example 1

```
LISTCAT ENTRIES(MMA.CUSTOMER.MASTER.FILE) -
        ALL
```

Example 2

```
DEFINE CLUSTER ( NAME(AR.TRANS) -
                 INDEXED -
                 RECORDSIZE(150 200) -
                 KEYS(12 0) ) -
        DATA   ( NAME(AR.TRANS.DATA) -
                 VOLUMES(VOL261 VOL262) -
                 CYLINDERS(50 50) ) -
        INDEX  ( NAME(AR.TRANS.INDEX) -
                 VOLUMES(VOL271) )
```

Example 3

```
DEFINE CLUSTER ( NAME(AR.TRANS)              -
                 INDEXED                     -
                 RECORDSIZE(150 200)         -
                 KEYS(12 0) )                -
        DATA   ( NAME(AR.TRANS.DATA)         -
                 VOLUMES(VOL261 VOL262)      -
                 CYLINDERS(50 50) )          -
        INDEX  ( NAME(AR.TRANS.INDEX)        -
                 VOLUMES(VOL271) )
```

Example 4

```
/* ACCOUNTS RECEIVABLE TRANSACTION FILE */
DEFINE CLUSTER (
                 NAME(AR.TRANS)              -
                 INDEXED                     -
                 RECORDSIZE(150 200)         -
                 KEYS(12 0)   /* ACCOUNT NO */ -
                 )                           -
        DATA   (                            -
                 NAME(AR.TRANS.DATA)         -
                 VOLUMES(VOL261 VOL262)      -
                 CYLINDERS(50 50)            -
                 )                           -
        INDEX  (                            -
                 NAME(AR.TRANS.INDEX)        -
                 VOLUMES(VOL271)             -
                 )
```

Example 5

```
PRINT MMA.CUSTOMER.MASTER.FILE/MM42JJ81
```

Figure 5-2   Examples of valid AMS commands

In the examples in this book, I separate parameters and subparameters with spaces.

Some parameters allow multiple sets of subparameters, each enclosed in parentheses. For example, consider this parameter:

```
KEYRANGES((0001 4000) (4001 7000) (7001 9999))
```

Here, three sets of subparameters, each consisting of two numbers, are coded within the KEYRANGES parameter. Each set is enclosed in parentheses, and the entire KEYRANGE subparameter list is enclosed in parentheses as well.

Parameter groups and parentheses   Parentheses are often used in AMS commands to delimit groups of parameters. To illustrate, consider example 2 in figure 5-2. Here, the first four parameters—NAME, INDEXED, RECORDSIZE, and KEYS—are grouped together within parentheses. That's a requirement of the DEFINE CLUSTER command. If you omit the parentheses, AMS will reject the command. Following the first group of parameters, you can code two other groups on a DEFINE CLUSTER command, labelled DATA and INDEX. In the example, I coded both, and the parameters coded at both levels are also enclosed within parentheses. Notice that each parameter group ends with two adjacent right parentheses. The first marks the end of the last parameter in the group; the second marks the end of the parameter group itself.

Quite frankly, the use of parentheses in AMS commands is confusing and will probably be the cause of most of your coding errors. To simplify things, some programmers use separate lines for the parentheses that begin and end a group of parameters, as in example 4 of figure 5-2. If that helps you reduce coding errors, by all means do it. For me, it just confuses things even more. The point is, be careful about how you use parentheses in your AMS commands.

Comments   Example 4 also illustrates how you can use *comments* along with AMS commands. A comment begins with the characters /* and ends with */. (If you've programmed in PL/I, you should see the similarity.) Example 4 contains two comments. One is on its own line, before the DEFINE command. The second is within the command, following the KEYS parameter. Notice that the continuation character comes *after* the comment.

Names and passwords   Most AMS commands require that you supply the name of a VSAM object, like a cluster or a catalog. Figure 5-3 gives the rules you must follow when you form a VSAM name. And figure 5-4 shows you how to avoid some common naming errors.

If a VSAM object is password protected, you'll have to supply a one- to eight-character password following the object's name. Example 5 in figure 5-2 shows how you do that. Here, I want to print the contents of a VSAM file named MMA.CUSTOMER.MASTER.FILE. The file's password is MM42JJ81. Notice that you must separate the object's name from its

Length	1 to 44 characters
Characters	The 26 letters (A-Z) The 10 digits (0-9) The 3 national characters (@, # and $) The hyphen (-) The 12-0 overpunch (hex C0)
Segments	VSAM names with more than eight characters must be broken into segments that each contain between one and eight characters. Separate segments from one another with periods.
First character	The first character of a VSAM name and of all segments within a name must be a letter or a national character.
Last character	The last character of a VSAM name may not be a period.

Figure 5-3   Rules for forming VSAM names

Invalid VSAM names

ACCOUNTS.RECEIVABLE.USER.CATALOG
  (Second segment too long.)

AR.TRANS.1984
  (Third segment starts
  with a digit.)

AR.TRANS.MAY + APR.YEAR1984
  (Third segment contains
  an invalid character.)

INVMAST.
  (Name ends with a period.)

ARCHIVE.GL.TRANS.FILE.7
  (Fifth segment starts
  with a digit.)

Valid VSAM names

ACCOUNTS.RECEIVBL.USER.CATALOG

AR.TRANS.YEAR1984
AR.TRANS84

AR.TRANS.APRIL.MAY.YEAR1984
AR.TRANS.APR-84.MAY-84

INVMAST

ARCHIVE.GL.TRANS.FILE.#7
ARCHIVE.GL.TRANS.FILE7
ARCHIVE.GL.TRANS.FILE.NO7

Figure 5-4   Invalid VSAM names with valid alternatives

---

password with a slash. As a result, you shouldn't use passwords that begin with an asterisk; that would require you to code an asterisk following the slash, which AMS interprets as the beginning of a comment. Although there are special coding rules to let you get around that problem, it's best just not to use an asterisk as the first character of a password.

Condition code	Meaning
0	The command executed correctly; no errors were encountered.
4	A minor problem was encountered, but AMS was able to complete the command.
8	A major problem was encountered, but AMS may have completed the command.
12	A major problem was encountered, and AMS couldn't complete the command.
16	A major problem was encountered, and AMS was unable to continue execution. The rest of the commands in the input stream are ignored.

Figure 5-5   Condition codes and their meanings

Modal commands

Access Method Services provides a set of modal commands you can use to control how your functional commands are executed. At the outset, I want you to realize that you probably won't use modal commands in most of the AMS jobs you code. However, there are a few cases in which you can save yourself headaches later on by including one or more of these commands at strategic points in your jobs.

There are three modal commands: IF, SET, and PARM. IF and SET let you control the flow of command execution by testing and altering condition codes returned by functional commands. PARM lets you set option values that affect the way AMS executes. First, I'll describe condition codes and the IF and SET commands. Then, I'll describe the PARM command.

Condition codes   Each AMS functional command issues a *condition code* that tells you whether or not the command was successfully executed. Figure 5-5 lists the condition codes and their meanings. Normally, a command returns a condition code of zero. That means the command executed successfully. Higher codes mean that errors of increasing severity were encountered.

Codes 4 and 8 often result from duplicate or missing file names. For example, if you issue a LISTCAT command for a file that doesn't exist, AMS returns condition code 4. If you try to delete a file that doesn't exist, AMS issues condition code 8. You'll also see warning messages that explain the problem in the AMS output (SYSPRINT on OS systems, SYSLST on DOS).

For condition codes 4 and 8, AMS is often able to complete your command, omitting the parts that caused the problem. For example, suppose a LISTCAT command specifies several files, one of which doesn't exist. In this case, the LISTCAT command will list information for the files that do exist and issue a completion code of 4 because of the one that doesn't.

Condition code 12 is more serious. It typically means you coded the AMS command wrong; you omitted a required parameter, misspelled one, or coded parentheses incorrectly. Because of the error, AMS isn't able to process your command at all.

Whenever AMS issues a condition code of 0, 4, 8, or 12, it issues an appropriate message and then continues processing the job stream. Sometimes, however, an error is so serious that AMS cannot continue. In that case, condition code 16 is issued and the job step is terminated; all remaining AMS commands in the step are ignored.

As it executes, AMS maintains two condition codes: LASTCC and MAXCC. *LASTCC* always represents the condition code issued by the most recently executed AMS command. And *MAXCC* represents the highest condition code returned by any command in the AMS job step. LASTCC changes with each AMS command executed, but MAXCC changes only when a command returns a condition code that's higher than the previous MAXCC.

The IF and SET commands   AMS provides two modal commands that use condition codes: IF and SET. The IF command, shown in figure 5-6, provides conditional processing based on LASTCC or MAXCC. And the SET command, shown in figure 5-7, lets you modify LASTCC or MAXCC at any time.

The Access Method Services manual for your system describes how you can code complex IF-THEN-ELSE sequences with multiple AMS commands within DO-END groups and up to 10 levels of nesting. Quite frankly, I've found few applications that require complex IF commands. As a result, I won't describe those elements in detail here. If you need more detailed information about the IF command, refer to the AMS reference manual for your system.

I have, however, found that I use one sequence of IF and SET commands often:

```
IF LASTCC > 0 THEN SET MAXCC = 16
```

Here, an IF command tests the condition code set by the last functional command. If it's greater than zero, indicating that the command failed, the SET command sets the maximum condition code to 16. That causes AMS to terminate, bypassing the rest of the AMS commands in the input stream. In effect, these two commands conditionally terminate AMS.

Why would you want to terminate AMS like this? Consider figure 5-8. Here, I show part of an AMS job stream for a batch transaction processing system. This job appends a file of daily transactions to a monthly transaction file using a REPRO command. Then, it deletes the daily transaction file. After the REPRO command, I coded an IF command to terminate the job if the REPRO command fails. That way, the daily transaction file won't be deleted if it's not copied to the monthly file properly.

As you can imagine, safeguards like this can be crucial in a production system. In figure 5-8, the REPRO command could fail for a variety of reasons.

The IF command

```
IF   { LASTCC | MAXCC } comparand number
       THEN [ command | command-set ]
     [ ELSE [ command | command-set ] ]
```

Explanation

LASTCC	The condition code set by the previous AMS command.
MAXCC	The highest condition code set by any previous command during this execution of AMS.
comparand	A relational operator, which can be:

EQ or =	Equal to
NE	Not equal to
GT or >	Greater than
LT or <	Less than
GE	Greater than or equal to
LE	Less than or equal to

number	A decimal value to which LASTCC or MAXCC is compared. Although you can code up to 10 digits, any value over 16 is assumed to be 16.
THEN	Specifies a command or group of commands to be executed if the specified condition is true.
ELSE	Specifies a command or group of commands to be executed if the specified condition is false.
command-set	One or more commands preceded by the word DO and followed by the word END.

Figure 5-6　　　　The IF command

For example, a file may be missing, a required volume may not mounted, or an I/O error may occur for either the input or the output file. If the job were allowed to continue under one of those conditions, the original copy of the transaction file would be lost. So I recommend you check condition codes at strategic points in your AMS command streams and terminate the job if necessary.

The PARM command　　　The PARM command, shown in figure 5-9, lets you alter AMS processing options. Frankly, you'll seldom need to do that. Figure 5-9 shows only the PARM command parameters that you're most likely to use. You can refer to the AMS reference manual for your system if you'd like to know more about the PARM command.

The SET command

```
SET    { LASTCC | MAXCC } = number
```

Explanation

LASTCC   The condition code set by the previous AMS command.

MAXCC   The highest condition code set by any previous command during this execution
                of AMS.

number   A decimal value to which LASTCC or MAXCC is set. Although you can code up to
                10 digits, any value over 16 is assumed to be 16. AMS terminates if you set
                LASTCC or MAXCC to 16.

Figure 5-7   The SET command

```
REPRO INDATASET(MMA2.DAILY.TRANS.FILE)        -
      OUTDATASET(MMA2.MONTHLY.TRANS.FILE)
IF LASTCC > 0 THEN SET MAXCC = 16
DELETE MMA2.DAILY.TRANS.FILE
```

Figure 5-8   An IF and SET command to conditionally terminate an AMS job

The PARM command

```
PARM    [ MARGINS(left right) ]
        [ SYNCHK ]
```

Explanation

left   Sets the left margin. When AMS begins, the left margin is set to 2.

right   Sets the right margin. When AMS begins, the right margin is set to 72.

SYNCHK   Specifies that commands are to be checked for correct syntax but not executed
                (DOS/VSE only).

Figure 5-9   The PARM command

The MARGINS option lets you change the default left and right margins for AMS command input. Normally, these defaults are set to 2 and 72. The IBM manual suggests that you might alter these margins to include or exclude comment indicators (/* and */). For example, you might code a LISTCAT command in a production job, marking it as a comment so it's not executed. If you want to occasionally run the job so the LISTCAT command executes, you could redefine the margins so that the comment indicators fall outside them. Then, the LISTCAT command will be executed. Frankly, that's an uncommon requirement. I've never done it, and I doubt that you will either.

The other PARM option, SYNCHK, is available on DOS systems only. It tells AMS to check the syntax of your commands but not to execute them. That way, you can make sure your commands are coded correctly before you execute them. Of course, AMS can't determine if your commands work the way you expect them to. But it can catch misspelled parameters or punctuation errors. This feature can come in handy for critical AMS jobs, where you don't want a missing parenthesis to terminate the job step.

How to invoke AMS

Now that you know how to code AMS commands, you're ready to learn how to code the necessary job control statements or commands to invoke AMS in your particular operating system environment. There are five such environments: OS, TSO, DOS, ICCF, and VM/CMS. Figure 5-10 shows how to invoke AMS under each of these environments.

OS JCL to invoke AMS   Example 1 in figure 5-10 shows the OS (VS1 or MVS) version of a LISTCAT job. Under OS, you specify IDCAMS as the program name in an EXEC statement. Then, you provide two DD statements: SYSPRINT and SYSIN. SYSPRINT directs AMS printed output, and SYSIN identifies the file that contains the AMS control statements. Usually, you'll code the control statements in the job stream, as in this example. When you code control statements in the job stream, be sure to follow them with an end-of-data statement (/*). If the control statements you code require that AMS process a VSAM data set, you may have to provide a DD statement for it too.

AMS under TSO   Example 2 in figure 5-10 shows how you can invoke AMS from a TSO terminal. Here, the lower-case text represents data entered by the terminal operator and the upper-case text is a TSO message. You don't need to enter any specific command to invoke AMS under TSO; TSO recognizes AMS commands and automatically invokes AMS to process them. Notice in this example that I combined the LISTCAT command parameters onto a single line. In a batch job, I recommend that you code each parameter on a separate line. But that just doesn't make sense when you're working at a terminal. If your AMS commands require access to a data set, you'll also have to issue an ALLOCATE command for it before you issue the IDCAMS command.

Example 1: OS

```
//LISTCAT   JOB   ...
//          EXEC  PGM=IDCAMS
//SYSPRINT DD   SYSOUT=A
//SYSIN    DD   *
    LISTCAT ENTRIES(AR.OPEN.ITEMS)          -
           VOLUME
/*
//
```

Example 2: TSO

```
READY
listcat entries(ar.open.items) volume
.
.
.
```

Example 3: DOS

```
// JOB      LISTCAT
// EXEC     IDCAMS,SIZE=AUTO
   LISTCAT ENTRIES(AR.OPEN.ITEMS)           -
           CATALOG(AR.USER.CATALOG)         -
           VOLUME
/*
/&
```

Example 4: ICCF

```
/LOAD IDCAMS
/OPTION GETVIS=AUTO
 LISTCAT ENTRIES(AR.OPEN.ITEMS)             -
         CATALOG(AR.USER.CATALOG)           -
         VOLUME
```

Example 5: VM/CMS

```
CP:
edit listcat amserv
NEW FILE:
EDIT:
input
    listcat entries(ar.open.items)          -
            catalog(ar.user.catalog)        -
            volume
file
CP:
amserv listcat (print
.
.
.
```

Figure 5-10   Invoking AMS under OS, TSO, DOS, ICCF, and VM/CMS

DOS JCL to invoke AMS   Example 3 in figure 5-10 shows how to invoke AMS under DOS. Here, you code an EXEC statement to invoke IDCAMS, followed by AMS commands. (Notice that I coded SIZE = AUTO on the EXEC statement.) After the AMS commands you code an end-of-data statement (/★). If the AMS commands you code actually process a data set, you must also provide a DLBL statement. You'll see examples of when and how to do that later in this book.

AMS under ICCF   If you're using ICCF on a DOS/VSE system, you can invoke AMS for execution in an interactive partition. To do that, you create a member like the one in example 4 of figure 5-10. Here, I coded two job entry statements: the /LOAD statement invokes IDCAMS, and the /OPTION statement specifies GETVIS=AUTO. (That's the same as coding SIZE=AUTO on an EXEC statement in a batch job.) The AMS control statements follow the /OPTION statement. To invoke this job, you enter the /EXEC system command, specifying the name of the ICCF library member that contains the job.

AMS under VM/CMS   If you're using VSAM under VM/CMS, you issue an AMSERV command to invoke AMS, as example 5 in figure 5-10 shows. Again, the lower-case text represents data entered by the terminal operator and the upper-case text is VM/CMS messages. On the AMSERV command, you specify the name of a file that contains the commands you want AMS to process. In figure 5-10, I used the editor to create a file named LISTCAT that contains the LISTCAT command I want to process. The (PRINT option tells AMS to direct its printed output to a printer.

Terminology

functional command
modal command
verb
parameter
subparameter list
comment
condition code
LASTCC
MAXCC

Objectives

1. List and briefly state the function of the AMS functional commands covered in this book.

2. Given several AMS commands, indicate whether they are coded correctly or incorrectly. For the ones coded incorrectly, make appropriate corrections.

3. Code an IF and SET command to terminate AMS conditionally.

4. Code the JCL or commands necessary to invoke AMS in your operating environment.

Chapter 6

Basic AMS commands

In the four topics of this chapter, you'll learn how to code basic AMS commands to define and manipulate VSAM objects. Topic 1 shows you how to define VSAM and ICF catalogs, catalog aliases, and VSAM data spaces. Then, topic 2 presents the DEFINE CLUSTER command to define VSAM data sets. In topic 3, you'll learn how to use AMS commands for alternate indexes. Finally, topic 4 shows you how to use a variety of other AMS commands for basic utility functions like copying and printing data sets.

As you read the topics in this chapter, you'll realize that I've deferred describing many of the advanced parameters for the commands covered here. That's because I want you first to learn how to use the basic forms of each AMS command. Then, in later chapters, I'll show you how to use additional parameters and commands that affect performance (chapter 7), recovery (chapter 8), and security (chapter 9).

■ □ □ □   ## Topic 1 How to define catalogs and space

In this topic, you'll learn how to use three AMS commands—DEFINE USERCATALOG, DEFINE ALIAS, and DEFINE SPACE—to define VSAM and ICF catalogs, aliases, and data space. These commands are generally used only by system programmers, so you may never find occasion to use them if you're an application programmer. If that's the case, feel free to skip this topic.

This topic is divided into two sections. The first shows you how to define a VSAM user catalog, a catalog alias, and a VSAM data space. The second shows you how to define an ICF catalog.

HOW TO DEFINE A VSAM CATALOG, ALIAS, AND SPACE

To define a user catalog, catalog alias, and space under standard VSAM (not ICF), you use three commands: DEFINE USERCATALOG, DEFINE ALIAS, and DEFINE SPACE.

The DEFINE USERCATALOG command

To define a VSAM user catalog, you invoke AMS and supply a DEFINE USERCATALOG command, shown in figure 6-1. By the way, to define a master catalog, you use the DEFINE MASTERCATALOG command, which is much like the DEFINE USERCATALOG command. Since each installation has just one master catalog, you're unlikely to ever use it.

As you can see in figure 6-1, the DEFINE USERCATALOG command has two sets of parameters. The first parameter set is coded in parentheses after the word USERCATALOG. Because they apply to the entire catalog, parameters you code there are called catalog-level parameters.

The second parameter set is coded in parentheses after the word DATA. The parameters you code there apply only to the catalog's data component. (Remember that a catalog is a special kind of key-sequenced data set with index and data components.) You can also code an INDEX parameter set to specify options that affect only the catalog's index component, but there's seldom reason to do that.

You code the last parameter in figure 6-1, CATALOG, to identify the master catalog. The CATALOG parameter doesn't belong to the catalog or DATA parameter sets; it stands by itself. You must code the CATALOG parameter when you define a user catalog if the master catalog is password protected, which it usually is.

Catalog-level parameters   At the catalog level, you must specify at least three parameters: NAME, VOLUME, and an allocation parameter. In

The DEFINE USERCATALOG command for VSAM catalogs

```
DEFINE USERCATALOG (     NAME(entry-name)

                         VOLUME(vol-ser)

                    [ OWNER(owner-id) ]

                    [ FOR(days) | TO(date) ]

                        ⎧CYLINDERS⎫
                    [   ⎨TRACKS   ⎬  (primary [secondary]) ]
                        ⎪BLOCKS   ⎪
                        ⎩RECORDS  ⎭

                    [ DEDICATE ]

                    [ ORIGIN(location) ]  )

                             ⎧CYLINDERS⎫
     [ DATA      ( [         ⎨TRACKS   ⎬  (primary [secondary]) ] )  ]
                             ⎪BLOCKS   ⎪
                             ⎩RECORDS  ⎭

     [ CATALOG(name[/password]) ]
```

Explanation

NAME(entry-name)	Required. Specifies the name of the catalog.
VOLUME(vol-ser)	Required. Identifies the volume which will contain the catalog.
OWNER(owner-id)	Optional. Specifies a one- to eight-character owner-id for the catalog.
FOR(days) TO(date)	Optional. Specifies a retention period (in the format dddd) or an expiration date (in the format yyddd) for the catalog.
primary	Required. Specifies how much space to allocate initially to the catalog or component, expressed in cylinders, tracks, records, or blocks.
secondary	Optional. Specifies the secondary space allocation. Ignored under DOS.
DEDICATE	Optional. Specifies that all available space on the volume should be allocated to the catalog and its space. (DOS only)
ORIGIN(location)	Optional. Identifies the starting point for the catalog space. Specify a relative track number (CKD devices) or a relative block number (FBA devices). (DOS only)
CATALOG(name[/password])	Optional. Specifies the name and password of the master catalog. Required to define a user catalog if the master catalog is password protected.

Figure 6-1   The DEFINE USERCATALOG command for VSAM catalogs

addition, you can code the OWNER parameter and either the FOR or TO parameter. I'll describe each of those parameters except the allocation parameter now. I'll describe the allocation parameter in a moment.

The NAME parameter supplies the name for the catalog. For example,

```
NAME(AR.USER.CATALOG)
```

specifies that the name of the catalog will be AR.USER.CATALOG.

The VOLUME parameter identifies the volume serial number of the DASD volume that will contain the catalog. For example,

```
VOLUME(VOL500)
```

tells AMS to put the catalog on VOL500.

The OWNER parameter supplies a one- to eight-character value that indicates who's responsible for the catalog. Typically, the owner-id is the user-id of the system programmer who defined the catalog. Or, it's a code that represents an application or group of applications.

The FOR and TO parameters indicate how long the catalog should be retained. If you omit both of these parameters, the catalog can be deleted at any time. If you code FOR, the value you code is the number of days (from 0 to 9999) the catalog should be retained. If you code TO, the value you specify is an expiration date in the form yyddd, where yy is the year (00-99) and ddd is the day (001-366).

Allocating space to a catalog   To specify how much space to allocate to a catalog, you code an allocation parameter using the format:

```
allocation-unit (primary secondary)
```

where allocation-unit can be CYLINDERS, TRACKS, RECORDS, or BLOCKS. Primary specifies the number of allocation units initially assigned to the catalog, and secondary specifies the size of any required secondary extents (OS systems only). For example, if you code

```
TRACKS(60 15)
```

VSAM initially allocates 60 tracks of DASD space to the catalog. Then, if the catalog grows beyond that initial allocation, secondary extents of 15 tracks each are allocated.

For CKD devices, VSAM always allocates catalog space in terms of tracks, whether you code TRACKS, CYLINDERS, or RECORDS. In other words, if you code CYLINDERS or RECORDS, VSAM converts the value you specify for primary and secondary space to an equivalent number of tracks. In addition, VSAM rounds the amount of space you specify down to the nearest control area boundary. For 3330, 3350, 3375, and 3380 devices, catalog control areas are always three tracks each. So, for these devices, VSAM rounds the track allocation down to the nearest multiple of three. For 3340 devices, control areas are five tracks each, so VSAM rounds the track allocation down to

Device	Records/CA
3330	40
3340	48
3350	54
3375	80
3380	92

Figure 6-2   Catalog control area capacity of various DASD units

the nearest multiple of five. As a result, I suggest that you specify TRACKS as the allocation unit and use a multiple of three or five (depending on the device) for both primary and secondary space.

For FBA devices under DOS, you can specify RECORDS or BLOCKS. Both have the same effect. VSAM rounds your allocation down to the nearest control area just as it does for CKD devices. For 3310s, the control areas are 96 blocks each. For 3370s, the control areas are 186 blocks each.

Quite frankly, it's difficult to calculate the exact amount of space a catalog will require. But you can make a rough estimate easily enough. First, determine how many records your catalog will contain. Figure three records for each key-sequenced data set or alternate index; add another record if the alternate index is upgradable. Figure two catalog records for each entry-sequenced or relative-record data set, and one for each path, space, and volume. Because the catalog will contain additional records for other types of records, add a generous amount to your estimate.

Once you've determined how many catalog records you need, use the table in figure 6-2 to see how many control areas the catalog's low-keyrange data component will require. For example, if your catalog will contain 1,000 records and will reside on a 3350, you'll need 19 control areas (1,000/54) for the low-keyrange data component. To allow for the high-keyrange data component and the index component, multiply the low-keyrange data component size by 1.12 and round the result up. So, for the 1,000-record catalog on a 3350, the total space allocation should be 22 control areas (19 × 1.12). Finally, to determine how many tracks to allocate to the catalog, multiply the number of control areas you need by the number of tracks per catalog control area (three or five, depending on the device type). So, for the 1,000-record catalog on a 3350, the total space allocation should be 66 tracks (22 × 3).

The technique I just described for calculating catalog space requirements is approximate. It doesn't take into account all of the types of entries your catalog might contain, and it doesn't consider all of the factors that might affect the size of the high-keyrange data component or the index component. In most cases, though, I think this technique will give you a good estimation of your catalog's space requirements. If you need a more exact estimate, the IBM manual for your system contains a detailed worksheet you can use.

Under DOS, the ORIGIN parameter lets you control where VSAM locates the catalog. If you omit the ORIGIN parameter, VSAM searches for the first disk extent that's large enough to contain your catalog. If you code the

ORIGIN parameter, however, VSAM uses the disk address you specify as the starting point for the catalog extent. For CKD devices, code a relative track number; for FBA devices, code a relative block number.

Suballocating a catalog space   If you code an allocation parameter only at the catalog level, the catalog is created as a unique file; it occupies its own data space. The amount of space you specify is allocated to that data space, and the user catalog fills it. However, if you code an allocation parameter at both the catalog level *and* the DATA level, the catalog is suballocated out of a data space whose size is specified in the allocation parameter you code at the catalog level. The size of the catalog itself is taken from the allocation parameter at the DATA level. Any space remaining can be used for additional VSAM files or to extend the catalog if necessary.

On OS systems, you'll usually define user catalogs in unique space. Under DOS, however, unique files, including catalogs, cannot be extended. So on DOS systems, it's a good idea to suballocate user catalogs out of VSAM data space. That way, secondary extents can be allocated to the catalog if necessary.

Under DOS, you can code the DEDICATE parameter at the catalog level to tell VSAM to acquire as much space on the DASD volume as possible for the catalog's data space. VSAM will allocate up to 16 extents for the space, acquiring the entire volume if possible. Then, the catalog will be allocated from this space. Using DEDICATE is a good way to reserve an entire DASD volume for VSAM files.

Because DEDICATE allocates a maximum of 16 extents, I suggest you use the LVTOC utility to list the volume's VTOC before you define the catalog. Then, you can examine the free extents on the volume. If there are 16 or fewer, all of the free space on the volume will be allocated to VSAM. If there are more than 16 free extents, however, only the first 16 will be allocated.

If you code the DEDICATE parameter, you'll want to code an allocation parameter at the DATA level. If you don't, VSAM will allocate the smallest possible catalog for you. For most devices, that allows just two tracks for catalog records, hardly enough for any serious usage.

DEFINE USERCATALOG examples   Figures 6-3, 6-4, and 6-5 show three examples of the DEFINE USERCATALOG command. The top part of each figure shows a DEFINE USERCATALOG command, and the bottom part shows how the command allocates space on the volume. For each of the examples, you can use the standard JCL statements required to invoke AMS, as described in chapter 5.

The top part of figure 6-3 shows a simple DEFINE USERCATALOG command that defines a catalog named AR.USER.CATALOG on a volume named VOL400. Here, the catalog's primary allocation is 60 tracks, with secondary extents allocated 15 tracks at a time. I coded the CATALOG parameter so I could supply the master catalog's password. (Of course, XXXXXXXX is an unlikely master catalog password.) The bottom part of the figure shows how the 60-track catalog might be allocated on VOL400.

Command

```
DEFINE USERCATALOG ( NAME(AR.USER.CATALOG)           -
                     VOLUME(VOL400)                  -
                     TRACKS(60 15) )                 -
          CATALOG(VSAM.MASTER.CATALOG/XXXXXXXX)
```

Resulting allocation

Volume VOL400

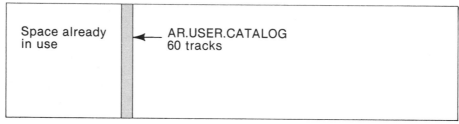

Figure 6-3   Defining a user catalog in a unique space

Command

```
DEFINE USERCATALOG ( NAME(AR.USER.CATALOG)           -
                     VOLUME(VOL400)                  -
                     CYLINDERS(200 20) )             -
          DATA       ( TRACKS(60 15) )              -
          CATALOG(VSAM.MASTER.CATALOG/XXXXXXXX)
```

Resulting allocation

Volume VOL400

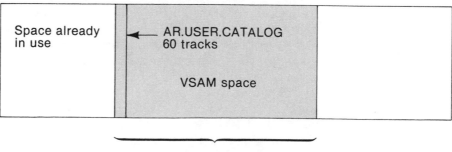

Figure 6-4   Defining a user catalog in suballocated space

Command

```
DEFINE USERCATALOG ( NAME(AR.USER.CATALOG)         -
                     VOLUME(VOL400)                -
                     DEDICATE )                    -
        DATA       ( TRACKS(60 15) )               -
        CATALOG(VSAM.MASTER.CATALOG/XXXXXXXX)
```

Resulting allocation

Volume VOL400

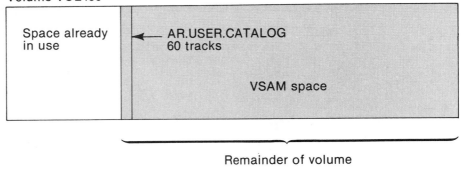

Figure 6-5   Defining a user catalog in dedicated suballocated space (DOS only)

Figure 6-4 shows how to create a suballocated catalog. Here, the data space created on volume VOL400 is initially 200 cylinders, extendable in 20 cylinder units. The allocation for the user catalog itself is the same as in figure 6-3: 60 tracks primary, 15 tracks secondary. In the bottom part of the figure, you can see that the total size of the allocated data space is 200 cylinders; the 60-track catalog is allocated out of that space.

Figure 6-5 shows how to use the DEDICATE parameter under DOS. Here, VSAM acquires as much space as possible (up to 16 extents on the volume). The 60-track catalog is allocated from that space.

The DEFINE ALIAS command

On OS systems, it's common to assign alternate names, or aliases, to user catalogs. To do that, you use the DEFINE ALIAS command, shown in figure 6-6. The DEFINE ALIAS command has three parameters: NAME, RELATE, and CATALOG. NAME supplies the name for the alias you're creating. RELATE supplies the name of an existing user catalog for which you wish to create an alias. And CATALOG identifies the master catalog and its password.

The DEFINE ALIAS command

```
DEFINE ALIAS ( NAME(entry-name)

             RELATE(entry-name[/password]) )

   [ CATALOG(name[/password]) ]
```

Explanation

NAME(entry-name)	Required. Specifies the name of the alias to be created.
RELATE(entry-name[/password])	Required. Specifies the name and password of an existing catalog with which the alias name is to be associated.
CATALOG(name[/password])	Optional. Specifies the name and password of the master catalog. Required only if the master catalog is password protected.

Figure 6-6   The DEFINE ALIAS command (OS only)

To illustrate how to define an alias, consider this command:

```
DEFINE ALIAS ( NAME(AR)                            -
               RELATE(AR.USER.CATALOG) )           -
       CATALOG(VSAM.MASTER.CATALOG/XXXXXXXX)
```

Here, AR is defined as an alias for an existing user catalog named AR.USER.CATALOG. As a result, AR can be used as the high-level qualifier for data sets cataloged in AR.USER.CATALOG.

There's no limit to the number of aliases you can create for a particular user catalog. For example, you could issue another DEFINE ALIAS command like this:

```
DEFINE ALIAS ( NAME(BILLING)                       -
               RELATE(AR.USER.CATALOG) )           -
       CATALOG(VSAM.MASTER.CATALOG/XXXXXXXX)
```

Then, files that use BILLING as their high-level qualifier are cataloged in AR.USER.CATALOG too.

The DEFINE SPACE command

To create VSAM data space, you use the DEFINE SPACE command, shown in figure 6-7. On it, you must specify two things: the name of the volume(s) on which the space is allocated and the amount of space to be allocated. If you want the space to be owned by a catalog other than the job or step catalog (if one is in effect), you should also code the CATALOG parameter.

The DEFINE SPACE command

```
DEFINE SPACE (    VOLUMES(vol-ser...)

            ⎧ CYLINDERS ⎫
        [   ⎨ TRACKS    ⎬   (primary [secondary]) ]
            ⎪ BLOCKS    ⎪
            ⎩ RECORDS   ⎭

        [ RECORDSIZE(avg max) ]

        [ DEDICATE | CANDIDATE ]

        [ ORIGIN(location) ] )

    [ CATALOG(name[/password]) ]
```

Explanation

VOLUMES(vol-ser...)	Required. Specifies one or more volumes on which space is to be defined.
primary	Required. Specifies how much DASD space to allocate initially to the space, expressed in cylinders, tracks, blocks, or records.
secondary	Optional. Specifies the secondary space allocation for the space. Ignored under DOS.
DEDICATE	Optional. Specifies that all available space on the volume should be allocated to the space. If you code DEDICATE, don't code a primary/secondary allocation. (DOS only)
CANDIDATE	Optional. Specifies that no space is allocated on the volume, but the volume is marked as owned by the defining catalog. If you code CANDIDATE, don't code a primary/secondary allocation.
RECORDSIZE(avg max)	Optional. Required only if RECORDS is specified as the allocation unit. Identifies the average and maximum record length used to determine how much space to allocate.
ORIGIN(location)	Optional. Identifies the starting point for the space. Specify a relative track number (CKD devices) or a relative block number (FBA devices). (DOS only)
CATALOG(name[/password])	Optional. Specifies the name of the catalog that will contain the space, and, if necessary, the catalog's password. If omitted, the jobcat or stepcat is used.

Figure 6-7   The DEFINE SPACE command

Figure 6-8 shows four examples of the DEFINE SPACE command. Again, you can use the standard JCL statements presented in chapter 5 to invoke AMS for these jobs. No additional DD or DLBL statements are required.

Example 1

```
DEFINE SPACE ( VOLUMES(VOL400)                    -
               CYLINDERS(200 20) )                -
        CATALOG(AR.USER.CATALOG)
```

Example 2

```
DEFINE SPACE ( VOLUMES(VOL400 VOL500)             -
               CYLINDERS(200 20) )                -
        CATALOG(AR.USER.CATALOG)
```

Example 3

```
DEFINE SPACE ( VOLUMES(VOL400 VOL500)             -
               CANDIDATE )                        -
        CATALOG(AR.USER.CATALOG)
```

Example 4 (DOS only)

```
DEFINE SPACE ( VOLUMES(VOL400)                    -
               DEDICATE )                         -
        CATALOG(AR.USER.CATALOG)
```

Figure 6-8   Examples of the DEFINE SPACE command

In example 1, a 200 cylinder space is created on a volume named VOL400. The secondary allocation is 20 cylinders. And the space will be owned by AR.USER.CATALOG.

Although you can specify TRACKS or RECORDS as the allocation unit when you define a space on a CKD device, I recommend you always specify CYLINDERS. Unless your allocation is less than one cylinder, VSAM allocates space in units of whole cylinders, rounding your TRACKS or RECORDS specification up if necessary. I think it's just as easy to specify CYLINDERS in the first place.

On OS systems, the secondary quantity you specify is used to allocate up to 15 secondary extents if necessary. On DOS systems, you can code a secondary quantity if you wish, but the space can't be extended. The value you code is stored in the catalog for compatibility with OS systems.

Example 2 in figure 6-8 shows how to define space on two volumes at once. Here, the primary space allocation is 200 cylinders, and the secondary allocation is 20 cylinders. In the VOLUMES parameter, I listed two volumes: VOL400 and VOL500. Space is allocated on both volumes using the primary amount. In other words, this command allocates two data spaces: a 200-cylinder space on VOL400, and a 200-cylinder space on VOL500.

Example 3 in figure 6-8 shows how you can use the CANDIDATE parameter rather than an allocation parameter to indicate that the specified volume (or, in this case, volumes) should be reserved for use by a particular catalog, even though no space is yet defined on the volume. The volume is then called a *candidate volume*; only the catalog that owns the volume can own VSAM space on it.

Example 4 shows how you can use the DEDICATE parameter on a DEFINE SPACE command to reserve an entire DOS volume for VSAM's use. Here, as much of VOL400 as possible (up to 16 extents) is allocated as VSAM data space. Before you issue a DEFINE SPACE command with the DEDICATE parameter, it's a good idea to run an LVTOC job to list the volume's VTOC. Then, you can see if the volume contains more than 16 free extents.

HOW TO DEFINE AN ICF CATALOG

Because of their different structure, ICF catalogs are defined differently than VSAM catalogs. Here, I'll describe how you create a Basic Catalog Structure (BCS) and a VSAM Volume Data Set (VVDS). You create an alias for an ICF catalog using the DEFINE ALIAS command, just as for a VSAM catalog. As for the DEFINE SPACE command, you don't use it under ICF because ICF doesn't support VSAM data space.

How to define a Basic Catalog Structure

To define a Basic Catalog Structure, you issue a DEFINE USERCATALOG command using a format that's different from the one you use for VSAM catalogs. Figure 6-9 shows the format of the DEFINE USERCATALOG command as you use it for ICF. To specify that you're defining an ICF catalog rather than a VSAM catalog, you must code ICFCATALOG.

Because a BCS is a standard key-sequenced data set, without the unusual structure of a VSAM catalog, the DEFINE USERCATALOG command for ICF catalogs is similar to the DEFINE CLUSTER command. In fact, I've omitted many parameters in figure 6-9 that are identical to DEFINE CLUSTER options you'll learn about in the next topic and in chapters 7 and 9. For example, you can specify free space or indexing options for an ICF catalog in the same way you can for a key-sequenced data set.

Rather than describe all of the parameters in figure 6-9, I'll describe just the allocation parameter since it's the one that's most likely to confuse you. The first point I want you to understand is this: because ICF doesn't use VSAM data space, the allocation parameter here is *not* used to create a suballocatable data space for a catalog, as it can be when you define a VSAM catalog. Instead, how you code the allocation parameter for an ICF catalog

The DEFINE USERCATALOG command for ICF catalogs

```
DEFINE USERCATALOG (    NAME(entry-name)

                        ICFCATALOG

                      [ VOLUMES(vol-ser...) ]

                      [ OWNER(owner-id) ]

                      [ FOR(days) | TO(date) ]
                        ⎧CYLINDERS⎫
                      [ ⎨TRACKS   ⎬ (primary [secondary]) ]
                        ⎪BLOCKS   ⎪
                        ⎩RECORDS  ⎭

                      [ RECORDSIZE (avg max) ] )
       [ DATA       ( [ VOLUMES(vol-ser...) ]
                        ⎧CYLINDERS⎫
                      [ ⎨TRACKS   ⎬ (primary [secondary]) ]
                        ⎪BLOCKS   ⎪
                        ⎩RECORDS  ⎭

                      [ RECORDSIZE(avg max) ] ) ]
       [ INDEX      ( [ VOLUMES(vol-ser...) ]
                        ⎧CYLINDERS⎫
                      [ ⎨TRACKS   ⎬ (primary) ] ) ]
                        ⎪BLOCKS   ⎪
                        ⎩RECORDS  ⎭

    [ CATALOG(name[/password]) ]
```

Figure 6-9   The DEFINE USERCATALOG command for ICF catalogs (part 1 of 2)

affects how DASD space is allocated to the catalog as a whole or to its individual data and index components.

You can code the allocation parameter at three levels: catalog, DATA, and INDEX. If you code it only at the catalog level, the amount of space you allocate applies to the entire catalog. VSAM determines how to divide that space between the catalog's data and index components.

If you code an allocation parameter at both the catalog and the DATA levels, the amount you specify at the catalog level is ignored. (You can't omit it, though, because the command's syntax requires an allocation parameter at the catalog level.) The entire amount you specify at the data level is used for the catalog's data component. VSAM determines how large the index component will be, and allocates an additional amount of DASD space for the index component.

You can also code an allocation parameter at the INDEX level to tell VSAM how much space to allocate to the catalog's index component.

Explanation

NAME(entry-name)	Required. Specifies the name of the catalog.
ICFCATALOG	Required. Distinguishes the command from a DEFINE USER-CATALOG command for a VSAM catalog.
VOLUMES(vol-ser...)	Required. Specifies one or more volumes that will contain the catalog or component.
OWNER(owner-id)	Optional. Specifies a one- to eight-character owner-id for the catalog.
FOR(days) TO(date)	Optional. Specifies a retention period (in the format dddd) or an expiration date (in the format yyddd) for the catalog.
primary	Required. Specifies how much space to initially allocate to the catalog, data, or index component, expressed in cylinders, tracks, records, or blocks.
secondary	Optional. Specifies the secondary space allocation for the catalog or data component.
RECORDSIZE(avg max)	Optional. Specifies the average and maximum length of the catalog's records. If omitted, (4086 32400) is assumed. The smallest value you can specify for the maximum record size is 4086.
CATALOG(name[/password])	Optional. Specifies the master catalog and its password.

Figure 6-9   The DEFINE USERCATALOG command for ICF catalogs (part 2 of 2)

```
DEFINE USERCATALOG ( NAME(AR.USER.CATALOG)      -
                     ICFCATALOG                 -
                     VOLUMES(VOL400)            -
                     CYLINDERS(5 1) )           -
              DATA   ( CYLINDERS(5 1) )          -
              INDEX  ( TRACKS(1) )
```

Figure 6-10   Defining an ICF user catalog

Normally, one track of primary space is enough for the index component. Notice that you can't specify a secondary amount at the INDEX level.

Figure 6-10 shows an example of a DEFINE USERCATALOG command to create a BCS. Here, I specified the allocation parameter at the DATA level, providing five cylinders of primary space and one cylinder of secondary space. At the INDEX level, I allocated one track to the index component.

How to define a VSAM Volume Data Set

There are two ways to define a VSAM Volume Data Set: implicitly or explicitly. A VVDS is implicitly defined whenever you define a VSAM data set on a volume that doesn't already contain a VVDS. In that case, VSAM automatically creates a VVDS using default values for space allocation and other attributes of the VVDS.

To define a VVDS explicitly, you issue a DEFINE CLUSTER command, which you'll learn about in the next topic. To tell VSAM you're defining a VVDS, you code the file's name in a special format: SYS1.VVDS.Vvolser, where *volser* is the serial number of the volume on which the VVDS will reside. For example, the VVDS for a volume named VOL400 is SYS1.VVDS.VVOL400. The only reason you would want to explicitly define a VVDS is to override the space allocation given to an implicitly defined VVDS. In most cases, that's not necessary.

Terminology

candidate volume

Objective

Given specifications for a VSAM or ICF user catalog, a catalog alias, or a VSAM data space, code an AMS job to define it.

■ ■ □ □   ## Topic 2   The DEFINE CLUSTER command

In this topic, you'll learn how to use the DEFINE CLUSTER command to define a VSAM key-sequenced, entry-sequenced, or relative-record data set. Before I begin, I want you to realize that this topic presents only a subset of the complete DEFINE CLUSTER command. In chapters 7 and 9, you'll learn about other DEFINE CLUSTER parameters that affect performance and security.

Figure 6-11 is a partial format of the DEFINE CLUSTER command. As you can see, the command consists of three sets of parameters, labeled CLUSTER, DATA, and INDEX; the CATALOG parameter stands by itself. Parameters you code at the CLUSTER level apply to the entire cluster. Parameters you code at the DATA or INDEX level apply only to the cluster's data or index component. Although you can code many of the DEFINE CLUSTER command's parameters at the CLUSTER, DATA, or INDEX level, I recommend you code most of the parameters I describe in this topic at the CLUSTER level. As I describe the parameters, I'll point out which ones you should code at the DATA and INDEX levels.

Quite frankly, the syntax of the DEFINE CLUSTER command is confusing. To help you understand it, figure 6-12 shows three examples of the DEFINE CLUSTER command. The first example defines a key-sequenced data set. Here, I coded parameters at the CLUSTER, DATA, and INDEX levels. The second and third examples define an entry-sequenced and a relative-record data set. Because those data sets don't have an index component, these commands have parameters at only the CLUSTER and DATA levels. As I describe the individual parameters of the DEFINE CLUSTER command, I'll refer to both the syntax diagram in figure 6-11 and the three examples in figure 6-12.

PARAMETERS THAT IDENTIFY THE FILE

Three of the DEFINE CLUSTER parameters listed in figure 6-11 simply identify the file you're defining by supplying its name (NAME), who's responsible for it (OWNER), and what catalog will own it (CATALOG).

The NAME parameter

The NAME parameter lets you supply a name for your file. The name you specify must follow the VSAM naming rules I described in chapter 5. When you code a value for the NAME parameter at the CLUSTER level, that name applies only to the cluster entry. Then, if you don't specify otherwise, VSAM creates a name for the data component (and, for a KSDS, for the index component) that's long and cryptic. As a result, I suggest you code the NAME parameter at all levels of your DEFINE CLUSTER command: CLUSTER, DATA, and, for a KSDS, INDEX. That way, you'll be able to identify

The DEFINE CLUSTER command

```
DEFINE CLUSTER (   NAME(entry-name)

               [ OWNER(owner-id) ]

               [ FOR(days) | TO(date) ]

               [ INDEXED | NONINDEXED | NUMBERED ]

               [ RECORDSIZE(avg max) ]

               [ SPANNED | NONSPANNED ]

               [ KEYS(length offset) ]

               [ REUSE | NOREUSE ]

               [ VOLUMES(vol-ser...) ]

                 ⎧CYLINDERS⎫
               [ ⎨TRACKS   ⎬ (primary [secondary]) ]
                 ⎪BLOCKS   ⎪
                 ⎩RECORDS  ⎭

               [ UNIQUE | SUBALLOCATION ]

               [ FILE(ddname) ]

               [ SHAREOPTIONS(a b) ]

               [ MODEL(entry-name[/password]) ]   )

   [ DATA    ( [ NAME(entry-name) ]

               [ VOLUMES(vol-ser...) ]

                 ⎧CYLINDERS⎫
               [ ⎨TRACKS   ⎬ (primary [secondary]) ] ) ]
                 ⎪BLOCKS   ⎪
                 ⎩RECORDS  ⎭

   [ INDEX   ( [ NAME(entry-name) ]

               [ VOLUMES(vol-ser...) ]

                 ⎧CYLINDERS⎫
               [ ⎨TRACKS   ⎬ (primary [secondary]) ] ) ]
                 ⎪BLOCKS   ⎪
                 ⎩RECORDS  ⎭

   [ CATALOG(name[/password]) ]
```

Figure 6-11   The DEFINE CLUSTER command: basic parameters (part 1 of 2)

individual components in LISTCAT output listings. And, for unique files, the names you code at the DATA and INDEX levels will appear in the volume's VTOC entries for the file. In figure 6-12, you can see that I coded a NAME parameter at each level of all three DEFINE CLUSTER commands. To form the data and index component names, I suggest you add DATA and INDEX to the cluster name, as I did in figure 6-12.

Explanation

NAME(entry-name)	Required. Specifies the name of the cluster or component.
OWNER(owner-id)	Optional. Specifies a one- to eight-character owner-id for the file.
FOR(days) TO(date)	Optional. Specifies a retention period (in the format dddd) or an expiration date (in the format yyddd) for the file.
INDEXED NONINDEXED NUMBERED	Optional. Specifies whether you're defining a KSDS (INDEXED), ESDS (NONINDEXED), or RRDS (NUMBERED) file. INDEXED is the default. Valid at the cluster level only.
RECORDSIZE(avg max)	Optional. Specifies the average and maximum length of the file's records. If omitted, (4089 4089) is assumed for nonspanned records; (4086 32600) is assumed for spanned records.
SPANNED NONSPANNED	Optional. Specifies whether logical records can span control intervals. NONSPANNED is the default.
KEYS(length offset)	Optional. Specifies, for a KSDS, the length and offset of the primary key.
REUSE NOREUSE	Optional. Specifies whether a file is reusable. NOREUSE is the default.
VOLUMES(vol-ser...)	Required. Specifies one or more volumes that will contain the cluster or component.
primary	Required. Specifies how much space to allocate initially to the cluster or component, expressed in cylinders, tracks, records, or blocks.
secondary	Optional. Specifies the secondary space allocation for the cluster. Ignored for unique files under DOS.
UNIQUE SUBALLOCATION	Optional. Specifies whether the file is unique (occupies its own data space) or suballocated (shares space with other files). SUBALLOCATION is the default.
FILE(ddname)	Optional. Specifies the ddname of a DD statement that allocates the volume. For OS, required only if volume is not permanantly mounted.
SHAREOPTIONS(a b)	Optional. Specifies how the file may be shared among regions (a) and among systems (b). See figure 6-17 for the values you can code for a and b.
MODEL(entry-name[/password])	Optional. Specifies the name of an existing cluster on which this cluster is to be modeled.
CATALOG(name[/password])	Specifies the name and password of the catalog that will own the cluster. If omitted, the stepcat, jobcat, master catalog, or high-level qualifier (MVS only) of the cluster name identifies the catalog.

Figure 6-11   The DEFINE CLUSTER command: basic parameters (part 2 of 2)

Example 1:   Define a key-sequenced data set

```
DEFINE CLUSTER ( NAME(MMA2.CUSTOMER.MASTER)              -
                 OWNER(DLOWE2)                           -
                 INDEXED                                 -
                 RECORDSIZE(200 200)                     -
                 KEYS(6 0)                               -
                 VOLUMES(MPS800)                         -
                 UNIQUE )                                -
        DATA   ( NAME(MMA2.CUSTOMER.MASTER.DATA)         -
                 CYLINDERS(50 5) )                       -
        INDEX  ( NAME(MMA2.CUSTOMER.MASTER.INDEX) )
```

Example 2:   Define an entry-sequenced data set

```
DEFINE CLUSTER ( NAME(MMA2.AR.TRAN)                      -
                 OWNER(DLOWE2)                           -
                 NONINDEXED                              -
                 RECORDSIZE(190 280)                     -
                 VOLUMES(MPS800) )                       -
        DATA   ( NAME(MMA2.AR.TRAN.DATA)                 -
                 CYLINDERS(10 1) )
```

Example 3:   Define a relative-record data set

```
DEFINE CLUSTER ( NAME(MMA2.GL.ACCOUNT.MASTER)           -
                 OWNER(ACCT1)                            -
                 NUMBERED                                -
                 RECORDSIZE(502 502)                     -
                 VOLUMES(MPS800)                         -
                 UNIQUE )                                -
        DATA   ( NAME(MMA2.GL.ACCOUNT.MASTER.DATA)       -
                 CYLINDERS(10 1) )
```

| **Figure 6-12** | Examples of the DEFINE CLUSTER command |

The OWNER parameter

The OWNER parameter supplies an eight-character value that indicates who's responsible for the file. The owner-id you supply is used for documentation only; it doesn't affect the way VSAM processes the file. If you issue the DEFINE CLUSTER command from a TSO terminal, VSAM uses your TSO user-id for the owner-id if you omit the OWNER parameter. The first two examples in figure 6-12 specify DLOWE2 as the owner-id; the third specifies ACCT1.

The CATALOG parameter

The last parameter in figure 6-11, CATALOG, lets you specify the catalog that will own the cluster you're defining. As I've already mentioned, the CATALOG parameter is the only DEFINE CLUSTER parameter that's not coded at the CLUSTER, DATA, or INDEX level. As a result, when you use the CATALOG parameter, you'll always code it as the last parameter on the DEFINE CLUSTER command.

If you omit the CATALOG parameter under MVS, the high-level qualifier of the cluster name is used to identify the catalog that owns it. Under OS/VS1, a STEPCAT or JOBCAT is used if you omit the CATALOG parameter. Under DOS, the job catalog is used if you omit the CATALOG parameter. For all operating systems, the master catalog is used if a user catalog can't be identified.

None of the examples in figure 6-12 use the CATALOG parameter. Instead, each cluster name begins with MMA2. Since these examples were run on an MVS system, the files will be cataloged in a user catalog identified by MMA2. (MMA2 is an alias for the user catalog that owns the file.)

PARAMETERS THAT DESCRIBE THE FILE'S CHARACTERISTICS

The next group of DEFINE CLUSTER parameters I'll explain describe the characteristics of the file: its organization, record size, and so on.

The file-type parameter

To indicate what type of cluster you're defining, you code INDEXED, NONINDEXED, or NUMBERED. As the examples in figure 6-12 indicate, you code INDEXED to define a KSDS, NONINDEXED to define an ESDS, and NUMBERED to define an RRDS. If you omit this parameter, AMS defaults to INDEXED.

The RECORDSIZE parameter

The RECORDSIZE parameter specifies the length of the logical records in your file. On it, you code two values: the average record length and the maximum record length. The average length indicates the length of most of the records in the file. The maximum length indicates the length of the largest record.

In most cases, the value you code for the average record length doesn't matter. The only case in which it does is when you allocate space to the file based on how many records the file will contain rather than on how many tracks, cylinders, or blocks it will require. But, as you'll learn in a few moments, I recommend you don't do that.

It's easy to get the idea from the IBM manuals that coding the same value for average and maximum record length will restrict the file to fixed-length records. But that's not the case. Whether you code the same or different values for average and maximum record size, the file can contain records that vary in length up to the maximum you specify. In other words, VSAM doesn't require that the records all have the same length, even if you do specify the same value for average and maximum length. (To define a relative-record file, however, you should code the same value for the average and maximum length.)

If you omit the RECORDSIZE parameter, VSAM's default depends on whether or not you specify the SPANNED parameter, which I'll describe next. If you omit SPANNED and RECORDSIZE, VSAM assumes 4089 for both the average and the maximum record length. If you specify SPANNED and omit RECORDSIZE, VSAM assumes 4086 average and 32600 maximum. The examples in figure 6-12 show a variety of average and maximum record lengths.

The SPANNED parameter

If your file will contain records that are longer than one control interval, you need to code the SPANNED parameter. Otherwise, you can let the parameter default to NONSPANNED. Since spanned records are uncommon, I don't think you'll use the SPANNED parameter often.

The KEYS parameter

You code the KEYS parameter at the CLUSTER or DATA level to identify a key-sequenced data set's primary key. On the KEYS parameter, you supply the key's length and displacement, like this:

    KEYS(6 0)

Here, the primary key occupies the first six positions of each record.

PARAMETERS THAT SPECIFY THE FILE'S SPACE ALLOCATION

The next group of parameters I'll describe specifies how space is allocated to the file. The VOLUMES parameter specifies the DASD volume or volumes on which to allocate the file. Depending on the type of volume or volumes named in the VOLUMES parameter, you may have to code a FILE parameter. The UNIQUE/SUBALLOCATION parameter specifies whether a file will be allocated to a unique space or will be suballocated out of existing VSAM space. Finally, the space allocation parameter specifies the amount of space that should be allocated to the file.

The VOLUMES parameter

When you code the VOLUMES parameter at the CLUSTER level, you name the volume or volumes (up to 123) on which the cluster will reside. In each of the examples in figure 6-12, the file resides on a single volume named MPS800.

If you code more than one volume name in the VOLUMES parameter, the additional volumes can be used if the file requires more space than is available on a single volume. For example, suppose you code the VOLUMES parameter like this:

```
VOLUMES(MPS800 MPS801 MPS802)
```

Here, the file can reside on one, two, or all three of the volumes named MPS800, MPS801, and MPS802. Normally, you'll code just one vol-ser in the VOLUMES parameter.

If you code two VOLUMES parameters, one at the DATA level and one at the INDEX level, VSAM puts the file's data and index components on the volumes you name. In some cases, that might improve performance for the file. However, unless you want to split the data and index components like that, I recommend you code just one VOLUMES parameter, at the CLUSTER level.

The FILE parameter

The FILE parameter lets you associate the file you're defining with one or more JCL statements that allocate the volume on which the file will reside. In early releases of VSAM, the FILE parameter was required for many DEFINE commands. In more recent releases, however, the FILE parameter isn't required.

Under OS, the FILE parameter provides the ddname of a DD statement that specifies the volume on which the cluster or component resides. You must code FILE only when the volume isn't permanantly mounted. Since most DASD units are permanantly mounted, you can usually omit FILE. But if your file resides on a 3330 or on a Mass Storage System volume, you should code FILE.

To illustrate, figure 6-13 shows a complete job stream that defines a KSDS on a Mass Storage System volume. The DEFINE CLUSTER command here is nearly the same as the one in example 1 of figure 6-12; the only differences are that I specified the vol-ser of an MSS volume in the VOLUMES parameter, and I coded a FILE parameter to identify the DD statement named MSSVOL. The MSSVOL DD statement, in turn, provides the information needed to locate the MSS volume on which the file resides.

```
//DLOWE2V   JOB   ...
//          EXEC  PGM=IDCAMS
//SYSPRINT  DD    SYSOUT=*
//MSSVOL    DD    UNIT=3330V,VOL=SER=MPS8BV,DISP=OLD
//SYSIN     DD  *
 DEFINE CLUSTER ( NAME(MMA2.CUSTOMER.MASTER)            -
                  OWNER(DLOWE2)                         -
                  INDEXED                               -
                  RECORDSIZE(200 200)                   -
                  KEYS(6 0)                             -
                  VOLUMES(MPS8BV)                       -
                  FILE(MSSVOL)                          -
                  UNIQUE )                              -
        DATA    ( NAME(MMA2.CUSTOMER.MASTER.DATA)       -
                  CYLINDERS(50 10) )                    -
        INDEX   ( NAME(MMA2.CUSTOMER.MASTER.INDEX) )
 /*
 //
```

Figure 6-13   Defining a VSAM file on a Mass Storage System volume

The UNIQUE/SUBALLOCATION parameter

This parameter lets you specify whether a file should be suballocated out of existing VSAM space or created in its own space. If you specify SUBALLOCATION (or let it default as in example 2 of figure 6-12), the file is suballocated out of VSAM space. As a result, the volume must contain enough VSAM space to hold your file. If you specify UNIQUE as in examples 1 and 3 of figure 6-12, the file is unique. So there must be enough non-VSAM space on the volume to contain your file. Remember that under OS, the minimum size of a unique file is one cylinder.

The space allocation parameter

You use the space allocation parameter to specify how much space to allocate to your file. The space allocation parameter has this general format:

```
    allocation-unit (primary   secondary)
```

where the allocation-unit can be CYLINDERS, TRACKS, RECORDS, or BLOCKS. The primary value specifies the number of units initially allocated to your file. The secondary value specifies the size of any secondary extents that may be required. In each of the examples in figure 6-12, I coded the allocation parameter at the DATA level. I'll explain what happens when you code it at other levels in a moment.

In example 1 of figure 6-12, I coded the allocation parameter like this:

```
CYLINDERS(50 5)
```

Here, the initial space allocation for the file will be 50 cylinders. If the data set grows beyond that initial allocation, secondary extents of 5 cylinders each are allocated. Up to 122 secondary extents can be allocated to the file before it must be reorganized.

For most files, you should allocate space in terms of cylinders. That's because if you specify CYLINDERS as the allocation unit, the file's control areas will be one cylinder each. For key-sequenced data sets, that allows the index component to be structured most efficiently. (You'll learn more about this in the next chapter.)

For suballocated files that require less than one cylinder of disk space, I suggest you allocate space in terms of records or tracks rather than cylinders. However, if a unique file requires less than one cylinder, you may as well allocate a whole cylinder to it. That's because a unique file can't be smaller than one cylinder anyway.

For FBA devices, you must specify RECORDS or BLOCKS as the allocation unit. For most files, I recommend you specify BLOCKS. Then, round your primary and secondary allocation amounts up to the next higher multiple of 194 for 3310 devices or 744 for 3370s. That's the easiest way to insure your file's control areas will be full cylinders. (194 and 744 are the number of blocks in a cylinder for 3310 and 3370 DASDs.)

As you can see in figure 6-11, you can code an allocation parameter at the CLUSTER, DATA, and INDEX level of a DEFINE CLUSTER command. When you define an entry-sequenced or relative-record data set, it doesn't matter whether you specify the allocation parameter at the CLUSTER or DATA level. Either way, the amount of space you specify is allocated to your file's data component. For a key-sequenced data set, however, you can code the allocation parameter in three ways: at the CLUSTER level only, at the DATA level only, or at both the DATA and INDEX levels.

If you specify an allocation parameter at the cluster level when you define a KSDS, VSAM uses that space for both the data component and the index component. VSAM determines how much space to allocate to the index component, and gives the rest to the data component. If the space remaining for the data component isn't a multiple of a control area (usually a cylinder), VSAM rounds the amount up.

For example, suppose you specify CYLINDER(5 1) at the CLUSTER level. For this file, VSAM will probably allocate just one track to the index component. Because the amount of space left for the file's data component is four cylinders plus several tracks, VSAM rounds the data component space allocation up to five cylinders. As a result, the total space initially allocated to this new KSDS is more than the requested five cylinders.

If you code an allocation parameter only at the DATA level when you define a KSDS, VSAM allocates the amount you specify to the file's data component and calculates an *additional* amount to allocate to the index component.

Number of records	10,000
Record size	400
Control interval size	4,096
Records per CI	10
Device type	3350
CIs per CA	116
Records per CA	1160
Cylinders required	9

Figure 6-14   Calculating a file's space allocation

For example, if you specify CYLINDERS(5 1) at the DATA level, VSAM allocates five cylinders to the data component. Then, it allocates an additional amount of space (again, probably just one track) for the index component.

In most cases, the end result is the same whether you code the allocation parameter at the CLUSTER or DATA level. Either way, the full amount of space you specify is allocated to your file's data component, and an additional amount of less than one cylinder is allocated to the index component. Only in rare cases does the index component require more than one cylinder.

Whether you code the allocation parameter at the CLUSTER or DATA level, VSAM calculates how much space to allocate to the index component. If you wish, you can code an allocation parameter at the INDEX level to override VSAM's calculation. However, because VSAM's index space calculation is almost always correct, I suggest you don't code an allocation parameter at the INDEX level.

How to calculate a file's space allocation   To determine how much space to allocate to a file, you need to know how many records the file will contain, the size of the records, the size of the file's control intervals, and the number of control intervals per control area for the type of device on which the file is allocated (assuming each control area is one cylinder). Figure 6-14 shows how I used this information to determine how many cylinders of a 3350 DASD to allocate to a KSDS that will contain 10,000 400-byte records.

In chapter 7, you'll learn how to determine a file's control interval size. For now, assume the file has 4096-byte control intervals. To determine how many fixed-length records fit in each control interval, first subtract 10 bytes from the CI size to allow for control information. Then, divide the record size into the control interval size and round the result down. In figure 6-14, ten 400-byte records fit in one 4096-byte control interval. For variable-length records, use the average record length and allow for additional bytes of control information in each control interval.

The number of control intervals that fit in a control area depends on the device on which the file is allocated, the size of each control interval, and whether or not the IMBED parameter is specified. (You'll learn about the IMBED parameter in chapter 7.) Figure 6-15 shows how many control intervals fit in each control area for the most common DASD units and control interval sizes. For each device type and control interval size, the first number

CI size	CIs per cylinder with IMBED/NOIMBED				
	3330	3340	3350	3375	3380
512	360/380	132/144	783/810	440/480	644/690
1024	198/209	77/84	435/450	275/300	434/456
2048	108/114	33/36	232/240	154/168	252/270
4096	54/57	33/36	116/120	88/96	140/150
6144	36/38	11/12	77/80	51/56	84/90
8192	26/28	16/18	58/60	44/48	70/75

Figure 6-15   Control area (cylinder) capacity for various control interval sizes on modern IBM DASD units

indicates the number of CIs per CA when the IMBED parameter is specified; the second indicates the number of CIs per CA when the IMBED parameter is omitted.

In the example in figure 6-14, the device type is 3350, the control interval size is 4096, and the IMBED parameter is specified. As a result, 116 control intervals fit in each control area. Since each control interval contains 10 records, each control area contains 1,160 records (116 × 10).

Once you've determined how many records will fit in each control area, divide that amount into the total number of records your file requires. Then, round the result to the next higher integer, if necessary. In figure 6-14, 10,000 divided by 1,160 is about 8.6. Rounding up, I'll allocate 9 control areas (cylinders) of primary space to the file.

Another factor you must consider when you allocate space to your file is how much distributed free space the file will contain. I'll have more to say about free space in chapter 7. For now, just realize that you must account for free space when you calculate the file's space requirements.

How space is allocated on multiple volumes   If you specify more than one volume on the VOLUMES parameter, VSAM allocates space on them differently than you might expect. First, all of the primary space allocation must fit on a single volume; VSAM won't split the primary space over several volumes. When your file needs to be extended, VSAM first tries to allocate a secondary extent on the same volume as the primary extent, using the secondary allocation amount. If there's no room on that volume, VSAM looks at the other volumes. But instead of allocating space using the secondary allocation amount, VSAM uses the primary allocation amount again for the first extent on another volume. In other words, the first allocation made on each volume uses the primary allocation, even if the allocation is for a secondary extent.

In some cases, that can cause unexpected results. Suppose, for example, that a file requires 1,000 cylinders of 3380 DASD space. A single 3380 volume contains 884 cylinders (that allows one cylinder for the VTOC), so you can't specify 1,000 as the primary allocation amount because VSAM can't allocate 1,000 cylinders on a single volume. So, your file will have to occupy space on two volumes. On first thought, the obvious way to allocate space for this file would be:

```
CYLINDERS(884 116)
```

Here, you would expect the first allocation to occupy all of a 3380 volume: 884 cylinders. Then, the secondary allocation of 116 cylinders—made on another volume—would bring the total allocation up to 1,000 cylinders. Unfortunately, though, VSAM uses the primary allocation amount of 884 for the first extent on the second volume. So the total amount of space allocated for this file is 1,768 cylinders.

There's no good way around this problem. You could specify 500 cylinders as the primary and secondary allocation amount, so that the file uses 500 cylinders of each volume. Or, you could specify 116 cylinders of primary space and 768 cylinders of secondary space. Then, the first allocation on the first volume will be 116 cylinders. When that space is used up, the secondary allocation of 768 cylinders will be made using up the rest of the first volume. Then, when that space is used up, an allocation of 116 cylinders will be made on the second volume, bringing the total allocation of the file to 1,000 cylinders. The disadvantage of both of these techniques is that if the file grows even further, the next secondary allocation will probably be too large: 500 cylinders in the first example, 768 cylinders in the second.

OTHER DEFINE CLUSTER PARAMETERS

The parameters you've learned so far make up a basic subset of the DEFINE CLUSTER command. Using them, you can define any of the three types of VSAM files. There are, however, other parameters you can, and often should, code on a DEFINE CLUSTER command. For example, you can use the FOR or TO parameter to specify a retention period or an expiration date for your file. Now, I'll describe the REUSE, FOR and TO, and SHAREOPTIONS parameters in detail. Then, I'll briefly describe two other categories of parameters: those that affect a file's performance and those that affect its security. I'll describe those parameters more fully in chapters 7 and 9, but I want you to know about them now.

To help you understand how these parameters are coded, figure 6-16 shows three DEFINE CLUSTER commands. These three commands are similar to the three commands in figure 6-12, but include some new parameters, which are shaded.

The REUSE parameter

In chapter 2, you learned how reusable files can be used for applications that require temporary work files. For example, a data-collection application might collect transactions in a reusable file. Then, when the transactions are posted to a master file, the reusable file is reset, deleting any records it contains.

To define a reusable work file, you specify REUSE on the DEFINE CLUSTER command at the CLUSTER or DATA level. If you omit REUSE, or if you code NOREUSE, the file will *not* be reusable. Whenever you open a reusable file for output, any records in the file are logically deleted. But you can process the file as usual by opening it for input or I/O.

The FOR and TO parameters

You can code FOR or TO to specify how long the file you're defining should remain current. If you omit both of these parameters, a DELETE command can delete the cluster at any time. If you do code one of these parameters, you can still delete the file at any time. But you have to code a special parameter on the DELETE command to delete a file while it's still current.

If you code FOR, the value you code is the number of days (0-9999) that the file should be retained. If you code TO, the value you include is an expiration date in the format yyddd, where yy is the year (00-99) and ddd is the day (001-366).

In figure 6-16, examples 1 and 3 specify TO(86365). That way, the files will be current until the last day of 1986. In example 2, I specified FOR(365) to indicate that the file should remain current for one year.

The SHAREOPTIONS parameter

The SHAREOPTIONS parameter tells VSAM whether you want to let two or more jobs process your file at the same time. You code two values in the SHAREOPTIONS parameter. The first specifies the *cross-region share option*. This option lets you control how two or more jobs on a single system can share a file. The second value—meaningful for MVS only—specifies the *cross-system share option*, which controls how jobs on different systems of a multi-processor complex can share a file. Examples 1 and 3 in figure 6-16 use the SHAREOPTIONS parameter. Figure 6-17 summarizes the meaning of each type of share option.

The cross-region share option   To specify a cross-region share option, code 1, 2, 3, or 4 as the first value of the SHAREOPTIONS parameter. In figure 6-16, the cross-region share option in example 1 is 2; in example 3, it's 1.

Example 1: Define a key-sequenced data set

```
DEFINE CLUSTER ( NAME(MMA2.CUSTOMER.MASTER)         -
                 OWNER(DLOWE2)                       -
                 INDEXED                             -
                 RECORDSIZE(200 200)                 -
                 KEYS(6 0)                           -
                 VOLUMES(MPS800)                     -
                 UNIQUE                              -
                 TO(86365)                           -
                 SHAREOPTIONS(2 3)                   -
                 IMBED )                             -
        DATA   ( NAME(MMA2.CUSTOMER.MASTER.DATA)     -
                 CYLINDERS(50 5)                     -
                 CISZ(4096) )                        -
        INDEX  ( NAME(MMA2.CUSTOMER.MASTER.INDEX) )
```

Example 2: Define an entry-sequenced data set

```
DEFINE CLUSTER ( NAME(MMA2.AR.TRAN)                 -
                 OWNER(DLOWE2)                       -
                 NONINDEXED                          -
                 RECORDSIZE(190 280)                 -
                 VOLUMES(MPS800)                     -
                 FOR(365)                            -
                 REUSE )                             -
        DATA   ( NAME(MMA2.AR.TRAN.DATA)            -
                 CYLINDERS(10 1) )
```

Example 3: Define a relative-record data set

```
DEFINE CLUSTER ( NAME(MMA2.GL.ACCOUNT.MASTER)       -
                 OWNER(ACCT1)                        -
                 NUMBERED                            -
                 RECORDSIZE(502 502)                 -
                 VOLUMES(MPS800)                     -
                 UNIQUE                              -
                 TO(86365)                           -
                 SHAREOPTIONS(1 3) )                 -
        DATA   ( NAME(MMA2.GL.ACCOUNT.MASTER.DATA)   -
                 CYLINDERS(10 1) )
```

Figure 6-16   Three DEFINE CLUSTER commands that use the FOR/TO, SHAREOPTIONS, REUSE, and performance parameters

Cross-region share option 1 lets any number of jobs open a file simultaneously, as long as they use it for input only. Or, a single job can open the file for output. Cross-region share option 2 is similar, but it lets one job open the file for output and an unlimited number of jobs open the file for input at the same time. Cross-region share option 3 provides no restrictions on file sharing; any number of jobs can open the file for any access they wish. And cross-region option 4 lets any number of jobs open the file, but places some

Cross-region share option (a)

1   The file can be processed simultaneously by multiple jobs as long as all jobs open the file for input only. If a job opens the file for output, no other job can open the file.

2   The file can be processed simultaneously by multiple jobs as long as only one job opens the file for output; all other jobs must open the file for input only.

3   Any number of jobs can process the file simultaneously for input or output; VSAM does nothing to insure the integrity of the file.

4   Any number of jobs can process the file simultaneously for input or output; VSAM imposes these restrictions:

- direct retrieval always reads data from disk even if the desired index or data records are already in a VSAM buffer

- data may not be added to the end of the file

- a control area split is not allowed

Cross-system share options (b)

3   Any number of jobs on any system can process the file simultaneously for input or output; VSAM does nothing to insure the integrity of the file.

4   Any number of jobs on any system can process the file simultaneously for input or output; VSAM imposes the same restrictions as for cross-region share option 4.

Figure 6-17   Cross-region and cross-system share options

restrictions on what those jobs can do with the file. For example, under cross-region share option 4, you can't add records to the end of the file.

For files that are used only by batch programs, you'll usually specify cross-region share option 1 or 2. That protects the file against simultaneous updating by more than one job, and may or may not allow other jobs to process the file in input mode while another job is updating the file.

For CICS applications, it's more common to specify cross-region share option 2 or 3. Share option 2 lets CICS open the file for output while programs running in other regions or partitions can open the file for input. In many cases, that's appropriate; it lets on-line users update the file and insures that batch jobs don't update the file at the same time. In some installations, though, share option 2 causes operational problems, especially if CICS must operate 24 hours a day. Those installations use share option 3 for VSAM files that are processed by CICS applications and use other procedures to insure the integrity of those files.

If you define a file with alternate indexes that will be processed by a COBOL program, you should code share option 3, even if the file isn't going to be shared. Because a COBOL program tries to open the base cluster more than once when alternate indexes are used, the OPEN statement will fail unless sharing is specified. With option 3, the base cluster can be opened as many times as necessary for input or output. In figure 6-5, you can see that I specified share option 3 for the key-sequenced data set so one or more alternate indexes can be used with this file.

If you're using an MVS system, you should realize that the cross-region share options are similar to those of the DISP parameter in a DD statement. Share options 1 and 2 are similar to DISP=OLD. Share option 3 is similar to DISP=SHR. The difference is that the DISP operand is checked when your job step is initialized, but the share option is checked when your file is opened. You should also realize that the share options have no meaning unless DISP=SHR is coded for a file. If DISP=OLD is coded, the file is locked out to other jobs no matter what share option is specified.

The cross-system share option The cross-system share option has just two values, 3 and 4, that correspond to cross-region share options 3 and 4. If you specify cross-system share option 3, jobs on separate systems can process the file without restrictions. Cross-system share option 4 enforces the same restrictions as cross-region share option 4. Under DOS, any value you code for cross-system sharing is ignored.

Quite frankly, the issue of sharing VSAM files in a multiprocessor network is a complex one that's beyond the scope of this book. But you should realize that the cross-system share option you specify in a DEFINE CLUSTER command doesn't provide nearly the level of file-sharing support needed by a large multi-CPU system. As a result, most multi-processor installations use facilities of the operating system or job scheduling subsystem to help manage file sharing, as well as non-IBM software products.

Performance and security parameters

Figure 6-18 shows two other categories of parameters you can code on a DEFINE CLUSTER command. I won't describe the details of these parameters here; instead, I'll describe the performance parameters in detail in chapter 7 and the security parameters in chapter 9. But I want you to see the parameters now. All of them can be coded at the CLUSTER level.

Of the performance parameters, CONTROLINTERVALSIZE, FREESPACE, and IMBED are the most important; you'll code them on most of the DEFINE CLUSTER commands you code. (FREESPACE and IMBED apply only to key-sequenced data sets, though.) CONTROLINTER-VALSIZE (abbreviated CISZ) specifies the size of the file's control intervals. FREESPACE lets you specify a percentage that's used to reserve free space in

Performance parameters (chapter 7)	Security parameters (chapter 9)
`CONTROLINTERVALSIZE(cisize)`	`READPW(password)`
`FREESPACE(ci-space ca-space)`	`UPDATEPW(password)`
`IMBED`	`CONTROLPW(password)`
`REPLICATE`	`MASTERPW(password)`
`BUFFERSPACE(bufferspace)`	`CODE(code)`
`KEYRANGES((lowkey highkey)...)`	`ATTEMPTS(number)`
`ORDERED`	`AUTHORIZATION(entryname [string])`
`SPEED	RECOVERY`	
`WRITECHECK`	

Figure 6-18   Performance and security parameters of the DEFINE CLUSTER command

the file's control intervals and control areas. And IMBED changes the structure of the file's index in a way that usually improves performance. The other performance options listed in figure 6-18 are used less frequently.

Of the security options listed in figure 6-18, the first four specify passwords that permit various levels of access to the file. The others specify options that affect how those passwords are used. Most MVS installations use RACF security protection, which ignores VSAM passwords. So you'll seldom code the security parameters in figure 6-18.

HOW TO USE A MODEL CLUSTER

Many VSAM file parameters—particularly the performance parameters I'll cover in chapter 7—have installation standards that should be specified for most, if not all, DEFINE CLUSTER commands. To simplify this requirement, you can code the MODEL parameter to *model* your cluster after an existing cluster. To do that, just specify the name of an existing cluster in the MODEL parameter. Then, any file attributes not specified in your DEFINE CLUSTER command will be copied from the model cluster.

Often, special data sets are defined simply to be used as models. For example, you might define a KSDS named KSDS.MODEL to use as a model for all your key-sequenced files. Then, whenever you define a KSDS, you code this parameter at the CLUSTER level:

```
MODEL(KSDS.MODEL)
```

Any parameters you don't code directly on your DEFINE CLUSTER command are then taken from KSDS.MODEL.

Under DOS, you can create *default models*: files with no space allocated to them that are used only as models for other clusters. Default model clusters have the following reserved cluster names:

```
DEFAULT.MODEL.KSDS
DEFAULT.MODEL.ESDS
DEFAULT.MODEL.RRDS
```

If one of these default model clusters exists, you don't have to code a MODEL parameter in your DEFINE CLUSTER commands. VSAM automatically uses these entries as models.

DISCUSSION

As I pointed out at the start of this topic, the syntax of the DEFINE CLUSTER command is complex; it has many parameters, and most of them can be coded at more than one level. However, despite its complex syntax, you'll usually code the DEFINE CLUSTER command in a form similar to one of the examples in figures 6-12 or 6-16. In any event, mastering the DEFINE CLUSTER command is an essential part of your VSAM training. So if you're not comfortable with the DEFINE CLUSTER command at this point, I suggest you reread this topic before you move on to the next one.

I've also mentioned several times that you'll learn about more DEFINE CLUSTER parameters in chapters 7 and 9. In particular, you'll learn about performance parameters in chapter 7 and security parameters in chapter 9.

Terminology

cross-region share option
cross-system share option
model

Objective

Given specifications for a VSAM KSDS, ESDS, or RRDS, code an AMS job to define the cluster.

■ ■ ■ □   # Topic 3   AMS commands for alternate indexes

In this topic, you'll learn how to use AMS facilities to define and build alternate indexes. To define an alternate index for a previously defined base cluster, you issue two DEFINE commands, one to define the alternate index itself, the other to define a special entry called a *path* that lets you process a base cluster via its alternate index. Then, to build an alternate index—that is, to create the index entries that let you access base cluster records using the alternate key—you issue a BLDINDEX command.

HOW TO DEFINE AN ALTERNATE INDEX AND PATH

To define an alternate index and its path, you invoke IDCAMS and supply two AMS commands: a DEFINE ALTERNATEINDEX command to define the alternate index, and a DEFINE PATH command to define the path. You don't have to code any special DD or DLBL statements.

The DEFINE ALTERNATEINDEX command

Figure 6-19 gives the format of the DEFINE ALTERNATEINDEX command. As you can see, its format is similar to the format of the DEFINE CLUSTER command. That's because an alternate index is actually a key-sequenced data set. So many of the parameters you code to define a KSDS can also be coded to define an alternate index. In this topic, I'll describe just the parameters that have special meaning for alternate indexes. You already know how to code the rest of the parameters.

Because the word ALTERNATEINDEX is long and easy to misspell, I usually code its abbreviation, AIX. In the rest of this topic, then, I'll refer to the DEFINE ALTERNATEINDEX command as the DEFINE AIX command.

The NAME parameter   You code the NAME parameter on a DEFINE AIX command to name the alternate index you're creating. To name an alternate index, I usually use a combination of the base cluster name, the alternate key field, and the word AIX. For example, to access a customer master file by a district number, I might name the alternate index MMA2.CUST-MAST.DISTRICT.AIX. (Under MVS, the high-level qualifier MMA2 identifies the user catalog that owns the alternate index, which must be the same as the catalog that owns the base cluster. Under DOS, you code the CATALOG parameter or use a job catalog to identify the catalog. Again, this catalog must also own the base cluster.)

I suggest you also code the NAME parameter at the DATA and INDEX levels of a DEFINE AIX command. That way, you can identify the data and

The DEFINE ALTERNATEINDEX command

```
DEFINE ALTERNATEINDEX (      NAME(entry-name)

                             RELATE(entry-name/password)

                           [ OWNER(owner-id) ]

                           [ FOR(days) | TO(date) ]

                           [ KEYS(length offset) ]

                           [ UNIQUEKEY | NONUNIQUEKEY ]

                           [ UPGRADE | NOUPGRADE ]

                             VOLUMES(vol-ser...)

                               ⎧CYLINDERS⎫
                               ⎪TRACKS   ⎪
                           [   ⎨RECORDS  ⎬  (primary [secondary]) ]
                               ⎩BLOCKS   ⎭

                           [ UNIQUE | SUBALLOCATION ]

                           [ FILE(ddname) ]

                           [ REUSE | NOREUSE ]

                           [ SHAREOPTIONS(a b) ]

                           [ MODEL(entry-name[/password]) ] )

    [ DATA          ( [ NAME(entry-name) ]

                    [ VOLUMES(vol-ser...) ]

                        ⎧CYLINDERS⎫
                        ⎪TRACKS   ⎪
                    [   ⎨RECORDS  ⎬  (primary [secondary]) ] ) ]
                        ⎩BLOCKS   ⎭

    [ INDEX         ( [ NAME(entry-name) ]

                    [ VOLUMES(vol-ser...) ]

                        ⎧CYLINDERS⎫
                        ⎪TRACKS   ⎪
                    [   ⎨RECORDS  ⎬  (primary [secondary]) ] ) ]
                        ⎩BLOCKS   ⎭

    [ CATALOG(name[/password]) ]
```

Figure 6-19   The DEFINE ALTERNATEINDEX command (part 1 of 2)

index components of an alternate index in a LISTCAT output listing. For the district number alternate index, I'd name the data and index components MMA2.CUSTMAST.DISTRICT.AIX.DATA and MMA2.CUSTMAST.DISTRICT.AIX.INDEX.

Explanation

NAME(entry-name)	Required. Specifies the name of the alternate index or component.
RELATE(entry-name/password)	Required. Specifies the name and, if required, password of the base cluster to which this alternate index is related.
OWNER(owner-id)	Optional. Specifies the one- to eight-character owner-id for the file.
FOR(days) TO(date)	Optional. Specifies a retention period (in the format dddd) or an expiration date (in the format yyddd) for the alternate index.
KEYS(length offset)	Optional. Specifies the length and offset of the alternate key within the base cluster.
UNIQUEKEY NONUNIQUEKEY	Optional. Specifies whether duplicate key values are allowed. NONUNIQUEKEY is the default.
UPGRADE NOUPGRADE	Optional. Specifies whether the alternate index is a part of the base cluster's upgrade set. UPGRADE is the default.
VOLUMES(vol-ser...)	Required. Specifies one or more volumes that will contain the alternate index or component.
primary	Required. Specifies how much space to allocate initially to the alternate index or component, expressed in cylinders, tracks, records, or blocks.
secondary	Optional. Specifies the secondary space allocation amount. Ignored for unique alternate indexes under DOS.
UNIQUE SUBALLOCATION	Optional. Specifies whether the alternate index is unique (occupies its own data space) or suballocated (shares space with other files). SUBALLOCATION is the default.
FILE(ddname)	Optional. For OS, required only if volume is not permanantly mounted. For DOS, required if UNIQUE is specified.
REUSE NOREUSE	Optional. Specifies whether the alternate index is reusable. NOREUSE is the default.
SHAREOPTIONS(a b)	Optional. Specifies what level of sharing is allowed between regions (a) and systems (b). (1 3) is the default.
MODEL(entry-name[/password])	Optional. Specifies the name of an existing alternate index to use as a model.
CATALOG(name[/password])	Optional. Specifies the name of the catalog that will own the alternate index. If omitted, the stepcat, jobcat, master catalog, or high-level qualifier (MVS only) of the alternate index name identifies the catalog.

Figure 6-19   The DEFINE ALTERNATEINDEX command (part 2 of 2)

The RELATE parameter   You code the RELATE parameter to associate an alternate index with its base cluster. Here, you code the name of the base cluster along with its password, if required. The base cluster must be an existing key-sequenced or entry-sequenced data set.

The KEYS and UNIQUEKEY/NONUNIQUEKEY parameters
These parameters identify the alternate key and specify whether or not duplicate keys are allowed. The KEYS parameter specifies the length and offset of the alternate key. For example, if a five-byte alternate key is in positions 10-14 of the base cluster record, you would code this:

    KEYS(5 9)

Remember, offsets start with zero. So the tenth byte of a record is offset 9.
    UNIQUEKEY and NONUNIQUEKEY specify whether the alternate keys must be unique or may be duplicated. The default is NONUNIQUEKEY, so if you do *not* want duplicate keys in your alternate index, specify UNIQUEKEY.

The UPGRADE and NOUPGRADE parameters   In chapter 2, you learned that an alternate index may or may not be upgradable. If you want the alternate index to be upgradable, code the UPGRADE option on the DEFINE AIX command, or allow it to default. If you do *not* want the alternate index to be upgradable, code NOUPGRADE.

Space allocation parameters   The parameters you code to allocate space to an alternate index are the same as the ones you use in a DEFINE CLUSTER command. You code the VOLUMES parameter to specify the volume or volumes that will contain the alternate index; you can code VOLUMES at the AIX level or at the DATA and INDEX levels. To indicate whether you want the alternate index to have its own space or be suballocated out of existing VSAM space, code the UNIQUE or SUBALLOCATION parameter. And the allocation parameter itself is the same as for a DEFINE CLUSTER command; it specifies primary and secondary allocation in terms of RECORDS, TRACKS, CYLINDERS, or, for FBA devices, BLOCKS.
    It's easy to calculate how much space to allocate to an alternate index. Since an AIX is actually a key-sequenced data set, you can use the techniques I described in topic 2 to calculate its space requirements. The only difference is that you must determine the average record length for the data component of the AIX before you can calculate how much space to allocate to the file. That calculation depends on whether the file has unique or nonunique keys.
    For unique keys, each alternate index record contains two fields: an alternate key value and its corresponding primary key value. In addition, each record contains five bytes of control information. So, the length of each record is the sum of the lengths of the alternate and primary keys plus five bytes. If the base cluster's primary key is 12 bytes long, and the alternate key is 8 bytes long, the alternate index records are 25 bytes each (12 + 8 + 5).

Alternate indexes with nonunique keys have variable-length records; each record consists of one alternate key value, a variable number of associated primary key values, and five bytes of control information. To determine the average record length for this type of alternate index, you need to estimate, on average, how many primary keys are associated with each alternate key value. For example, suppose a base cluster's primary key is 12 bytes long, its alternate key is 20 bytes long, and each alternate key value has an average of four primary keys associated with it. Then, the average alternate index record length is 73, the sum of one alternate key and four primary keys (20 + (4 × 12) + 5).

Once you've determined the size of the alternate index records, you can determine how many records will fit in a control interval, how many control intervals will fit in a cylinder (control area), and how many cylinders are required to hold the data component of your alternate index. Then, you specify the space allocation at the AIX or DATA level of the DEFINE AIX command, letting VSAM determine how much space to allocate to the index component.

The REUSE and NOREUSE parameters   In topic 2, you learned how to define a reusable cluster that can be used as a work file. You can specify the REUSE parameter for an alternate index too. When you do, you can use the BLDINDEX command, presented later in this topic, over and over again to recreate the records of the alternate index without deleting and redefining the alternate index each time. When the BLDINDEX command opens the alternate index, any existing records are ignored and the index is built again from scratch. Since the BLDINDEX command needs to be used periodically whether or not an alternate index is part of the base cluster's upgrade set, I suggest you specify REUSE whenever you define a suballocated alternate index. (Reusable alternate indexes are always suballocated, so don't code the REUSE and UNIQUE parameters together on a DEFINE AIX command.)

The DEFINE PATH command

To process the records of a base cluster via the alternate keys stored in an alternate index, you don't access the base cluster or the alternate index directly. Instead, you access them together using another catalog entry called a path. It's the path that lets you access base cluster records via the alternate index.

To create a path, you issue a DEFINE PATH command, shown in figure 6-20. There are just three important parameters of the DEFINE PATH command: NAME, PATHENTRY, and UPDATE/NOUPDATE. The NAME parameter supplies the name of the path you're defining. And the PATHENTRY parameter supplies the name of the alternate index for which you are creating a path. You don't have to supply the name of the base cluster in the DEFINE PATH command because it was identified in the RELATE parameter when the alternate index was defined.

The DEFINE PATH command

```
DEFINE PATH (    NAME(entry-name)

                 PATHENTRY(entry-name[/password])

           [ UPDATE | NOUPDATE ]

           [ FOR(days) | TO(date) ]

           [ MODEL(entry-name[/password]) ] )

      [ CATALOG(name[/password]) ]
```

Explanation

NAME(entry-name)	Required. Specifies the name of the path.
PATHENTRY(entry-name[/password])	Required. Specifies the name of the alternate index to which this path is related.
UPDATE NOUPDATE	Optional. Specifies whether the upgrade set should be updated when this path is processed. UPDATE is the default.
FOR(days) TO(date)	Optional. Specifies a retention period (in the format dddd) or an expiration date (in the format yyddd) for the path.
MODEL(entry-name[/password])	Optional. Specifies the name of a path to use as a model.
CATALOG(name[/password])	Optional. Specifies the name of the catalog that contains the alternate index. If omitted, the stepcat, jobcat, master catalog, or high-level qualifier (MVS only) of the alternate index name identifies the catalog.

Figure 6-20   The DEFINE PATH command

The UPDATE/NOUPDATE parameter tells AMS whether or not you want the base cluster's upgrade set to be maintained when you process the base cluster via the path. (A base cluster's *upgrade set* is all of its upgradable alternate indexes.) If you specify UPDATE, all of the alternate indexes in the base cluster's upgrade set are opened when you open the path. If you code NOUPDATE, the upgrade set is *not* maintained when you process the file via the path.

Don't be confused by the relationship between the UPGRADE/ NOUPGRADE parameter of DEFINE AIX and the UPDATE/ NOUPDATE parameter of DEFINE PATH. Specifying UPGRADE on a DEFINE AIX command causes the alternate index to be included in the base cluster's upgrade set. The upgrade set is *always* maintained when the base cluster is processed directly—that is, via its primary key. The UPDATE/NOUPDATE parameter of the DEFINE PATH command gives

```
DEFINE AIX      ( NAME(MMA2.EMPMAST.SSN.AIX)          -
                  RELATE(MMA2.EMPLOYEE.MASTER)        -
                  OWNER(DLCWE2)                       -
                  TO(86365)                           -
                  KEYS(9 12)                          -
                  UNIQUEKEY                           -
                  NOUPGRADE                           -
                  VOLUMES(MPS80C)                     -
                  UNIQUE )                            -
        DATA    ( NAME(MMA2.EMPMAST.SSN.AIX.DATA)     -
                  CYLINDERS(1 1) )                    -
        INDEX   ( NAME(MMA2.EMPMAST.SSN.AIX.INDEX) )
DEFINE PATH     ( NAME(MMA2.EMPMAST.SSN.PATH)         -
                  PATHENTRY(MMA2.EMPMAST.SSN.AIX)     -
                  UPDATE )
```

Figure 6-21	A DEFINE ALTERNATEINDEX and DEFINE PATH command

you additional control over whether or not the upgrade set is maintained when you process the base cluster via a path—that is, via an alternate key.

In most cases, I suggest you code UPDATE on your DEFINE PATH commands. Then, you can control whether alternate indexes are upgraded by coding UPGRADE or NOUPGRADE in your DEFINE AIX commands. That way, the alternate indexes, if any, in the base cluster's upgrade set will always be maintained, whether the cluster is processed directly or via a path.

An example of the DEFINE AIX and DEFINE PATH commands

Figure 6-21 shows an example of how you use the DEFINE AIX and DEFINE PATH commands together to define an alternate index and path. Here, you can use the standard JCL to invoke IDCAMS under OS or DOS. No data sets need to be allocated to the job, so you don't need to add any special DD or DLBL statements.

The DEFINE AIX command in figure 6-21 defines an alternate index named MMA2.EMPMAST.SSN.AIX for a base cluster named MMA2.EMPLOYEE.MASTER. The alternate keys are nine bytes long, starting in the thirteenth byte (displacement 12) of each record. (The alternate key values are employee social security numbers.) Duplicates are not allowed (UNIQUEKEY), and this alternate index is *not* a part of the base cluster's upgrade set (NOUPGRADE).

The DEFINE PATH command in figure 6-21 is simple enough; it defines a path named MMA2.EMPMAST.SSN.PATH for the alternate index named MMA2.EMPMAST.SSN.AIX. Because I coded the UPDATE parameter, the base cluster's upgrade set is maintained when I process the base cluster via this path, even though the alternate index isn't part of the upgrade set.

HOW TO BUILD AN ALTERNATE INDEX

Once you've defined an alternate index and its path, you can issue a BLDINDEX command to create the alternate key entries needed to access the base cluster. In addition, you'll need to issue the BLDINDEX command to rebuild your alternate indexes periodically, even if the index is upgradable. That's because, as I mentioned in chapter 2, additions to an alternate index are made in the order in which they occur rather than in prime key sequence. So, with time, most alternate indexes need reorganization.

The operation of the BLDINDEX command is simple. First, BLDINDEX reads all of the records in your base cluster. From those records, it extracts the data it needs to build your alternate index: key-pointer pairs that consist of one alternate key value and the prime key or RBA of the corresponding base cluster record. Those key-pointer pairs are then sorted into ascending sequence. And finally, they're written to your alternate index. If your alternate index allows only unique keys, each key-pointer pair becomes one alternate index record, and duplicates are flagged as errors. If your alternate index allows nonunique keys, BLDINDEX combines duplicates into a single alternate index record.

The BLDINDEX command

Figure 6-22 gives the format of the BLDINDEX command. Unlike the DEFINE commands, the BLDINDEX command has no parameter levels; you code all of its parameters right after the word BLDINDEX, with no parentheses.

Specifying the input and output files   To use the BLDINDEX command, you need to identify two VSAM files: an input file and an output file. The input file is the base cluster. Although the output file is always an alternate index, you can specify either an alternate index or its path. Either way, the alternate index is processed as the output file.

You can identify the input and output files in two ways. First, you can identify the base cluster or alternate index directly by coding its name in the INDATASET or OUTDATASET parameter. Second, you can code an INFILE or OUTFILE parameter that refers to a DD or DLBL statement that identifies the base cluster or alternate index. I prefer to use the INDATASET and OUTDATASET parameters so I don't have to code additional JCL.

Under MVS, the high-level qualifier of the input and output file names identify the user catalog that owns them. Under DOS, you must specify a job catalog to indicate the correct user catalog. If you don't, the master catalog is assumed. The CATALOG parameter, which I'll describe in a moment, does *not* identify the catalog that owns the input and output files.

The BLDINDEX command

```
BLDINDEX  {INFILE(ddname[/password])           }
          {INDATASET(entry-name[/password]))   }

          {OUTFILE(ddname[/password]...)        }
          {OUTDATASET(entry-name[/password]...))}

          [ EXTERNALSORT | INTERNALSORT ]

          {WORKFILES(ddname ddname)}
          {WORKVOLUMES(vol-ser...) }

          [ CATALOG(name[/password]) ]
```

Explanation

INFILE(ddname[/password])
INDATASET(entry-name[/password])

Required. INFILE specifies the name of a DD or DLBL statement that identifies the base cluster. INDATASET identifies the name of the base cluster itself.

OUTFILE(ddname/password...)
OUTDATASET(entry-name[/password]...)

Required. OUTFILE specifies the name of a DD or DLBL statement that identifies the alternate indexes or paths to be built. OUTDATASET identifies the names of the alternate indexes or paths directly.

EXTERNALSORT
INTERNALSORT

Optional. Specifies whether VSAM is to sort the alternate index records in virtual storage (INTERNALSORT) or using disk storage (EXTERNALSORT). If you specify INTERNALSORT and enough virtual storage isn't available to sort the records, an external sort is performed. INTERNALSORT is the default.

WORKFILES(ddname ddname)
WORKVOLUMES(vol-ser...)

Optional. WORKFILES (OS only) supplies the ddnames for the work files used by an external sort. DD statements for these files must be provided. If omitted, IDCUT1 and ID-CUT2 are used. WORKVOLUMES (DOS only) specifies the volumes (up to ten) that will contain the two work files. No DLBL statements are required.

CATALOG(name[/password])

Optional. Specifies the name and password of the catalog that will own the sort work files. If omitted, the stepcat or jobcat is used if available; otherwise, the master catalog is used. On MVS systems, if data set names are supplied on the DD statements for the work files, the high-level qualifiers of those names identify the catalog.

Figure 6-22   The BLDINDEX command

BLDINDEX sort options   As I've already mentioned, BLDINDEX performs a sort operation as a part of building an alternate index. The remaining parameters in figure 6-22 have to do with how BLDINDEX does that sort.

Normally, VSAM checks to see if enough virtual storage is available to perform the sort internally. If there isn't, VSAM allocates two sort work files and does an external sort. If you want VSAM to *always* do an external sort, you could code the EXTERNALSORT option. I don't see much point in that, however, so I suggest you specify INTERNALSORT or allow it to default. That way, VSAM will try to do an internal sort. If there's not enough room, the sort is done externally anyway.

As for the sort work files, they're allocated in slightly different ways under OS and DOS. For both operating systems, VSAM automatically defines the work files as entry-sequenced data sets in VSAM space. When the sort is completed, the files are automatically deleted. The difference is that under OS, you must supply DD statements for these files to identify the volumes on which they should reside. Under DOS, you identify the volumes in the BLDINDEX command.

Under OS, you can code the WORKFILES parameter and supply your own names for the DD statements that define the sort work files. But I suggest you omit the WORKFILES parameter and use the VSAM default ddnames: IDCUT1 and IDCUT2. On the DD statements, you just identify the volumes that will contain the work files like this:

```
//IDCUT1    DD    UNIT=SYSDA,VOL=SER=MPS800,DISP=SHR
//IDCUT2    DD    UNIT=SYSDA,VOL=SER=MPS800,DISP=SHR
```

In this case, if there's not enough virtual storage for an internal sort, the work files will be allocated on a volume named MPS800.

Under DOS, you code the WORKVOLUMES parameter and list up to ten volumes on which the work files can be defined. In many cases, you'll list just one vol-ser; others are needed only if there isn't enough space for both work files on the first volume. Again, the files are defined only if there's not enough virtual storage to perform the sort internally. And when the sort is complete, the files are automatically deleted.

The CATALOG parameter tells VSAM which catalog to use when it defines the work files. If you omit the CATALOG parameter, VSAM uses its typical search order to determine which catalog to use. If there is an active job or step catalog, it's used. Under MVS, the high-level qualifier of the work file data set name (if you coded a DSN parameter in the DD statement for the work file) can identify the catalog. If all else fails, VSAM defines your work files in the master catalog.

Examples of the BLDINDEX command

Figure 6-23 shows two job steps that build an alternate index: one for an OS system, the other for a DOS system. In the OS job step, you can see the DD

OS job step to build an alternate index

```
//          EXEC PGM=IDCAMS
//SYSPRINT DD  SYSOUT=A
//IDCUT1   DD  UNIT=SYSDA,VOL=SER=MPS800,DISP=OLD
//IDCUT2   DD  UNIT=SYSDA,VOL=SER=MPS800,DISP=OLD
//SYSIN    DD  *
 BLDINDEX INDATASET(MMA2.EMPLOYEE.MASTER)    -
          OUTDATASET(MMA2.EMPMAST.SSN.AIX)   -
          CATALOG(MMA2)
/*
```

DOS job step to build an alternate index

```
// DLBL IJSYSUC,'MMA.USER.CATALOG',,VSAM,CAT=IJSYSCT
// EXEC IDCAMS,SIZE=AUTO
 BLDINDEX INDATASET(MMA2.EMPLOYEE.MASTER)    -
          OUTDATASET(MMA2.EMPMAST.SSN.AIX)   -
          WORKVOLUMES(SYSWK2)                -
          CATALOG(MMA.USER.CATALOG)
/*
```

Figure 6-23	OS and DOS job steps to build an alternate index

statements required for the sort work files. Because I coded the CATALOG parameter, the work files will be cataloged in a use catalog names MMA2. Depending on your installation, you may also need to specify a data set name for these work files.

In the DOS example, the WORKVOLUMES parameter tells VSAM to place the work files on a volume named SYSWK2. The IJSYSUC DLBL statement identifies the user catalog that owns the input and output files, and the CATALOG parameter specifies the user catalog that will contain the work files. In this case, the job catalog is the same as the catalog named in the CATALOG parameter. Notice that under DOS, you don't have to code any special JCL to allocate the work volumes.

Terminology

path
upgrade set

Objective

Given specifications for a key-sequenced or entry-sequenced data set that requires an alternate index, code the required AMS commands to define the alternate index, define the path, and build the alternate index.

■ ■ ■ ■   Topic 4   Other basic AMS commands

In this topic, you'll learn how to use a variety of AMS commands to maintain catalogs and to print and copy files. In particular, you'll learn how to use the LISTCAT, ALTER, and DELETE commands to maintain catalogs. And you'll learn how to use the PRINT and REPRO commands to print and copy VSAM data sets.

HOW TO USE AMS TO MAINTAIN VSAM CATALOGS

You should know how to use three AMS commands for maintaining catalogs: LISTCAT, ALTER, and DELETE. The LISTCAT command lets you list the contents of a catalog. The ALTER command lets you change the characteristics of an existing VSAM file. And the DELETE command lets you delete a VSAM file by removing its catalog entry.

The LISTCAT command

Often, you need to know what VSAM files are defined in a particular user catalog. Or you need to know the characteristics of a particular file. To get that information, you use the LISTCAT command, whose format is given in figure 6-24. The parameters you code on the LISTCAT command identify the catalog, the names of the entries to be listed, the types of objects to be listed, and the amount of information about each object to be listed.

Identifying the catalog   The first LISTCAT parameter, CATALOG, names the catalog whose contents you want to list. If you omit the CATALOG parameter, VSAM uses its standard search order to determine which catalog to use: on MVS systems, the high-level qualifier of a file name (if one is supplied in a subsequent ENTRY or LEVEL parameter) is used; otherwise, a step catalog (OS only) or job catalog is used. If no job or step catalog is in effect, the master catalog is used.

Under DOS, I recommend you always code the CATALOG parameter on your LISTCAT commands. That way, you'll know for sure what catalog you're listing. Under MVS, however, you'll normally omit the CATALOG parameter. MVS uses the high-level qualifier of each file name you supply to determine the correct user catalog.

Identifying the entries to be listed   The next two parameters, ENTRIES and LEVEL, identify the catalog entries you want to list. Under OS, you can code ENTRIES or LEVEL to identify the catalog entries, and you can code generic entry names to cause more than one entry to be listed. Under DOS, however, you can't code the LEVEL parameter or generic names; only the ENTRIES parameter is allowed.

The LISTCAT command

```
LISTCAT [ CATALOG(name[/password]) ]

        {ENTRIES(entry-name[/password]...)}
        {LEVEL(level)                      }

        [ entry-type ]

        (NAME      )
        (HISTORY   )
        {VOLUMES   }
        (ALLOCATION)
        (ALL       )

        [ NOTUSABLE ]

        [ CREATION(days) ]

        [ EXPIRATION(days) ]

        [ OUTFILE(ddname) ]
```

Parameters

CATALOG(name[/password])	Optional. Specifies the name and, if required, password of the catalog from which entries are to be listed.
ENTRIES(entry-name[/password]...)	Optional. Specifies the names of the entries you want to list. Under OS, entry names may be generic (see text). If omitted, all entries in the specified catalog are listed.
LEVEL(level)	Optional. Specifies one or more levels of qualification. Any data sets whose names match those levels are listed. (OS only)
entry-type	Optional. Specifies the type of entries you want listed. The values you can code depend on your system; see figure 6-26 for more information. If both ENTRIES/LEVEL and entry-type are omitted, all entries of all types in the specified catalog are listed.

Figure 6-24   The LISTCAT command (part 1 of 2)

If you omit the ENTRIES or LEVEL parameters, VSAM lists *all* of the objects in the catalog. You'll rarely want to do that however, since user catalogs can contain hundreds of entries.

The ENTRIES parameter lets you specify one or more names for the catalog entries you want listed. For example, if you want to list the catalog entry for a VSAM file named MMA2.CUSTOMER.MASTER, you would code this:

```
ENTRIES(MMA2.CUSTOMER.MASTER)
```

NAME	Optional. Specifies that only the names and types of the specified entries are to be listed. NAME is the default.
HISTORY	Optional. Specifies that the information listed by NAME, plus the history information (such as creation and expiration dates), is to be listed. (OS only)
VOLUME	Optional. Specifies that the information listed by HISTORY, plus the volume locations of the specified entries, is to be listed.
ALLOCATION	Optional. Specifies that the information listed by volume, plus detailed extent information, is to be listed.
ALL	Optional. Specifies that all available catalog information for the specified entries is to be listed.
NOTUSABLE	Optional. Specifies that only damaged catalog entries are to be listed.
CREATION(days)	Optional. Specifies that only entries which were created on or before the specified number of days before the current date should be listed. (OS only)
EXPIRATION(days)	Optional. Specifies that only entries which will expire on or before the specified number of days after the current date should be listed. (OS only)
OUTFILE(ddname)	Optional. Specifies the name of a DD statement that should receive the output from the LISTCAT command. If omitted, output is sent to SYSPRINT. (OS only)

Figure 6-24   The LISTCAT command (part 2 of 2)

To list information for more than one file, just code several file names in a single ENTRIES parameter, like this:

```
ENTRIES(MMA2.CUSTOMER.MASTER      -
        MMA2.EMPLOYEE.MASTER      -
        MMA2.DAILY.TRANS )
```

Here, three catalog entries will be listed.

On OS systems, you can specify a *generic entry name* by replacing one or more levels of the file name with an asterisk. For example, if you code

```
ENTRIES(MMA2.*.MASTER)
```

all files whose names consist of three levels, with MMA2 as the first level and MASTER as the third level, are listed. MMA2.CUSTOMER.MASTER and MMA2.EMPLOYEE.MASTER meet these criteria, so they would be listed. The level represented by the asterisk in a generic name must be present for an entry to be listed, however. So, in this example, MMA2.MASTER would *not* be listed, because the second level of the entry name is missing.

The LEVEL parameter is similar to generic entry names in an ENTRIES parameter. In the LEVEL parameter, you code a partial name consisting of one or more levels. VSAM then lists all the catalog entries whose names begin with the partial name. For example, if you code

```
LEVEL(MMA2)
```

all catalog entries whose first level is MMA2 are listed. In this example, it doesn't matter how many levels are actually present in the entry name, as long as the *first* level is MMA2.

Similarly, if you code

```
LEVEL(MMA2.EMPLOYEE)
```

any entry whose name begins with MMA2.EMPLOYEE is listed, regardless of how many additional levels are in its name.

To understand how the ENTRIES and LEVEL parameters work, look at figure 6-25. Here, I've listed five LISTCAT commands that use the ENTRIES or LEVEL parameter. Then, I've shown which of five VSAM file names would be selected by each of the five commands. If you study this figure for a moment, I think you'll understand the difference between the ENTRIES and LEVEL parameters.

Identifying the entry types to be listed   The third LISTCAT parameter, entry-type, lets you specify that only certain types of catalog entries are to be listed (such as clusters, alternate indexes, and so on). If you omit the entry-type parameter, all entries that match the ENTRIES or LEVEL parameter will be listed.

The values you can code for the entry-type parameter for OS/MVS, ICF, and DOS/VSE are given in figure 6-26. As you can see, not all values are allowed under all versions of VSAM. For example, you can't code ALIAS under DOS, because VSE/VSAM doesn't support aliases. Similarly, you can't code SPACE under ICF, because ICF doesn't support VSAM data spaces.

You can code more than one of these values on a LISTCAT command. For example, if you want to list clusters and alternate indexes, you could code both CLUSTER and ALTERNATEINDEX on the LISTCAT command.

Component name	Example				
	1	2	3	4	5
MMA2.CUSTOMER	X				X
MMA2.CUSTOMER.MASTER			X		X
MMA2.EMPLOYEE				X	X
MMA2.EMPLOYEE.MASTER		X	X	X	X
MMA2.EMPLOYEE.FILE		X		X	X

Example 1

```
LISTCAT ENTRIES(MMA2.CUSTOMER)
```

Example 2

```
LISTCAT ENTRIES(MMA2.EMPLOYEE.*)
```

Example 3

```
LISTCAT ENTRIES(MMA2.*.MASTER)
```

Example 4

```
LISTCAT LEVEL(MMA2.EMPLOYEE)
```

Example 5

```
LISTCAT LEVEL(MMA2)
```

Figure 6-25   Examples of the ENTRIES and LEVEL parameters of the LISTCAT command

Limiting the amount of catalog information to be listed   The next
LISTCAT parameter lets you limit the amount of catalog information to be
listed for each entry. If you specify NAME, or let it default, VSAM lists just
the entry's name, type, and owning catalog. To illustrate, figure 6-27 shows
the output from this command:

```
LISTCAT LEVEL(MMA2) -
        NAME
```

Parameters available under all versions of VSAM

```
ALTERNATEINDEX
CLUSTER
DATA
INDEX
NONVSAM
PATH
USERCATALOG
```

Additional parameters available under

OS/MVS	ICF	DOS/VSE
``` ALIAS GENERATIONDATAGROUP PAGESPACE SPACE ```	``` ALIAS GENERATIONDATAGROUP PAGESPACE ```	``` SPACE ```

Figure 6-26   Valid entry types for the LISTCAT command

As you can see, several files whose names begin with MMA2 are listed as a result of this command. Under DOS, this output would look slightly different, but would contain the same information.

Figure 6-28 shows what happens if you list an entry for a specific file (MMA2.CUSTOMER.MASTER) and specify the HISTORY parameter (not available under DOS). Here, the entry's name and type are listed, along with its history information: owner-id, creation and expiration dates, and the VSAM release under which the entry was created. In addition, the HISTORY parameter causes VSAM to list any entries that are associated with the entry you specify. In this example, the cluster is a key-sequenced data set. So VSAM lists the DATA and INDEX component entries too. If the cluster had any associated paths or alternate indexes, they would have been listed as well.

In figure 6-29, I specified the VOLUMES parameter rather than the HISTORY parameter. As a result, VSAM listed the same information listed for HISTORY, plus the names of the DASD volumes which contain the data and index components. In this case, both are contained on a volume named MPS800.

In addition to the volume serial number, the LISTCAT command in figure 6-29 also indicates the device type. Unfortunately, the device type is given in a coded format. To determine what type of device the file resides on, look up the device code in figure 6-30. The device type in the LISTCAT output in figure 6-29 is 3010200E. In figure 6-30, you can see that's the device code for a model 3380 disk drive.

```
IDCAMS   SYSTEM SERVICES


                    LISTCAT LEVEL(MMA2) -
                    NAME

CLUSTER ------- MMA2.CR
       IN-CAT --- VCAT.MPS800

DATA ---------- MMA2.CR.DATA
       IN-CAT --- VCAT.MPS800

CLUSTER ------- MMA2.CRPX
       IN-CAT --- VCAT.MPS800

DATA ---------- MMA2.CRPX.DATA
       IN-CAT --- VCAT.MPS800

INDEX --------- MMA2.CRPX.INDEX
       IN-CAT --- VCAT.MPS800

CLUSTER ------- MMA2.CRSX
       IN-CAT --- VCAT.MPS800

DATA ---------- MMA2.CRSX.DATA
       IN-CAT --- VCAT.MPS800

INDEX --------- MMA2.CRSX.INDEX
       IN-CAT --- VCAT.MPS800

CLUSTER ------- MMA2.CUSTOMER.MASTER
       IN-CAT --- VCAT.MPS800

DATA ---------- MMA2.CUSTOMER.MASTER.DATA
       IN-CAT --- VCAT.MPS800

INDEX --------- MMA2.CUSTOMER.MASTER.INDEX
       IN-CAT --- VCAT.MPS800

NONVSAM ------- MMA2.IMSVS.ACBLIB
       IN-CAT --- VCAT.MPS800

NONVSAM ------- MMA2.IMSVS.DBDLIB
       IN-CAT --- VCAT.MPS800

NONVSAM ------- MMA2.IMSVS.PGMLIB
       IN-CAT --- VCAT.MPS800

NONVSAM ------- MMA2.IMSVS.PSBLIB
       IN-CAT --- VCAT.MPS800
```

Figure 6-27   Output from a LISTCAT command with the NAME parameter

```
IDCAMS   SYSTEM SERVICES


              LISTCAT ENTRIES(MMA2.CUSTOMER.MASTER) -
                    HISTORY

CLUSTER ------- MMA2.CUSTOMER.MASTER
      IN-CAT --- VCAT.MPS800
      HISTORY
         OWNER-IDENT-------(NULL)      CREATION----------85.234
         RELEASE----------------2      EXPIRATION--------00.000

    DATA ------- MMA2.CUSTOMER.MASTER.DATA
      IN-CAT --- VCAT.MPS800
      HISTORY
         OWNER-IDENT-------(NULL)      CREATION----------85.234
         RELEASE----------------2      EXPIRATION--------00.000

    INDEX ------ MMA2.CUSTOMER.MASTER.INDEX
      IN-CAT --- VCAT.MPS800
      HISTORY
         OWNER-IDENT-------(NULL)      CREATION----------85.234
         RELEASE----------------2      EXPIRATION--------00.000
```

| **Figure 6-28** | Output from a LISTCAT command with the HISTORY parameter |

```
IDCAMS   SYSTEM SERVICES


              LISTCAT ENTRIES(MMA2.CUSTOMER.MASTER) -
                    VOLUMES

CLUSTER ------- MMA2.CUSTOMER.MASTER
      IN-CAT --- VCAT.MPS800
      HISTORY
         OWNER-IDENT-------(NULL)      CREATION----------85.234
         RELEASE----------------2      EXPIRATION--------00.000

    DATA ------- MMA2.CUSTOMER.MASTER.DATA
      IN-CAT --- VCAT.MPS800
      HISTORY
         OWNER-IDENT-------(NULL)      CREATION----------85.234
         RELEASE----------------2      EXPIRATION--------00.C00
      VOLUMES
         VOLSER-----------MPS800       DEVTYPE------X'3010200E'

    INDEX ------ MMA2.CUSTOMER.MASTER.INDEX
      IN-CAT --- VCAT.MPS800
      HISTORY
         OWNER-IDENT-------(NULL)      CREATION----------85.234
         RELEASE----------------2      EXPIRATION--------00.000
      VOLUMES
         VOLSER-----------MPS800       DEVTYPE------X'3010200E'
```

| **Figure 6-29** | Output from a LISTCAT command with the VOLUMES parameter |

Device code in LISTCAT output	Device type
30008001	9 track tape
3040200A	3340 (35 or 70 MB)
30502006	2305-1
30502007	2305-2
30502009	3330-1 or 3330-2
3050200B	3350
3050200D	3330-11
30582009	3330 MSS virtual volume
30808001	7 track tape
30C02008	2314 or 2319
3010200C	3375
3010200E	3380

Figure 6-30   Device codes that appear in LISTCAT output

If you specify ALLOCATION instead of VOLUMES, the output looks like figure 6-31. Here, detailed information about the file's disk extents is shown. For example, you can see that the data component occupies two extents. The first, allocated from the file's primary space allocation, fills 30 tracks, or two cylinders. The second, allocated from the file's secondary space allocation, fills 15 tracks, or one cylinder.

If you want to know all of the characteristics of a VSAM file, specify the ALL parameter. Then, the output looks like figure 6-32. Here, several new categories of information are listed. In the ATTRIBUTES group, you can see which attributes were specified for the file when it was defined. For example, in figure 6-32, you can see that SHAREOPTIONS(2 3) was specified for the file.

The STATISTICS group provides useful information about the file's growth and performance. Here, you can see how many records the file contains, as well as how many records have been deleted, inserted, updated, or retrieved since the file was loaded. In addition, you can see how many control interval and control area splits have occurred, as well as how much free space remains in the file. You should periodically review this information to see if the file's attributes need to be adjusted to meet different processing requirements.

As figure 6-32 illustrates, LISTCAT output can be lengthy. If you run a job to print all the entries in a typical user catalog, and you specify ALL, the

```
      LISTCAT ENTRIES(MMA2.CUSTOMER.MASTER) -
            ALLOCATION

CLUSTER ------ MMA2.CUSTOMER.MASTER
    IN-CAT --- VCAT.MPS800
    HISTORY
        OWNER-IDENT-----(NULL)          CREATION--------85.234
        RELEASE---------2               EXPIRATION------00.000

DATA ------- MMA2.CUSTOMER.MASTER.DATA
    IN-CAT --- VCAT.MPS800
    HISTORY
        OWNER-IDENT-----(NULL)          CREATION--------85.234
        RELEASE---------2               EXPIRATION------00.000
    ALLOCATION
        SPACE-TYPE-----CYLINDER         HI-ALLOC-RBA----1843200
        SPACE-PRI-------2               HI-USED-RBA-----1843200
        SPACE-SEC-------1
    VOLUME
        VOLSER---------MPS800           PHYREC-SIZE-----4096           HI-ALLOC-RBA------1843200   EXTENT-NUMBER------2
        DEVTYPE--------X'3010200E'      PHYRECS/TRK-----10             HI-USED-RBA-------1843200   EXTENT-TYPE-------X'0C'
        VOLFLAG--------PRIME            TRACKS/CA-------15
        EXTENTS:
        LOW-CCHH----X'005F0000'         LOW-RBA---------0              TRACKS-------------30
        HIGH-CCHH---X'0060000E'         HIGH-RBA--------1228799
        LOW-CCHH----X'03C60000'         LOW-RBA---------1228800        TRACKS-------------15
        HIGH-CCHH---X'0306000E'         HIGH-RBA--------1843199

INDEX ------ MMA2.CUSTOMER.MASTER.INDEX
    IN-CAT --- VCAT.MPS800
    HISTORY
        OWNER-IDENT-----(NULL)          CREATION--------85.234
        RELEASE---------2               EXPIRATION------00.000
    ALLOCATION
        SPACE-TYPE------TRACK           HI-ALLOC-RBA----36864
        SPACE-PRI-------1               HI-USED-RBA-----8192
        SPACE-SEC-------1
    VOLUME
        VOLSER---------MPS800           PHYREC-SIZE-----2048           HI-ALLOC-RBA------36864     EXTENT-NUMBER------1
        DEVTYPE--------X'3010200E'      PHYRECS/TRK-----18             HI-USED-RBA-------8192      EXTENT-TYPE-------X'0C'
        VOLFLAG--------PRIME            TRACKS/CA-------1
        EXTENTS:
        LOW-CCHH----X'00D40000'         LOW-RBA---------0              TRACKS-------------1
        HIGH-CCHH---X'00D40000'         HIGH-RBA--------36863
```

Figure 6-31   Output from a LISTCAT command with the ALLOCATION parameter

```
          LISTCAT  ENTRIES(MMA2.CUSTOMER.MASTER) -
                    ALL

CLUSTER ------ MMA2.CUSTOMER.MASTER
     IN-CAT --- VCAT.MPS8CO
     HISTORY
          OWNER-IDENT------(NULL)          CREATION---------85.234
          RELEASE-----------2              EXPIRATION-------00.000
          PROTECTION-PSWD----(NULL)        RACF------------(YES)
     ASSOCIATIONS
          DATA------MMA2.CUSTOMER.MASTER.DATA
          INDEX-----MMA2.CUSTOMER.MASTER.INDEX

DATA ------- MMA2.CUSTOMER.MASTER.DATA
     IN-CAT --- VCAT.MPS800
     HISTORY
          OWNER-IDENT------(NULL)          CREATION---------85.234
          RELEASE-----------2              EXPIRATION-------00.000
          PROTECTION-PSWD----(NULL)        RACF------------(YES)
     ASSOCIATIONS
          CLUSTER--MMA2.CUSTOMER.MASTER
     ATTRIBUTES
          KEYLEN-----------6     AVGLRECL-----------100     BUFSPACE--------10240     CISIZE---------4096
          RKP--------------0     MAXLRECL-----------100     EXCPEXIT-------(NULL)     CI/CA-----------150
          SHROPTNS(2,3)  RECOVERY   UNIQUE    NOERASE        INDEXED    NCWRITECHK     NOIMBED    NOREPLICAT
          UNORDERED      NOREUSE   NONSPANNED
     STATISTICS
          REC-TOTAL-----10693    SPLITS-CI---------54        EXCPS------------3691
          REC-DELETED----238     SPLITS-CA----------1        EXTENTS-------------2
          REC-INSERTED--1034     FREESPACE-%CI------5        SYSTEM-TIMESTAMP:
          REC-UPDATED----354     FREESPACE-%CA------5           X'999FD9E6D0092200'
          REC-RETRIEVED--592     FREESPC-BYTES--573440
     ALLOCATION
          SPACE-TYPE-----CYLINDER    HI-ALLOC-RBA----1843200     HI-ALLOC-RBA-----1843200
          SPACE-PRI----------2       HI-USED-RBA-----1843200     HI-USED-RBA------1843200
          SPACE-SEC----------1
     VOLUME
          VOLSER--------MPS800       PHYREC-SIZE------4096       HI-ALLOC-RBA-----1843200     EXTENT-NUMBER-------2
          DEVTYPE-----X'3010200E'    PHYRECS/TRK--------10       HI-USED-RBA------1843200     EXTENT-TYPE------X'OC'
          VOLFLAG-------PRIME        TRACKS/CA---------15
          EXTENTS:
          LOW-CCHH----X'005F0000'    LOW-RBA------------0        TRACKS-------------30
          HIGH-CCHH---X'0060000E'    HIGH-RBA-----1228799
          LOW-CCHH----X'03C6000C'    LOW-RBA-----1228800        TRACKS-------------15
          HIGH-CCHH---X'0306000E'    HIGH-RBA----1843199

INDEX ------ MMA2.CUSTOMER.MASTER.INDEX
     IN-CAT --- VCAT.MPS800
     HISTORY
          OWNER-IDENT------(NULL)        CREATION---------85.234
```

Figure 6-32   Output from a LISTCAT command with the ALL parameter (part 1 of 2)

```
IDCAMS  SYSTEM  SERVICES                           TIME: 19:16:06        08/22/85        PAGE    2

      RELEASE--------------2          EXPIRATION-------00.000
      PROTECTION-PSWD----(NULL)       RACF------------(YES)
  ASSOCIATIONS
      CLUSTER--MMA2.CUSTOMER.MASTER
  ATTRIBUTES
      KEYLEN-------------6            AVGLRECL----------0        BUFSPACE----------0        CISIZE---------2048
      RKP----------------0            MAXLRECL-------2041        EXCPEXIT-----(NULL)        CI/CA-----------18
      SHROPTNS(2,3)  RECOVERY         UNIQUE      NOERASE        NOWRITECHK  NOIMBED        NOREPLICAT  UNORDERED
      NOREUSE
  STATISTICS
      REC-TOTAL----------4            SPLITS-CI---------1        EXCPS----------3327        INDEX:
      REC-DELETED--------0            SPLITS-CA---------0        EXTENTS-----------1        LEVELS-----------2
      REC-INSERTED-------0            FREESPACE-%CI-----0        SYSTEM-TIMESTAMF:          ENTRIES/SECT----12
      REC-UPDATED-------61            FREESPACE-%CA-----0            X'999FD9E6D0092200'    SEQ-SET-RBA------0
      REC-RETRIEVED------0            FREESPC-BYTES-28672                                   HI-LEVEL-RBA--4096
  ALLOCATION
      SPACE-TYPE------TRACK           HI-ALLOC-RBA--36864
      SPACE-PRI----------1            HI-USED-RBA----8192
      SPACE-SEC----------1
  VOLUME
      VOLSER-------MPS800             PHYREC-SIZE----2048        HI-ALLOC-RBA----36864      EXTENT-NUMBER-----1
      DEVTYPE----X'3010200E'          PHYRECS/TRK------18        HI-USED-RBA------8192      EXTENT-TYPE---X'00'
      VOLFLAG------PRIME              TRACKS/CA---------1
  EXTENTS:
      LOW-CCHH----X'00D40000'         LOW-RBA-----------0        TRACKS------------1
      HIGH-CCHH---X'00D40000'         HIGH-RBA------36863
```

Figure 6-32   Output from a LISTCAT command with the ALL parameter (part 2 of 2)

output can easily be hundreds of pages long. So be as specific as you can about the information you need when you run an AMS LISTCAT job. The less output you request, the simpler it will be for you to read and the less system time it will take to create and print it.

Listing information about data spaces   To list information about data spaces rather than data sets, you code SPACE as an entry-type on the LISTCAT command. When you do, there are a few things I want you to realize. First, data spaces don't have names, so you can't specify them by name with ENTRIES or LEVEL parameters. However, you can code the ENTRIES parameter to print information about spaces that reside on specific volumes. Just code one or more vol-sers in the ENTRIES parameter. For example, suppose you code this command:

```
LISTCAT ENTRIES(MPS800)
        SPACE
```

Here, AMS lists information about all the spaces on the volume named MPS800.

Second, you'll probably need to use the CATALOG parameter or a job or step catalog to identify the catalog that owns the space. If you don't, AMS uses the master catalog. You can't rely on the high-level qualifier of the name you code in the entries parameter under MVS, because vol-sers aren't qualified.

Finally, the LISTCAT output for a space includes a listing of the names of the data sets contained in the space. As you'll learn later in this topic, that information can be useful if you want to delete a space.

The ALTER command

With the ALTER command, shown in figure 6-33, you can change a VSAM file's name, volume allocation, and other characteristics assigned to the file when you defined it. You can nullify certain protection attributes associated with the file. And you can inhibit the file so that it can be read but not updated.

Besides the parameters shown in figure 6-33, you can also code many DEFINE parameters on the ALTER command. For example, you can use an ALTER command to change the FREESPACE specification for a key-sequenced data set. Or, you can change a file's SHAREOPTIONS settings. Unfortunately, there are many restrictions on how you can code those parameters. As a result, I won't describe them in detail here. Instead, I suggest you consult the appropriate AMS reference manual to see how to use those parameters on your system when you need to.

Figure 6-34 gives five examples of the ALTER command. As I describe how to use ALTER to change a file's name, volume allocation, and DEFINE parameters, refer to the examples in this figure.

How to change an object's name   Example 1 in figure 6-34 shows how to change a VSAM object's name. To do that, you code two parameters on the

The ALTER command

```
ALTER    entry-name[/password]
     [ CATALOG(name[/password]) ]
     [ NEWNAME(entry-name) ]
     [ ADDVOLUMES(vol-ser...) ]
     [ REMOVEVOLUMES(vol-ser...) ]
     [ NULLIFY(security parameters) ]
     [ INHIBIT | UNINHIBIT ]
```

Explanation

entry-name[/password]	Required. Specifies the name and, if required, password of the object whose catalog entry is to be altered.
CATALOG(name[/password])	Optional. Identifies the catalog that contains the object to be altered. Required only if the catalog can't be located by the standard search sequence.
NEWNAME(entry-name)	Optional. Specifies a new entry name for the entry.
ADDVOLUMES(vol-ser...)	Optional. Adds the specified volumes to the list of volumes on which space may be allocated to the object.
REMOVEVOLUMES(vol-ser...)	Optional. Removes the specified volumes from the list of volumes on which space may be allocated to the object. Ignored if space has already been allocated on the specified volumes. See text for implications of REMOVEVOLUMES for the master catalog.
NULLIFY(security parameters)	Optional. Removes the protection provided by certain security parameters. See chapter 9 for details.
INHIBIT UNINHIBIT	Optional. INHIBIT sets the data set to read-only status; UNINHIBIT returns the data set to normal status.

Figure 6-33 The ALTER command

ALTER command: the name of the existing VSAM object and, in the NEWNAME parameter, the new name for the object. The object you're renaming can be a cluster, component, alternate index, path, or catalog.

How to change an object's volume allocation   When you define a VSAM object, you specify at least one volume on which space for the object can be allocated. If you specify more volumes than are necessary to hold the object, the excess volumes are available for future expansion of the object. In other words, they're candidate volumes for the object. With the ADD-VOLUMES and REMOVEVOLUMES parameter of the ALTER command, you can add or remove volumes from this list of candidate volumes.

Example 1

```
ALTER  MMA2.CUSTOMER.MASTER           -
        NEWNAME(MMA2.CUSTMAST)
```

Example 2

```
ALTER  MMA2.CUSTOMER.MASTER.DATA       -
        ADDVOLUMES(VOL291 VOL292)       -
        REMOVEVOLUMES(VOL281 VCL282)
```

Example 3

```
ALTER  MMA2.CUSTOMER.MASTER.DATA       -
        FREESPACE(10 10)
```

Example 4

```
ALTER  MMA2.CUSTMAST                    -
        NULLIFY(RETENTION)
```

Example 5

```
ALTER  MMA2.CUSTOMER.MASTER.DATA       -
        INHIBIT
```

Figure 6-34   Examples of the ALTER command

To illustrate, consider example 2 in figure 6-34. Here, I've decided to change the candidate volumes for a data component named MMA2.CUSTOMER.MASTER.DATA. Rather than using VOL281 and VOL282, I want the file to use VOL291 and VOL292 if necessary. So, I listed the volumes I want added in the ADDVOLUMES parameter. And I listed the volumes I want dropped in the REMOVEVOLUMES parameter. Notice that I specified the data component as the object to be altered; you can't code ADDVOLUMES or REMOVEVOLUMES for the cluster itself.

One restriction of the REMOVEVOLUMES parameter is that you can *not* remove a volume if the object already has space allocated for it on that volume. To see the volumes on which an object has space allocated, issue a LISTCAT command with the ALLOCATION or ALL parameter.

Also, you should realize that REMOVEVOLUMES works differently when you're altering the master catalog. In that case, AMS deletes all VSAM objects, including space, from the specified volumes. At first, that may sound like a good way to clean up a volume that has many unwanted VSAM files on it. But if the catalog that owns the objects on the volume resides on a different volume, VSAM does *not* update the catalog to reflect the new status of the volume. In some cases, that can have disasterous consequences. As a result, you should not use ALTER REMOVEVOLUMES for volume cleanup unless absolutely necessary. And if you do, realize that the catalog that owns the volume may become outdated.

How to change other DEFINE attributes   Example 3 in figure 6-34 shows how to change other DEFINE attributes for VSAM objects. Here, I changed the free space allocation for a KSDS cluster. Notice that the entry-name I coded on the ALTER command is the name of the file's data component, not the cluster itself. That's because the FREESPACE parameter applies to a file's data component only, even though you can code it at the CLUSTER or DATA level of the DEFINE CLUSTER command. (You'll learn more about the FREESPACE parameter in chapter 7.) In any event, there are many other DEFINE parameters you can change with the ALTER command. As I've already mentioned, you can find out about them in your AMS reference manual.

How to nullify protection attributes   When you define a cluster, you can specify protection parameters that establish security procedures for the cluster and you can associate a retention period with the cluster. To change one of those options, you can code the parameter again on an ALTER command. Alternatively, you can code the parameter as a subparameter of the NULLIFY parameter. In that case, the protection originally provided by the parameter is removed.

To understand this, consider example 4 in figure 6-34. Here, I coded NULLIFY(RETENTION) in an ALTER command. As a result, any retention period associated with the file is removed. So the effect of a FOR or TO parameter on the DEFINE command for this cluster is negated.

You can also nullify passwords and other security information with the NULLIFY parameter. You'll learn about passwords and security in chapter 9.

How to inhibit a VSAM object   The last ALTER parameters I want you to know about are INHIBIT and UNINHIBIT. Simply put, these parameters let you control whether or not a VSAM file can be updated. If a file is inhibited, it can be opened only for INPUT. When the file is uninhibited, it can be processed as usual. Frankly, I doubt that you'll find much use for this feature, but it's good to know about.

Example 5 in figure 6-34 shows how to code an ALTER command to inhibit a file. To uninhibit this file, just code UNINHIBIT instead of INHIBIT. You can also inhibit a file by coding INHIBITTARGET on an EXPORT command. You'll learn more about that in chapter 8.

The DELETE command

You use the DELETE command to remove entries from a VSAM catalog. Its format, shown in figure 6-35, is simple. To delete a VSAM file, all you normally need to include on the DELETE command is the name of the file. To delete more than one file, list the names in parentheses. If you want to delete the file regardless of whether its retention period has expired, code

The DELETE command

```
DELETE   {entry-name[/password]          }
         {( entry-name[/password]... )}

         [ CATALOG(name[/password]) ]

         [ entry-type ]

         [ FORCE | NOFORCE ]

         [ PURGE | NOPURGE ]

         [ ERASE | NOERASE ]
```

Explanation

entry-name[/password] (entry-name[/password]...)	Required. Specifies the name and password of the entry or entries to be deleted. If you specify more than one entry name, you must enclose the list in parentheses. To delete a space, specify a vol-ser as the entry name.
CATALOG(name[/password])	Optional. Specifies the name and password of the catalog that owns the entries to be deleted. Required only if the correct catalog can't be found using the standard search sequence.
entry-type	Optional. Specifies that only entries of the listed types should be deleted. The valid entry types are the same as for the LISTCAT command.
FORCE NOFORCE	Optional. When SPACE is specified as the entry-type along with FORCE, data spaces are deleted even if they contain data sets. If you specify NOFORCE, only empty spaces are deleted. NOFORCE is the default. (Doesn't apply to ICF.)
PURGE NOPURGE	Optional. PURGE means that an object should be deleted even if its retention period has not expired. NOPURGE means to delete entries only if their retention periods have expired. NOPURGE is the default.
ERASE NOERASE	Optional. ERASE means that the data component of a cluster or alternate index should be erased (overwritten with binary zeros). NOERASE means that the data component should not be erased. NOERASE is the default.

Figure 6-35   The DELETE command

PURGE as well. The CATALOG parameter lets you specify the catalog that owns the file to be deleted. If you omit it, AMS uses the high-level qualifier of the file name (OS only) or the step, job, or master catalog.

You can use a generic name in a DELETE command by replacing one level of the entry name with an asterisk, like this:

```
DELETE MMA2.CUSTOMER.*
```

Here, all entries whose names consist of three levels, with the first two levels being MMA2.CUSTOMER, will be deleted. That includes names like MMA2.CUSTOMER.MASTER and MMA2.CUSTOMER.HISTORY.

Although DELETE removes catalog records for an entry, it leaves the file itself on the disk until it's overwritten by another file. You can cause AMS to overwrite the data in a file you delete by coding the ERASE option on the DELETE command. Then, AMS writes binary zeros over the entire file. That way, once the file's deleted, it can't be accessed under any circumstances. Bear in mind, however, that erasing a file can take a lot of time, depending on the size of the file. So use ERASE only when the file contains sensitive data that actually should be erased when deleted.

The entry-type parameter lets you limit the delete operation to certain types of objects. The values you can code here are the same as the entry-types you can code in a LISTCAT command. Normally, you don't need to specify an entry-type since the names you specify indicate which objects you want deleted. But if you use a generic name, you might want to specify that just objects of certain types should be deleted.

To delete a space, you code the vol-ser of the volume that contains the space you want deleted. That causes all empty data spaces on the volume to be deleted. If you specify FORCE, all spaces are deleted from the volume, whether or not they contain data sets. DELETE with the FORCE parameter does *not* delete the catalog entries for data sets that resided in those spaces. As a result, I recommend you don't use the DELETE command with the FORCE option. Instead, issue a LISTCAT command with the entry-type SPACE to see what data sets reside in the space. Then, issue a DELETE command for each data set. Only then should you issue a DELETE command for the space.

Figure 6-36 shows four examples of the DELETE command. In example 1, I deleted a single file named MMA2.CUSTOMER.MASTER. Because I specified the PURGE parameter, this file will be deleted whether or not its expiration date has arrived.

Examples 2 and 3 show how to delete several files with a single DELETE command. In example 2, I listed three names on the command. In example 3, I used a generic file name to delete all alternate indexes whose names follow the form MMA2.CUSTMAST.*.AIX.

Example 4 shows how to delete space. Here, I listed VOL291 on the DELETE command; that's the volume from which I want space deleted. Although it's not required, I listed SPACE as the entry type. And because I didn't code FORCE, only empty spaces will be deleted.

COMMANDS THAT COPY AND PRINT FILES

Besides performing catalog maintenance functions, you'll often use AMS to print and copy files. To do that, you use the PRINT and REPRO commands. The format of both commands is similar. I'll cover PRINT first because it's a bit simpler than REPRO.

Example 1

```
DELETE MMA2.CUSTOMER.MASTER                    -
        PURGE
```

Example 2

```
DELETE (MMA2.CUSTOMER.MASTER                   -
        MMA2.CUSTMAST.DISTRICT.AIX             -
        MMA2.CUSTMAST.DISTRICT.PATH)
```

Example 3

```
DELETE MMA2.CUSTMAST.*.AIX                     -
        ALTERNATEINDEX
```

Example 4

```
DELETE VOL291                                  -
        SPACE
```

Figure 6-36	Examples of the DELETE command

The PRINT command

Figure 6-37 gives the format of the PRINT command. You must always code at least one parameter, INFILE or INDATASET, to identify the file you want to print. If you code INFILE, you specify the ddname of a file identified in the JCL with a DD or DLBL statement. If you code INDATASET, you supply the VSAM file name, and you don't have to provide a DD or DLBL statement for the file.

The CHARACTER, HEX, and DUMP parameters let you specify the format of the printed output. If you specify CHARACTER, AMS prints the actual characters contained in each file record. However, many files contain unprintable characters like packed-decimal fields. For those files, you should specify HEX or DUMP. HEX prints the hexadecimal value of each byte in the file's records, and DUMP prints both the character and the hex values. If you omit CHARACTER, HEX, and DUMP, the default format is DUMP.

The next two sets of parameters let you select specific records to be printed. If you don't specify otherwise, AMS starts printing with the first record in the data set. If you don't want to start printing at the beginning of the data set, you can code SKIP, FROMKEY, FROMNUMBER, or FROMADDRESS. SKIP lets you bypass a specified number of records. So to begin printing with the 50th record, code SKIP(49). You can use SKIP with

The PRINT command

```
PRINT    {INDATASET(entry-name[/password])}
         {INFILE(ddname[/password])      }

         {CHARACTER}
         {HEX      }
         {DUMP     }

         {SKIP(count)          }
      [  {FROMKEY(key)         }  ]
         {FROMNUMBER(number)   }
         {FROMADDRESS(address) }

         {COUNT(count)       }
      [  {TOKEY(key)         }  ]
         {TONUMBER(number)   }
         {TOADDRESS(address) }
```

Explanation

INDATASET(entry-name[/password])
INFILE(ddname[/password])

Required. INDATASET specifies the filename of the VSAM file to be printed. INFILE specifies the name of a DD or DLBL statement that identifies the file.

CHARACTER
HEX
DUMP

Optional. Specifies the format of the output. CHARACTER and HEX print the data in character or hex format. DUMP prints data in both character and hex format. DUMP is the default.

SKIP(count)
FROMKEY(key)
FROMNUMBER(number)
FROMADDRESS(address)

Optional. Specifies the first record of the file to be printed. For count, specify a numeric value to indicate the number of records to be skipped before the print operation begins. Valid for all file types. For key, specify the value of the key at which the print operation should begin. Valid only when printing a KSDS or an ISAM file. For number, specify the relative record number at which the print operation should begin. Valid only when printing an RRDS. For address, specify the RBA of the first record to be printed. Valid only when printing a KSDS or ESDS.

COUNT(count)
TOKEY(key)
TONUMBER(number)
TOADDRESS(address)

Optional. Specifies the last record of the file to be printed. For count, specify a numeric value to indicate the number of records to be printed. Valid for all file types. For key, specify the value of the key at which the print operation should end. Valid only when printing a KSDS or an ISAM file. For number, specify the relative record number at which the print operation should end. Valid only when printing an RRDS. For address, specify an RBA that lies within the last record to be printed. Valid only when printing a KSDS or ESDS.

Figure 6-37   The PRINT command

Example 1

```
PRINT INDATASET (MMA2.CUSTOMER.MASTER) -
      CHARACTER                        -
      SKIP(28)                         -
      COUNT(3)
```

Example 2

```
PRINT INDATASET (MMA2.CUSTOMER.MASTER) -
      HEX                              -
      SKIP(28)                         -
      COUNT(3)
```

Example 3

```
PRINT INDATASET (MMA2.CUSTOMER.MASTER) -
      DUMP                             -
      SKIP(28)                         -
      COUNT(3)
```

Figure 6-38   Examples of the PRINT commands

any type of file organization. For a KSDS, you can code FROMKEY with the key value of the first record you want to process. (If the key contains commas, semicolons, blanks, parentheses, or slashes, you must code the key between apostrophes.) For an RRDS, you can use the FROMNUMBER parameter to specify the relative record number of the first record you want printed. And, for an ESDS or a KSDS, you can specify a relative byte address in the FROMADDRESS parameter.

Printing continues until AMS reaches the end of the data set unless you code COUNT, TOKEY, TONUMBER, or TOADDRESS to specify where printing should end. COUNT indicates how many records should be processed; it's valid for any type of file. For a KSDS or RRDS, you use TOKEY or TONUMBER to indicate where in the file to stop printing. And for an ESDS or KSDS, you can specify an RBA in the TOADDRESS parameter.

To illustrate how to use the PRINT command, figure 6-38 presents three AMS job steps that print a customer master file. In each case, I coded SKIP(28) to bypass the first 28 records and COUNT(3) to print only three records. As a result, these jobs print the 29th, 30th, and 31st records in the file. Each PRINT command in figure 6-38 specifies a different print format: CHARACTER, HEX, or DUMP. Figures 6-39, 6-40, and 6-41 show the output produced by each PRINT command.

```
IDCAMS  SYSTEM  SERVICES

LISTING OF DATA SET -MMA2.CUSTOMER.MASTER

KEY OF RECORD - 28776J
28776JOHN WARDS AND ASSOC5600 N CLARKE        CHICAGO      IL603002027  010200...%...%...@

KEY OF RECORD - 29556N
29556NATIONAL INDUSTRIES 3879 NE FOOTE        WASHINGTON DC200190003   010210...........*

KEY OF RECORD - 29573U
29573UNIVERSAL SERVICES  2115 FULTON RD        POMONA       CA917680223  010220..........¯..

IDC0005I NUMBER OF RECORDS PROCESSED WAS 3

IDC0001I FUNCTION COMPLETED, HIGHEST CONDITION CODE WAS 0
```

Figure 6-39 Output produced by the PRINT command in example 1 of figure 6-38 (CHARACTER format)

IDCAMS SYSTEM SERVICES

TIME: 17:12:52   01/16/86   PAGE   2

LISTING OF DATA SET -MMA2.CUSTOMER.MASTER

KEY OF RECORD - F2F8F7F7F6D1
F2F8F7F7F6D1D6C8D540E6C1D9C4E240C1E2E2D6C3F5F6F0F040D540C3D3C1D9D2C540404040404040404040404040C3C8C9C3C1C7D6404040
40C9D3F6F0F3F0F0F2F2F740404040F1F0F2F0F0392706C0571316274040404040404C4040404040404C4040404040404C40404040404040
4040404040404040404C404040404040404C40404040

KEY OF RECORD - F2F9F5F5F6D5
F2F9F5F5F6D5C1E3C9D6D5C1D340C9D5C4E4E2E3D9C9C5E240F3F8F7F940D5C540C6D6D6E3C54040404040404040404040E6C1E2C8C9D5C7E3D6D5
40C4C3F2F0F0F1F9F0F0F0F0F0CF34040F0F1F0F2F1F004057 88C058 89543C073708 5C40404040404C40404040404C40404040404C40404040404040
4040404040404040404C4040404040404040404040

KEY OF RECORD - F2F9F5F5F7F3E4
F2F9F5F5F7F3E4D5C9E5C5D9E2C1D340E2C5D9E5C9C3C5E24040F2F1F1F540C6E4D3E3D6D5C440404040404C404040404040404040404040404040
40C3C1F9F1F7F6F8F0F2F2F340404040F1FCF2F2F004188 70C060727 0C0760543C4040404040404C4040404040404C4040404040404C40404040404040
4040404040404040404C4040404040404C4040404C40

IDC0005I NUMBER OF RECORDS PROCESSED WAS 3

IDC0001I FUNCTION COMPLETED, HIGHEST CONDITION CODE WAS 0

Figure 6-40   Output produced by the PRINT command in example 2 of figure 6-38 (HEX format)

LISTING OF DATA SET -MMA2.CUSTOMER.MASTER

```
KEY OF RECORD - F2F8F7F7F6D1
000000 F2F8F7F7 F6D1D6C8 D540E6C1 D9C4E240  C1D5C440 C1E2E2D6 C3F5F6F0 F040D54C  *28776JOHN WARDS AND ASSOC5600 N *
000020 C3D3C1D9 D2C54040 404C404C 40F2FOF0  40C03C8 C9C3C1C7 D6404040 40C9D3F6  *CLARKE    CHICAGO      IL6*
000040 F0F3FCF0 F2FOF2F7 4040F0F1 F0F2F0F0  0392706C 0571816C 0713627C 40404040  *030C2027 010200...%...a *
000060 40404040 40404040 40404040 40404040  40404040 40404040 40404040 40404040  *                              *
000080 40404040 40404040 40404040 40404040  40404040 40404040 40404040 40404040  *                              *
0000A0 40404040 40404040 40404040 40404040  40404040 40404040 40404040 40404040  *                              *
0000C0 40404C40 40404040                     40404040 40404C40                    *                              *

KEY OF RECORD - F2F9F5F5F6D5
000000 F2F9F5F5 F6D5C1E3 C9D6D5C1 D340C9D5  C4E4E2E3 D9C9C5E2 40F3F8F7 F940D5C5  *29956NATIONAL INDUSTRIES 3879 NE*
000020 40C6D6D6 E3C54040 40404040 40404040  404CE6C1 E2C8C9D5 C7E3D6D5 40C4C3F2  * FOOTE         WASHINGTON DC2*
000040 F0F0F1F9 F0F0F0F3 4040CF0F1 40404040  0405788C 0589543C 0737085C 40404040  *0019003 01021C..........* 
000060 40404040 40404040 40404040 4C404040  40404040 40404040 40404040 40404040  *                              *
000080 40404040 40404040 40404040 40404040  40404040 40404040 40404040 40404040  *                              *
0000A0 40404040 40404040 40404040 40404040  40404040 40404040 40404040 40404040  *                              *
0000C0 40404040 40404040                     40404040 40404040                    *                              *

KEY OF RECORD - F2F9F5F7F3E4
000000 F2F9F5F7 F3E4D5C9 E5C5D9E2 C1D340E2  C5D9E5C9 C3C5E240 40F2F1F1 F540C6E4  *29573UNIVERSAL SERVICES 2115 FU*
000020 D3E3D6D5 40D9C440 40404040 40404040  404CD7D6 D4D6D5C1 40404040 40C3C1F9  *LTON RD        PCMONA        CA9*
000040 F1F7F6F8 F0F2F2F3 4040F0F1 F0F2F2F0  041887CC 060727CC 0760543C 40404040  *17680223 010220..........* 
000060 40404C40 40404C4C 404C404C 4C404040  40404040 40404040 40404040 40404040  *                              *
000080 40404040 40404040 40404040 40404040  40404040 40404040 40404040 40404040  *                              *
0000A0 40404040 40404040 40404040 4C404040  40404040 40404040 40404040 40404040  *                              *
0000C0 40404040 40404040                     40404040 40404040                    *                              *
```

IDC0005I NUMBER OF RECORDS PROCESSED WAS 3

IDC0001I FUNCTION COMPLETED, HIGHEST CONDITION CODE WAS 0

Figure 6-41   Output produced by the PRINT command in example 3 of figure 6-38 (DUMP format)

The REPRO command

```
REPRO        {INDATASET(entry-name[/password])}
             {INFILE(ddname[/password])      }

             {OUTDATASET(entry-name[/password])}
             {OUTFILE(ddname[/password])       }

             {SKIP(count)          }
        [    {FROMKEY(key)         }    ]
             {FROMNUMBER(number)   }
             {FROMADDRESS(address) }

             {COUNT(count)         }
        [    {TOKEY(key)           }    ]
             {TONUMBER(number)     }
             {TOADDRESS(address)   }

        [    REUSE | NOREUSE    ]

        [    REPLACE | NOREPLACE    ]
```

Figure 6-42   The REPRO command (part 1 of 2)

The REPRO command

You use the REPRO command to copy the contents of a data set into another data set. Figure 6-42 gives the format of the REPRO command. Its format is similar to the PRINT command, with two important differences. First, you must specify an output file as well as an input file. You do that by coding the OUTFILE or OUTDATASET parameters. If you code OUTFILE, you must specify the name of a DD or DLBL statement that identifies the file. If you code OUTDATASET, you provide the VSAM file name. Second, the REPRO command doesn't support the CHARACTER/HEX/DUMP parameters.

The output file you specify in a REPRO command must exist. In other words, you must first define the output file using a DEFINE CLUSTER command. If the output file is empty, VSAM processes the file in load mode, and records are copied one by one from the input file to the output file. If the output file contains records when the REPRO command starts, records from the input file are merged with the records in the output file. Where the input records are placed depends on the output file's organization. For an ESDS, records are added at the end of the output file. For an RRDS or KSDS, records are added at the correct position based on relative record numbers or key values. Duplicates are handled according to how you code the REPLACE option. If you specify REPLACE, duplicates in the input file replace existing records in the output file; if you specify NOREPLACE, they do not.

Explanation

INDATASET(entry-name[/password])
INFILE(ddname[/password])

Required. INDATASET specifies the name of the data set to be copied. INFILE specifies the name of a DD or DLBL statement that identifies the file to be copied.

OUTDATASET(entry-name[/password])
OUTFILE(ddname[/password])

Required. OUTDATASET specifies the name of the data set to which the input file is to be copied. OUTFILE specifies the name of a DD or DLBL statement that identifies the file to which the input file is to be copied.

SKIP(count)
FROMKEY(key)
FROMNUMBER(number)
FROMADDRESS(address)

Optional. Specifies the first record of the file to be copied. For count, specify a numeric value to indicate the number of records to be skipped before the copy operation begins. Valid for all file types. For key, specify the value of the key at which the copy operation should begin. Valid only when copying a KSDS or an ISAM file. For number, specify the relative record number at which the copy operation should begin. Valid only when copying an RRDS. For address, specify the RBA of the first record to be copied. Valid only when copying a KSDS or ESDS.

COUNT(count)
TOKEY(key)
TONUMBER(number)
TOADDRESS(address)

Optional. Specifies the last record of the file to be copied. For count, specify a numeric value to indicate the number of records to be copied. Valid for all file types. For key, specify the value of the key at which the copy operation should end. Valid only when copying a KSDS or an ISAM file. For number, specify the relative record number at which the copy operation should end. Valid only when copying an RRDS. For address, specify an RBA that lies within the last record to be copied. Valid only when copying a KSDS or ESDS.

REUSE
NOREUSE

REUSE specifies that the output file should be reset if it is reusable. NOREUSE specifies that a reusable output file should not be reused. NOREUSE is the default.

REPLACE
NOREPLACE

Specifies how duplicate records should be handled. If you specify REPLACE, duplicate records are replaced; if you specify NOREPLACE, duplicates are treated as errors. NOREPLACE is the default.

Figure 6-42   The REPRO command (part 2 of 2)

The REUSE parameter lets you specify that the file should be loaded even though it already contains records. When you specify REUSE, VSAM resets the file's high-used RBA field to zero, effectively deleting all records in the file. You can only specify REUSE for files you defined with the REUSE attribute.

You can use the SKIP, FROMKEY, FROMNUMBER, and FROMADDRESS parameters along with the COUNT, TOKEY, TO-NUMBER, and TOADDRESS parameters to limit the number of records copied. You code these parameters just as you do for a PRINT command.

```
//          EXEC PGM=IDCAMS
//SYSPRINT DD   SYSOUT=A
//SYSIN    DD   *
 DEFINE CLUSTER ( NAME(MMA2.EMPMAST.REPRO)           -
                  MODEL(MMA2.EMPLOYEE.MASTER)         -
                  VOLUMES(MPS8BV) )                   -
         DATA    ( NAME(MMA2.EMPMAST.REPRO.DATA) -
                   CYLINDERS(5 1) )                   -
         INDEX   ( NAME(MMA2.EMPMAST.REPRO.INDEX) )
 REPRO   INDATASET(MMA2.EMPLOYEE.MASTER)             -
         OUTDATASET(MMA2.EMPMAST.REPRO)
 IF LASTCC > 4 THEN SET MAXCC = 16
 DELETE MMA2.EMPLOYEE.MASTER
 ALTER  MMA2.EMPMAST.REPRO                           -
        NEWNAME(MMA2.EMPLOYEE.MASTER)
 ALTER  MMA2.EMPMAST.REPRO.DATA                      -
        NEWNAME(MMA2.EMPLOYEE.MASTER.DATA)
 ALTER  MMA2.EMPMAST.REPRO.INDEX                     -
        NEWNAME(MMA2.EMPLOYEE.MASTER.INDEX)
 /*
```

Figure 6-43   A job step that reorganizes a VSAM key-sequenced data set

If you wish, the input and output files can be of different types. In other words, you can copy an ESDS input file to a RRDS output file. Or, you can copy an ISAM file to a KSDS. There's no restriction on the combination of input and output file types, except that you can't specify an ISAM file as the output file.

One of the most common uses of the REPRO command is for reorganizing key-sequenced data sets. Because REPRO opens a KSDS for output and loads it, the free space you originally allocated is restored, and the file is consolidated into a single extent if possible.

Figure 6-43 shows a typical AMS job step to reorganize a KSDS. First, a DEFINE CLUSTER command defines the new file, using the existing file as a model. Next, a REPRO command copies data from the old KSDS to the new one. Then, a DELETE command deletes the old KSDS. Finally, ALTER commands change the names of the new KSDS and its data and index components to the original names. Although the job stream is for an MVS system, the AMS commands for a DOS/VSE system are similar.

DISCUSSION

In this topic, I've presented a variety of AMS commands, some of which you'll use more often than others. Still, it's good to be familiar with all of the commands in this topic so that you'll know which commands to use in many situations.

Objective

Given specifications for an AMS job requiring the LISTCAT, ALTER, DELETE, PRINT, or REPRO commands, code an acceptable job stream using any of the facilities presented in this topic.

Chapter 7

Performance considerations

An important aspect of defining and maintaining VSAM files is insuring that they perform as efficiently as possible. As you might expect, evaluating VSAM file performance is not simple; there are many factors to consider. In this chapter, I'll describe those factors and recommend how to code the DEFINE parameters that affect performance.

The DEFINE parameters this chapter describes apply most directly to key-sequenced data sets. That's appropriate, because most of the data sets you'll use will be key-sequenced. Still, you can apply the concepts I present in this chapter to relative-record data sets, entry-sequenced data sets, and alternate indexes too.

CONTROL INTERVAL SIZE

One of the most important aspects of insuring good VSAM file performance is selecting an appropriate control interval size. As I mentioned in chapter 2, VSAM restricts control interval sizes to those listed in figure 7-1. Up to 8192 bytes, the control interval size must be a multiple of 512. Beyond that, up to the maximum of 32,768, you must select a multiple of 2048.

To specify a control interval size, you code the CONTROL-INTERVALSIZE parameter (usually abbreviated CISZ) on the DEFINE CLUSTER command, like this:

```
CISZ(4096)
```

Here, a control interval size of 4096 bytes is specified. Although you can code the CISZ parameter at the CLUSTER level, that's not a good idea because it assigns the same CI size to both the data and index components. Instead, specify CISZ at the DATA level, and let VSAM calculate the index CI size. Although VSAM will select a control interval size for both components if you omit the CISZ parameter, it often makes a poor choice for the data CI size. For the index component, VSAM's CI size choice is usually best.

When you select the control interval size for your file's data component, you need to consider a variety of factors. At the start, though, you can assume you'll use a control interval size of 4096 bytes. For most data sets, that size represents the best balance of the various factors to be considered.

Will the file be processed randomly, sequentially, or both? The first thing to consider when you select a control interval size is how the data set will be processed. In general, use a smaller CI size (4096 or less) when the file will be used mostly for random retrieval. A larger control interval size is more appropriate when you expect sequential processing.

The reasoning behind this is simple. When records are processed at random, you want to minimize the unnecessary data that's processed along with the record you want. That reduces both I/O time and the amount of virtual storage needed to hold the data. On the other hand, when sequential processing is used, you want to maximize the amount of data retrieved and processed at once, because that reduces the total number of I/O operations required to process the file.

Unfortunately, few files are used exclusively for either random or sequential processing. As a result, you must balance the importance of efficient random processing and efficient sequential processing. In most cases, random processing is done by on-line applications like CICS. When that's the case, you'll probably want to favor the on-line application and select a smaller control interval size. (Incidentally, when I describe buffering options later in this chapter, you'll see that even if you select a smaller CI size, you can regain lost sequential processing efficiency by specifying extra buffers for sequential applications.)

Increments of 512		Increments of 2048	
512	4608	10240	26624
1024	5120	12288	28672
1536	5632	14336	30720
2048	6144	16384	32768
2560	6656	18432	
3072	7168	20480	
3584	7680	22528	
4096	8192	24576	

Figure 7-1   Valid sizes for control intervals

CI size	Records/CI	Utilization
512	1	59 percent
1024	3	89 percent
2048	6	88 percent
4096	13	95 percent
6144	20	98 percent
8192	27	99 percent

Figure 7-2   How 300-byte records utilize space in a variety of control interval sizes

How well do the records fit in the control interval?   After considering the type of processing the file requires, you should consider how the file's records will fit in the control intervals. That can be simple or complex, depending on whether the file contains fixed- or variable-length records.

When fixed-length records are used, it's easy to figure out how the records will fit in the control intervals; all you do is divide the CI size by the record size, after allowing for the 10 bytes of control information required by fixed-length records. To illustrate, suppose you're defining a file with 300-byte records. Figure 7-2 shows how those 300-byte records fit in a variety of control interval sizes. Here, I divided the record size into the available space for each control interval size to see how many records will fit in each control interval and how many unused bytes will remain. Then, I calculated the percentage of control interval space utilized. As you can see, the utilization varies from 59 percent for 512-byte control intervals to 99 percent for 8192-byte control intervals. The recommended control interval size, 4096, gives 95 percent utilization for 300-byte records.

Of course, you'll have to calculate the utilization percentage for each file you define. Small changes in record size can make a big difference in space utilization. For example, 2043-byte records use all of the available space in a 4096-byte control interval. But a 2044-byte record uses only a littler more than half of the same control interval, wasting 2042 bytes.

For variable-length records, the calculation is more difficult. First of all, you must determine the average record size for the file. And, you must determine how much the records deviate from the average. In some cases, the deviation falls into predictable patterns. In others, it doesn't. Finally, when you calculate how many "average" records will fit in a control interval, you must allow for additional control bytes that will be needed.

How well does the selected control interval size fit on the device? One more item to consider when you select a control interval size is how well CIs of that size will fit on the particular DASD unit you're using. The key here is understanding how control intervals are actually stored on disk. Although VSAM always reads and writes entire control intervals with a single I/O operation, control intervals are actually stored on disk in *physical records* that may be smaller than the control intervals. For example, suppose you define a file on a 3330 DASD with 6144-byte control intervals. For this file, VSAM automatically picks a physical record size of 2K (2048). As a result, each control interval is stored in three physical records. And since each 3330 track can store 12K of data, six physical records (two control intervals) are stored per track.

VSAM uses only four sizes for physical records: 512, 1024, 2048, and 4096. VSAM selects the largest physical record size that divides evenly into your control interval size. That's why it picked 2048 as the physical record size for the file with 6144-byte control intervals. If you pick 7680 as a control interval size, VSAM uses fifteen 512-byte physical records for each CI.

In general, the larger the physical record, the better use it makes of the space in each track. As a result, you should try to use a control interval size that's a multiple of 4096. That gives you the best possible use of DASD space. (Incidentally, 2048-byte physical records work as well as 4096-byte records on a 3330 or 3350 DASD. For other devices, though, 4096 is best.)

FREE SPACE ALLOCATION

As you learned in chapter 2, you can reserve free space within the data component of a key sequenced file. To do that, you code the FREESPACE parameter on a DEFINE CLUSTER command. On the FREESPACE parameter, you code two values: one to indicate how much free space should be reserved within each control interval, the other to indicate how many control intervals within each control area should be reserved as free space. You specify both values as percentages, like this:

```
FREESPACE(20 10)
```

Here, 20 percent of the space in each control interval is reserved for insertions, while 10 percent of the control intervals in each control area are reserved.

Free space is distributed in your data set only during load processing. That happens when you copy data into a file using the REPRO command, when you open a file for OUTPUT in a COBOL program, or when you specify load processing in an assembler-language program. Then, during subsequent processing, that free space is used as required. Eventually, the free space will be used up, and the data set will have to be reloaded to regain the free space allocation. Of course, records may still be added to a data set if all of its free space has been used. However, CI and CA splits then occur.

Your objective when you determine how much free space to allocate is to minimize the number of CI and CA splits without wasting excessive DASD space. If you allocate too much free space, your file will waste DASD space and sequential processing will be degraded. But, more importantly, if you don't allocate enough free space, record insertions will cause control interval splits and, possibly, control area splits.

To determine the proper amount of free space to allocate, you must study the applications that process your data set to get an idea of how the file will grow. How many records will be inserted? Will they be inserted at random throughout the data set, will they cluster around certain key values, or will they always be inserted at the end of the data set? How often will the data set be reorganized, so that free space can be redistributed throughout the data set? Will records be deleted from the data set in a predictable pattern? If so, will inserted records be able to use space that's freed by deletions? These and other factors will help you decide how much free space to allocate to control intervals and control areas.

Control interval free space

When you calculate the percentage of free space to allocate within a data set's control intervals, probably the most important thing to remember is that free space is allocated in terms of bytes, not records. In other words, VSAM does *not* consider the size of your logical records when it reserves free space in the control intervals. For example, if you tell VSAM to reserve ten percent of the space in a 4096-byte control interval, VSAM reserves 410 bytes; that's ten percent of 4096, rounded up. However, depending on the length of your file's records, the effective free space percentage—that is, the percent of free space that's usable by new records—may be more or less than what you intended.

To illustrate, suppose your logical records are 100 bytes long and you specify 10 percent free space with 4096-byte control intervals. In this case, VSAM would initially load 36 records into the control interval, using 3600 bytes of the control interval for data, 10 bytes for control information, and leaving 486 bytes of free space. In that 486 bytes, VSAM will be able to insert four more logical records, for a total of 40 records in the control interval. As a result, the effective free space allocation within this control interval is ten percent: space for four records (out of a total capacity of 40) is reserved during load processing for later insertions.

On the other hand, suppose the logical records are 590 bytes in length. In this case, VSAM will load six records into the control interval before it reaches the free space amount. Those six records use 3540 bytes, leaving 546 bytes of free space after excluding the 10 bytes of control information in the CI. That's more than the requested ten percent, but not enough space to hold another record. As a result, VSAM cannot insert any records into this control interval. So even though you specified ten percent free space, the effective free space percentage is zero.

When your records are relatively large, more space than you might expect can be reserved in your control intervals. For example, suppose your logical records are 2000 bytes long, and you specify ten percent free space in a 4096 control interval. In this case, VSAM loads just one record into the control interval; the second record would cause the free space allocation to be less than requested. As a result, the number of free bytes in each control interval is 2086, enough to hold one more record. Even though you asked for 10 percent free space, VSAM gave you 50 percent.

The best way to avoid these unintended results is to calculate free space in terms of records, not bytes. First, determine what percentage of records you wish to reserve for free space. If your file will have a total of 100,000 records with 80,000 loaded initially and 20,000 inserted later, you'll have to allow for 20 percent free space. Next, determine how many records will fit in each control interval. Then, calculate how many bytes of free space will be reserved if you specify 20 percent free space, and see if the correct number of records will fit in that space. If not, adjust the free space percentage accordingly.

Some files have a high percentage of insertions that are almost always clustered around certain key values. In that case, it would be wasteful to allow a large percentage of free space in every control interval when only a few of the control intervals need the space. In a case like this, you can distribute the free space unevenly throughout the file by loading the file in stages, altering the free space percentage between each stage. For example, you might define the file with 10 percent CI free space, then load the first range of records. Then, you could use the ALTER command to change the free space allocation to 25 percent and load the next range of records (the records around which you expect the high rate of insertions). You could then alter the free space percentage again and load the next range of records. This process could go on and on, depending on your requirements.

Control area free space

Besides leaving free space in control intervals, VSAM lets you reserve control intervals within control areas as free space. When VSAM tries to insert a record into a control interval that doesn't have enough free space, it looks for a free control interval within the control area so that it can do a control interval split. If there are no free control intervals within the control area, VSAM splits the entire control area, extending the data set if necessary. As you can imagine, a control area split is one of the most inefficient VSAM operations. It requires multiple I/O operations to read and write control intervals. In addition, the data set's index must be updated. And additional overhead is required if the data set must be extended to accomodate the new control area.

In short, you should allow sufficient control area free space to eliminate control area splits. That helps insure that when a CI split occurs, VSAM will be able to find a free control interval within the control area, so no control area split will be required.

Right now, you might be wondering why you should plan for control interval splits when the purpose of allocating CI free space is to eliminate CI splits in the first place. While it's true that a good CI free space allocation can minimize CI splits, it's almost impossible to eliminate them altogether. Record insertions won't always occur in the patterns that you predict. So it's usually best to allow a small percentage of control area free space to reduce the likelyhood of a CA split.

Notice that I say to allocate a *small* amount of control area free space. Your main free space allocation should normally be in the control intervals. So if you allow for 25 percent free space in your control intervals, don't allow another 25 percent of CA free space. Remember that the purpose of CA free space is to accomodate the *unexpected* insertions that will cause CI splits. So you can usually get away with less CA free space, say, 10 percent. Then, if you find that control area splits are occurring, you can increase the CA free space allocation.

If your logical records are large and you expect a low insertion rate, you might rely on CA rather than CI free space. Earlier, I mentioned an example where 50 percent free space was reserved in each control interval even though only 10 percent was requested, because the records were large (2000 bytes) relative to the control interval size (4096 bytes). One solution to this problem would be to increase the control interval size. But that would probably have other degrading effects. In a case like this, you may be better off allocating no CI free space and 10 percent CA free space (or perhaps 15 percent to allow for a margin of error). Insertions will require control interval splits, but you won't be wasting 50 percent of your DASD space when only 10 percent is required.

INDEX OPTIONS

Two of the DEFINE CLUSTER performance parameters, IMBED and REPLICATE, let you change the way the index component of a key-sequenced data set is stored. In both cases, performance may or may not be improved, depending on a variety of factors that include contention from other applications for the DASD device on which the file resides and how you specify index buffering options, which I'll describe later in this chapter. You can code the IMBED and REPLICATE options at the CLUSTER or INDEX level. Either way, the effect is the same.

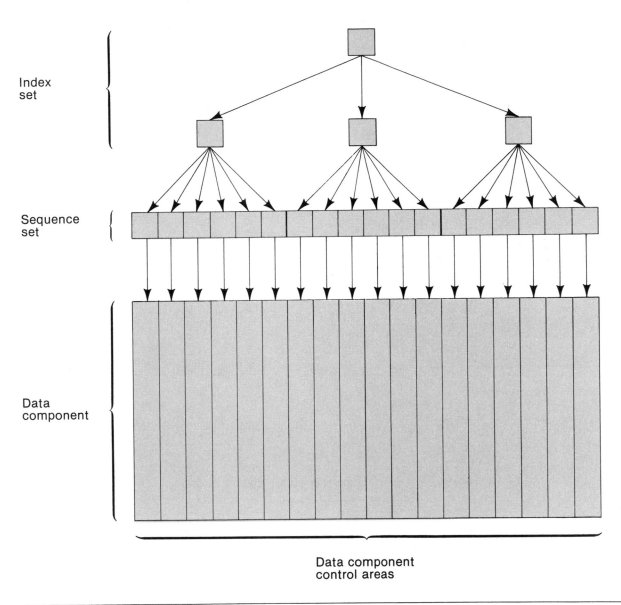

Index
set

Sequence
set

Data
component

Data component
control areas

Figure 7-3   Structure of a key-sequenced data set

To understand the IMBED and REPLICATE options, you need to understand the structure of a key-sequenced data set. Figure 7-3 illustrates that structure. As you know, a KSDS has two components: the index component and the data component. Space is allocated to them separately. In fact, they can even reside on different volumes if you wish. The index component itself has two parts: the index set and the sequence set. Each sequence set record contains index entries that provide access to all of the control intervals in a control area. As a result, there's a one-to-one correspondence between sequence set records and data component control areas.

For data sets that have more than one control area—and therefore have more than one sequence set record—VSAM may create additional levels in the index set. Each record in the lowest level of the index set contains entries for the sequence set records. If more than one index set record is required to index all of the sequence set records, additional index set levels are created. The highest level of the index set always contains one record. As I pointed out in chapter 2, few key-sequenced data sets require more than two levels in the index set.

The IMBED option

The IMBED option lets you improve KSDS performance by capitalizing on the fact that in nearly all key-sequenced data sets, each control area of the data component occupies one cylinder of DASD space. If you allocate space to the file in terms of cylinders, that's always the case. And you should allocate space in terms of records or tracks only in unusual cases.

The IMBED option simply moves sequence set records from the space allocated to the index set and places them in the space allocated to the data component. The first track of each control area is used to store the sequence set record that corresponds to that control area. As a result, a sequence set record and all of the control intervals it indexes can be accessed with a single movement, or *seek*, of the DASD's access mechanism. And that's a performance improvement; without the IMBED option, the access mechanism must first move to the index component to retrieve the sequence set record, then move to the cylinder in the data component that contains the desired control interval. The IMBED option eliminates the first seek.

In addition, the IMBED option causes the sequence set record to be duplicated as many times as possible on its track. That reduces rotational delay—how long the DASD has to wait for the desired record to pass under the read/write heads—when the sequence set record is read. Even though the performance benefit of fewer seeks and less rotational delay is measured in milliseconds, it can have a significant effect on the overall performance of your application.

Actually, the IMBED option improves performance only if you specify the file's index buffering options correctly. You'll learn how to do that later in this chapter. For now, I want you to realize that unless you provide enough index buffer space for the *entire* index set to reside in virtual storage, you lose the benefit of the IMBED option.

On DASD units that are highly utilized, the performance benefit of IMBED can be reduced by *stolen seeks*. Even when the IMBED option is used, two separate I/O operations may be required to retrieve a record: one to read the sequence set record, the other to read the data control interval. That happens when another program issues an I/O request to the device between the time your program reads the sequence set record and the data control interval and the access mechanism moves to another disk location. In effect, the first seek is "stolen," and another seek is required to move the access mechanism back to the cylinder that contains the data control interval.

The effect of stolen seeks can be difficult to detect. However, once detected, there are two common ways to handle the problem. One is to reduce contention for the DASD unit by moving the other high-use files to another unit. Another is to remove the IMBED option and move the index component to another volume. Which technique you choose depends on a lot of factors that are too complex to cover here.

There's one other point I want you to realize about the IMBED option: it adds to the space requirements for the data component of your file. That's because the first track of each control area isn't available for user data. As a result, you'll have to consider whether or not the IMBED option will be used when you determine your file's space requirements.

The REPLICATE option

The REPLICATE option causes VSAM to store each record of the index component, both index set and sequence set records, on a seperate track, duplicated as many times as possible. That results in less rotational delay and better overall performance. If REPLICATE is used with IMBED, REPLICATE causes the index set records to be duplicated; the sequence set records are duplicated automatically and stored along with the data component control areas because of the IMBED option.

In most cases, however, you won't want to use the REPLICATE option. Instead, you'll use the IMBED option and buffering techniques. The IMBED option automatically provides for replication of the sequence set records, and the buffering techniques eliminate DASD I/O altogether for the index set records by keeping the entire index set in virtual storage buffers.

However, there are some cases in which REPLICATE can be useful. For example, if stolen seeks cause you to isolate the index component on a separate DASD unit, REPLICATE might improve performance. Or, if you're using VSAM with another system component that doesn't give you complete control over index buffering options (like IMS or CICS), you might want to use REPLICATE because you can't guarantee that the entire index set will be available in virtual storage buffers. That way, any DASD I/O that's required to retrieve index set records will be as efficient as possible.

ALLOCATING BUFFERS FOR VSAM DATA SETS

One of the best ways to improve the performance of a VSAM file is to allocate additional buffers to it. Simply put, a *buffer* is an area of storage that VSAM uses to store a control interval after it's been read or before it's written. VSAM uses two types of buffers: *data buffers* for holding control intervals from the data component and *index buffers* for holding control intervals from the index component. Each data buffer is the same size as the file's data control intervals, and each index buffer is the same size as the file's index control intervals. Since each index control interval holds just one index record, each index buffer holds one index record too.

VSAM provides several ways to specify how much buffer space to use. You code the BUFFERSPACE option on a DEFINE command to specify the minimum amount of buffer space that will be allocated for the file. And, you can increase that amount when your program executes by coding the BUFSP parameter of the file's DLBL statement (DOS) or appropriate subparameters of the AMP parameter of the file's DD statement (OS).

VSAM's default buffer allocation

If you don't specify any buffer allocation, VSAM automatically allocates the smallest amount of buffer space it can operate with: two data buffers and one index buffer. For a typical data set with 4096-byte data control intervals and 2048-byte index control intervals, that's a total buffer space of 10K. However, in most cases, VSAM's default buffer allocation is unacceptable, and you should override it.

How to override VSAM's default buffer allocation

The most direct way to increase the total amount of buffer space is to code the BUFFERSPACE parameter at the CLUSTER level of a DEFINE CLUSTER command. When you do that, you specify a specific amount of buffer space, like this:

```
BUFFERSPACE(16384)
```

Here, 16K of buffer space is allocated. That means that whenever the data set is opened, a *minimum* of 16K will be allocated for buffers.

At execution time, you can increase the amount of buffer space allocated if you need to by specifying the BUFSP operand on the DD or DLBL statement for the file. For OS, code BUFSP as a subparameter of the AMP parameter on the DD statement, like this:

```
AMP=(BUFSP=20480)
```

For DOS, code the BUFSP parameter of the DLBL statement like this:

```
BUFSP=20480
```

In both cases, the buffer allocation is increased to 20K. Note that you can use the BUFSP operand only to *increase* the amount specified in the DEFINE CLUSTER command. If you specify a smaller amount, VSAM uses the BUFFERSPACE amount from the DEFINE command.

To determine how much buffer space to allocate, you first determine how many data and index buffers to use. (I'll describe how you do that in a moment.) Then, you determine how many bytes of storage are required to accomodate those buffers, and code that value on the BUFFERSPACE or BUFSP parameter. (Remember, each data buffer is the same size as a data control interval, and each index buffer is the same size as an index control interval.)

When you specify buffer space, you also need to know how VSAM will divide your space between data and index buffers. When you open your file for sequential processing, VSAM allocates one index buffer; the rest of the buffer space is allocated to data buffers. When you open the file for random processing, VSAM allocates two data buffers; the rest of the space goes to index buffers.

On OS systems, an easier way to specify buffer space is to specify BUFND and BUFNI in the AMP parameter on the file's DD statement. These options let you specify how many data (BUFND) and index (BUFNI) buffers to allocate. Then, you don't have to worry about translating how many buffers you need to a specific number of bytes, or how VSAM allocates buffer space between data and index buffers.

Allocating buffers for sequential processing

When you process a VSAM file sequentially, you don't need to worry about increasing VSAM's default index buffer allocation. Since the file's index set records aren't used at all, the buffers only need to provide for the sequence set records. And, because only one sequence set record is used at a time, there's no point in providing more than the one index buffer VSAM automatically allocates.

However, increasing the number of data buffers for sequential processing can give you two performance benefits. First, given enough data buffers, VSAM will overlap I/O and processing. In short, VSAM reads or writes data using one group of buffers while your program processes data in the other group. However many buffers you provide, VSAM divides them in half, using one set for processing and the other for I/O.

Second, VSAM reads or writes as many control intervals as it can in a single I/O operation using the number of buffers you provide. Given a sufficient number of buffers, VSAM will read or write up to an entire control area—a full cylinder of DASD space—with a single I/O operation. However, an entire cylinder is an excessive amount of buffer space for a normal application program. In general, you should allocate only enough buffer space for VSAM to read or write data one track at a time. And, to provide for overlap, you really need to allocate enough space for *two* tracks of data.

To determine how much buffer space to allocate for sequential processing, then, you must first determine how many control intervals are stored in each track. Earlier in this chapter, when I described how to select an appropriate control interval size, I explained how to do that. Once you've determined how many control intervals are in each track, double that amount to provide for overlap and add one to provide for the extra buffer VSAM needs to process control interval splits and do other internal processing. If you use BUFND to specify data buffers, that's the number you specify. If you use BUFFERSPACE or BUFSP, multiply that number by the data control interval size and add the index control interval size to allow for the index buffer for the sequence set record.

Figure 7-4 shows how buffers might be used to process a VSAM file sequentially. Here, I specified BUFNI = 1 and BUFND = 9. Since the file's index buffers are 2048 bytes each and its data buffers are 4096 each, that's a total of 38912 bytes of buffer space.

As you can see in figure 7-4, the index buffer contains a single sequence set record. VSAM uses eight of the nine data buffers for data control intervals, splitting them in half to overlap I/O and processing. The four buffers on the left contain control intervals that are currently available to the program; the program is processing records in the buffer that's shaded. At the same time, VSAM is using the four buffers on the right for control intervals being read from or written to the data set. The ninth data buffer is reserved for control interval split processing.

Incidentally, the rule that no additional index buffers are required applies only when processing is purely sequential. If you use the COBOL START statement, processing is actually a combination of sequential and random operations. In that case, you should consider adding additional index buffers.

Allocating buffers for random processing

For random processing, you need just two data buffers: one for the control interval being processed, the other for special operations such as control interval or control area splits. There's no point in allocating extra data buffers for random processing.

However, you can significantly improve random processing performance by allocating additional index buffers. In particular, you should allocate enough index buffers so the entire index set plus one sequence set record can be held in virtual storage at the same time. Then, if you specify the IMBED option, no extra access mechanism movement is needed to process the index records once the index set has been read into the buffers.

Figure 7-5 shows how those buffers might be processed. Here, three of the four index buffers contain index set records; the fourth index buffer contains a sequence set record. The shaded data buffer contains the data control interval currently being processed by the application program. The other data buffer is reserved for control interval splits.

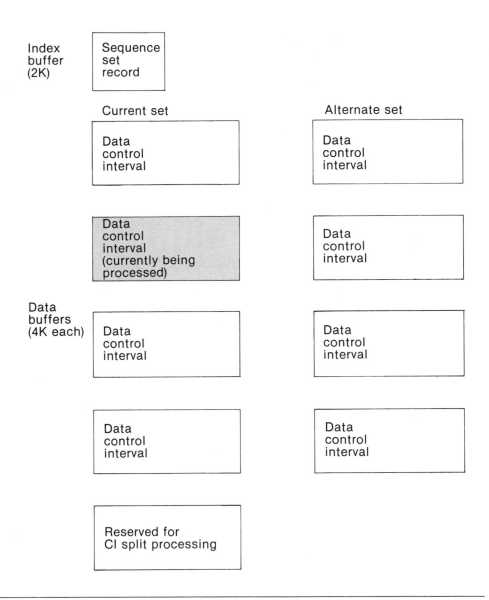

Figure 7-4   How buffers are used for sequential processing

To determine how many index buffers to allocate, you have to determine how many records are in the index set. Unfortunately, there's no direct way to do that. In the complete LISTCAT output for a data set, you'll find the number of records contained in its index component, but that includes sequence set as well as index set records. So you must subtract from that figure the number of sequence set records in the data set. Since there's one sequence set record per active cylinder, you can determine how many sequence set records there are by calculating how many cylinders are in use. To do that, you

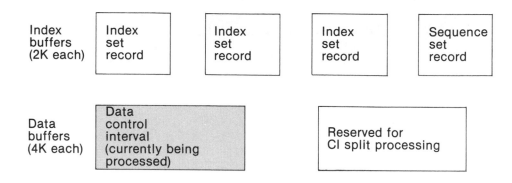

| Index buffers (2K each) | Index set record | Index set record | Index set record | Sequence set record |

| Data buffers (4K each) | Data control interval (currently being processed) | | Reserved for CI split processing |

Figure 7-5   How buffers are used for direct processing

need three other items from the data component portion of the LISTCAT output: the data control interval size (CISIZE), the number of control intervals per control area (CI/CA), and the high-used RBA in the data component (HI-USED-RBA). Figure 7-6 shows typical LISTCAT output with this information shaded.

Once you get this information, you multiply the control interval size by the number of CIs per CA. That gives you the number of bytes per control area. Then, divide that amount into the high-used RBA and round up. That gives you the number of control areas in use, and, as a result, the number of sequence set records.

For the data set whose LISTCAT output is shown in figure 7-6, there are 614,400 bytes in each control area (4096 × 150). Thus, three control areas are used (1,843,200 / 614,400). And, since there are four records in the index component, the index set contains just one record (4 - 3). To keep that index set record in virtual storage, I have to allocate two index buffers: one for a sequence set record, the other for the index set record. Thus, I would code BUFNI = 2 in the AMP parameter of the file's DD statement. Or, if I used BUFFERSPACE or BUFSP, I would increase the default buffer allocation by one index buffer, or 2048 bytes.

Allocating buffers for alternate indexes

When you process a base cluster via an alternate index, the buffer space you specify in the AMP parameter of the DD statement (or the BUFSP parameter of the DLBL statement) applies to the alternate index, not the base cluster. As a result, you can optimize the performance of the alternate index using the same techniques I described for sequential and random processing.

As for the base cluster, VSAM uses either the default or the amount you specify in the BUFFERSPACE parameter on the file's DEFINE command to allocate buffer space. And, since performance won't be satisfactory if the default is used, I suggest you always code the BUFFERSPACE parameter on a DEFINE command for a base cluster. Because the base cluster is always

```
IDCAMS   SYSTEM   SERVICES                                    TIME: 19:16:06      08/22/85      PAGE    1

         LISTCAT ENTRIES(MMA2.CUSTOMER.MASTER) -
              ALL

CLUSTER ------- MMA2.CUSTOMER.MASTER
  IN-CAT --- VCAT.MPS800
  HISTORY
    OWNER-IDENT------(NULL)        CREATION--------85.234
    RELEASE----------2             EXPIRATION------00.000
    PROTECTION-PSWD----(NULL)      RACF------------(YES)
  ASSOCIATIONS
    DATA-------MMA2.CUSTOMER.MASTER.DATA
    INDEX------MMA2.CUSTOMER.MASTER.INDEX

DATA ------- MMA2.CUSTOMER.MASTER.DATA
  IN-CAT --- VCAT.MPS800
  HISTORY
    OWNER-IDENT------(NULL)        CREATION--------85.234
    RELEASE----------2             EXPIRATION------00.000
    PROTECTION-PSWD----(NULL)      RACF------------(YES)
  ASSOCIATIONS
    CLUSTER--MMA2.CUSTOMER.MASTER
  ATTRIBUTES
    KEYLEN----------6     AVGLRECL------100    BUFSPACE-------10240    CISIZE-------4096
    RKP-------------0     MAXLRECL------100    EXCPEXIT------(NULL)    CI/CA--------150
    SHROPTNS(2,3)  RECOVERY        UNIQUE             INDEXED          NOIMBED        NOREPLICAT
    UNORDERED      NOREUSE         NONSPANNED         NOWRITECHK
                                   NOERASE
  STATISTICS
    REC-TOTAL-------10693    SPLITS-CI-------54    EXCPS----------3691
    REC-DELETED------238     SPLITS-CA--------1    EXTENTS-----------2
    REC-INSERTED----1034     FREESPACE-%CI----5    SYSTEM-TIMESTAMP:
    REC-UPDATED------354     FREESPACE-%CA----5         X'999FD9E6D0092200'
    REC-RETRIEVED----592     FREESPC-BYTES-573440
  ALLOCATION
    SPACE-TYPE----CYLINDER    HI-ALLOC-RBA----1843200
    SPACE-PRI---------2       HI-USED-RBA-----1843200
    SPACE-SEC---------1
  VOLUME
    VOLSER--------MPS800     PHYREC-SIZE----4096    HI-ALLOC-RBA----1843200    EXTENT-NUMBER------2
    DEVTYPE----X'3010200E'   PHYRECS/TRK------10    HI-USED-RBA-----1843200    EXTENT-TYPE----X'00'
    VOLFLAG-------PRIME      TRACKS/CA--------15
    EXTENTS:
    LOW-CCHH----X'005F0000'  LOW-RBA------------0    TRACKS-----------30
    HIGH-CCHH---X'0060000E'  HIGH-RBA-----1228799
    LOW-CCHH----X'03C60000'  LOW-RBA------1228800    TRACKS-----------15
    HIGH-CCHH---X'03C6000E'  HIGH-RBA-----1843199

INDEX ------- MMA2.CUSTOMER.MASTER.INDEX
  IN-CAT --- VCAT.MPS800
  HISTORY
    OWNER-IDENT------(NULL)        CREATION--------85.234
```

Figure 7-6 LISTCAT output used to calculate the number of sequence set records in a KSDS (part 1 of 2)

```
IDCAMS   SYSTEM SERVICES                           TIME: 19:16:06      08/22/85      PAGE    2

   RELEASE--------------2          EXPIRATION-----------00.000
   PROTECTION-PSWD-----(NULL)      RACF----------------(YES)
ASSOCIATIONS
   CLUSTER--MMA2.CUSTOMER.MASTER
ATTRIBUTES
   KEYLEN-------------6    AVGLRECL-----------0    BUFSPACE-----------0    CISIZE-----------2048
   RKP----------------0    MAXLRECL--------2041    EXCPEXIT--------(NULL)   CI/CA--------------18
   SHROPTNS(2,3)  RECOVERY    UNIQUE    NOERASE    NOWRITECHK   NOIMBED    NOREPLICAT   UNORDERED
   NOREUSE
STATISTICS
   REC-TOTAL----------4    SPLITS-CI----------1    EXCPS-----------3327    INDEX:
   REC-DELETED--------0    SPLITS-CA----------0    EXTENTS------------1    LEVELS-------------2
   REC-INSERTED-------0    FREESPACE-%CI------0    SYSTEM-TIMESTAMP:       ENTRIES/SECT------12
   REC-UPDATED-------61    FREESPACE-%CA------0        X'999FD9E6D0092200' SEQ-SET-RBA---------0
   REC-RETRIEVED------0    FREESPC-BYTES--28672                            HI-LEVEL-RBA-----4096
ALLOCATION
   SPACE-TYPE-----TRACK    HI-ALLOC-RBA----36864
   SPACE-PRI----------1    HI-USED-RBA------8192
   SPACE-SEC----------1
VOLUME
   VOLSER--------MPS800    PHYREC-SIZE-----2048    HI-ALLOC-RBA----36864   EXTENT-NUMBER------1
   DEVTYPE----X'3010200E'  PHYRECS/TRK-------18    HI-USED-RBA------8192   EXTENT-TYPE----X'OC'
   VOLFLAG-------PRIME     TRACKS/CA----------1    TRACKS-------------1
   EXTENTS:
   LOW-CCHH----X'00D40000' LOW-RBA------------0
   HIGH-CCHH---X'00D40000' HIGH-RBA-------36863
```

Figure 7-6 LISTCAT output used to calculate the number of sequence set records in a KSDS (part 2 of 2)

processed randomly whether you process the alternate index randomly or sequentially, you need to allocate enough buffer space for the base cluster to hold the entire index set, a sequence set record, and two data control intervals.

Allocating buffers for entry-sequenced and relative-record data sets

Although the concepts I've presented here apply most directly to key-sequenced data sets, they also apply to entry-sequenced and relative-record data sets. The only difference is that these data sets don't have an index component, so you don't have to worry about allocating index buffers. As a result, VSAM's default buffer allocation of two data buffers is sufficient for random processing of an ESDS or an RRDS. For sequential processing, allocate additional data buffers just as you would for a KSDS.

Allocating buffers for multiple strings

For most batch programs, VSAM files are processed using a single string. Simply put, a *string* consists of the buffers and control blocks necessary to handle one processing request for a VSAM file. Under CICS and some unusual assembler-language batch programs, multiple strings are used so several independent processing requests can be handled at once for a single VSAM file. It's easy to see why that's necessary under CICS: in on-line systems, it's common for several users to access the same file at once. Batch applications for multiple strings are less common but possible through special assembler-language options. Since the most common use of multiple string processing is for random access via CICS, I'll explain how buffers are allocated in that environment.

When multiple strings are used for random access, VSAM allocates one data and one index buffer for each string. One additional data buffer is set aside for CI or CA split processing. Any remaining index buffers are pooled together so they can be accessed by any string. The string-dependent index buffer is used for sequence set records, and the pooled index buffers are used for index set records. As a result, you should allocate enough buffers so that the entire index set can be held in the index buffer pool.

To illustrate, suppose three strings are active and the index set contains five records. In this case, you should allocate four data buffers: one for each string, plus one for CI/CA splits. And you should allocate eight index buffers: one for the sequence set record needed by each string, and five for the index set records in the buffer pool.

Local and global shared resources

VSAM provides two advanced buffering facilities called local shared resources and global shared resources. Both are used to reduce the total buffer space requirements of an on-line system such as CICS or IMS DC by allowing all open VSAM data sets to share buffers in a common pool. CICS, which runs multiple programs within a single address space, uses *local shared resources*, or *LSR*, to share buffers among data sets. IMS DC can use LSR or *global shared resources*, or *GSR*, to share buffers among on-line programs running in several address spaces at once.

When local or global shared resources is used, the buffer space allocation specified at define time or through JCL is ignored. Instead, VSAM creates a series of *buffer subpools* based on specifications made to CICS or IMS. Each buffer subpool contains a number of buffers of a specified size. For example, one buffer subpool might contain twenty 2048-byte buffers, while another contains twelve 4096-byte buffers. Whenever an I/O request is issued for a VSAM file, VSAM uses buffers from the appropriate subpools to store index and data control intervals. The only significant difference between LSR and GSR is that under LSR, buffer subpools are maintained in the user's address space or partition, while under GSR, buffer subpools are maintained in the Common System Area, an area of storage that's available to all regions in the system.

The important thing to realize about local and global shared resources is that buffers are allocated based on their sizes. Because there's no distinction between data and index buffers, a data control interval can replace a previously read index control interval in a buffer if both control intervals are the same size. As a result, it's common when LSR or GSR is used to restrict index and data control interval sizes to certain values, so data and index control intervals won't use the same buffer subpools. For example, an installation might specify that all index control intervals be 2048 bytes long, and not allow 2048-byte data control intervals. That way, the 2048-byte buffer subpool will effectively become an index buffer subpool, and its size can be calculated more easily. If control interval size restrictions aren't imposed, it's more difficult to calculate the best size for a particular buffer subpool.

At many CICS installations, only infrequently used data sets use LSR buffers. For high-use files, it's often better to allocate dedicated buffers so you can assure that the index set remains in the buffers at all times. In addition, data sets that are a part of an alternate index's upgrade set cannot use LSR. So those data sets must have dedicated buffers.

In any event, specifying the correct size for a buffer subpool when LSR or GSR is used is the responsibility of the systems programmer who maintains CICS or IMS. As a result, I won't cover LSR or GSR in more detail here. If you're interested in more information, I suggest you consult the appropriate CICS or IMS reference manuals.

OTHER PERFORMANCE OPTIONS

So far in this chapter, I've discussed the four major groups of performance options you should always consider when you define a data set: control interval size, free space, index options, and buffer allocation. Now, I'll describe a

```
DEFINE CLUSTER ( NAME(MMA2.CUSTOMER.MASTER)      -
                 OWNER(DLOWE2)                    -
                 INDEXED                          -
                 RECORDSIZE(620 620)              -
                 KEYS(8 0)                        -
                 KEYRANGES ( (00000 24999)        -
                             (25000 49999)        -
                             (50000 74999)        -
                             (75000 99999) )      -
                 VOLUMES(MPS800                    -
                         MPS801                    -
                         MPS802                    -
                         MPS803)                   -
                 ORDERED                          -
                 UNIQUE                           -
                 TO(86365)                        -
                 SHAREOPTIONS(2 3)                -
                 IMBED                            -
                 FREESPACE(20 10) )               -
         DATA    ( NAME(MMA2.CUSTOMER.MASTER.DATA) -
                 CYLINDERS(50 10)                 -
                 CISZ(4096) )                     -
         INDEX   ( NAME(MMA2.CUSTOMER.MASTER.INDEX) )
```

Figure 7-7	Defining a keyrange data set

few other performance options of the DEFINE CLUSTER command: keyrange data sets, the SPEED and RECOVERY options, and the WRITECHECK option.

Keyrange data sets

Basically, the function of a *keyrange data set* is to distribute the data component of a key-sequenced data set among several volumes. For heavily used files, that can improve performance by reducing contention for a single DASD unit. The parts of the data component are distributed across volumes based on ranges of key values. For example, you might specify that all records whose key values fall between 00000 and 49999 be placed on one volume, while all records with key values 50000 to 99999 be placed on another volume.

Figure 7-7 shows an example of how you might define a four-volume keyrange data set. Here, the KEYRANGE parameter specifies the four key ranges used to partition the file: 00000-24999, 25000-49999, 50000-74999, and 75000-99999. In the VOLUMES parameter, I listed the four DASD volumes that will contain the key ranges: MPS800, MPS801, MPS802, and MPS803.

The ORDERED parameter tells VSAM to use the volumes listed in the VOLUMES parameter in the order in which they're listed, one key range per volume. Since I specified ORDERED in figure 7-7, the first key range (00000-24999) will be allocated on MPS800, the second key range (25000-49999) on MPS801, and so on. When you omit the ORDERED parameter, VSAM determines the volumes on which to allocate the key ranges, and the results may not be what you expect; more than one key range may be allocated on some of the volumes, while other volumes may not be used. As a result, I suggest you always specify ORDERED when you use keyrange data sets.

The primary allocation amount you specify in the space allocation parameter (RECORDS, TRACKS, CYLINDERS, or BLOCKS) for a keyrange data set is allocated to *each* key range. As a result, if you specify a primary allocation of 50 cylinders for a file with four key ranges, a total of 200 cylinders is allocated. Remember that when you calculate the space requirements for your file.

Secondary extents for key range data sets are made without regard for the original key range order specified when the file was defined. In other words, if the second key range requires a secondary extent, that extent may or may not be made on the same volume. So to insure the relationship of key ranges to volumes, be sure to allocate enough primary space for the key ranges and select the key ranges so that each will contain roughly the same number of records.

The SPEED and RECOVERY parameters

You can code the SPEED or RECOVERY parameters at the CLUSTER or DATA level of a DEFINE CLUSTER command to affect how VSAM loads data into a new file. If you specify RECOVERY (or allow it to default), VSAM preformats each control area it allocates with binary zeros before it writes any control intervals to it. In contrast, if you specify SPEED, VSAM does no preformatting. Therefore, load processing is much faster when SPEED is in effect because the additional I/O required to preformat the control intervals is eliminated.

Theoretically, the advantage of using RECOVERY is that if load processing terminates abnormally, you can resume the load operation from the point of failure without starting over from the beginning. Unfortunately, in practice that's only possible for entry-sequenced data sets. That's because if the load program (or REPRO) terminates abnormally, the file is left unclosed and must be verified using the VERIFY command before load processing can resume. And the VERIFY command doesn't work for key-sequenced or relative-record files that were improperly closed while open for load mode.

Because RECOVERY lets you resume a terminated load operation only for an ESDS, I recommend you specify SPEED for a KSDS or RRDS. That way, your load processing won't be slowed by preformatting that does no good. Then, if the load does abend, you'll have to delete the cluster, redefine it, and start the load operation over from the beginning.

The WRITECHECK parameter

If you specify the WRITECHECK parameter in a DEFINE CLUSTER command, every write operation to your file will cause the DASD unit to

```
DEFINE CLUSTER ( NAME(MMA2.CUSTOMER.MASTER)        -
                 OWNER(DLOWE2)                     -
                 INDEXED                           -
                 RECORDSIZE(620 620)               -
                 KEYS(8 0)                         -
                 VOLUMES(MPS800)                   -
                 UNIQUE                            -
                 TO(86365)                         -
                 SHAREOPTIONS(2 3)                 -
                 IMBED                             -
                 FREESPACE(0 0)                    -
                 SPEED )                           -
        DATA   ( NAME(MMA2.CUSTOMER.MASTER.DATA)   -
                 CYLINDERS(180 18)                 -
                 CISZ(4096) )                      -
        INDEX  ( NAME(MMA2.CUSTOMER.MASTER.INDEX) )
```

Figure 7-8   A DEFINE CLUSTER command for a customer master file

reread the data that was written to make sure it was written correctly. Because of this, write checking significantly increases the time it takes to complete a write operation. Therefore, I recommend you don't code WRITECHECK and let the default, NOWRITECHECK, stand; with modern DASD technology, write checking is a waste of time.

EXAMPLES OF SELECTING PERFORMANCE OPTIONS FOR VSAM FILES

Now that I've explained the DEFINE CLUSTER options that affect file performance, I'll describe two typical VSAM files and explain which performance options are probably best for them.

Example 1: A customer master file

The first example is a large file that contains customer master records, each 620 bytes in length. The file will be loaded with 120,000 records and will reside on a 3350 volume named MPS800. Each customer is assigned a unique eight-digit customer number, which is stored in the first eight bytes of each record. Customer numbers are sequential, so new customers are always added at the end of the file. The file is heavily used for random retrieval by an on-line CICS application.

Figure 7-8 shows the DEFINE CLUSTER command for this file. The performance options I used are CISZ(4096), FREESPACE(0 0), SPEED,IM-BED, and NOREPLICATE. (I didn't explicitly code NOREPLICATE because it's the default.) Now, I'll explain why I chose those options.

I tested three control interval sizes—2048, 4096, and 6144—to see which would best fit the 620-byte record size. In each case, I found that approximately 90 percent of the control interval would be used by data, with only 10 percent unused space. Because the variation among the control interval sizes was small, I selected 4096, which allows space for six records. Next, I turned to figure 6-15 to find out that 116 4096-byte CI's fit in one cylinder of a 3350 (when IMBED is specified). As a result, each cylinder will hold 696 records, and 173 cylinders will be required to hold 120,000 customer records (120,000/696).

Because of the sequential nature of the file's key values, all additions are made at the end of the data set. Since it would be wasteful to provide any control interval or control area free space, I coded FREESPACE(0 0). However, I did allocate enough additional primary DASD space, seven cylinders, to allow for about 5,000 new customer records before a secondary extent would have to be allocated. That's seven cylinders. As a result, the total primary space allocation I specified for the file is 180 cylinders (173 + 7).

Because the file has no unusual processing requirements that would indicate otherwise, I coded the usual index options for it: IMBED and NOREPLICATE. That way, sequence set records and data control intervals can be retrieved with as little DASD overhead as possible. Because programs that process the file will provide enough buffer space to hold the entire index set, there's no need to specify REPLICATE.

Example 2: An inventory master file

The second example is an inventory master file of variable-length records. The records consist of a 600-byte segment followed by up to ten 100-byte segments. That means the records can vary in length from 700 to 1,600 bytes. Most of the records have five 100-byte segments, so the average record length is 1,100 bytes.

The file will be loaded on a 3380 DASD volume with 9,000 records. About 2,000 records will be added to the file between reorganizations. However, there's no predictable pattern to where new records will be inserted.

Figure 7-9 shows the DEFINE CLUSTER command for this file. The performance options I used are CISZ(6144), FREESPACE(20 10), SPEED, IMBED, and NOREPLICATE. Again, I used the usual index options, IMBED and NOREPLICATE, just as I did for the customer master file, so I won't cover them again here. But let me explain why I chose the other options.

I allocated 20 percent of each control interval to free space to allow for the 2,000 expected insertions without forcing control interval splits. Then, to reduce the control area splits that might occur when control interval splits do happen, I allocated an additional ten percent of each control area to free space.

The reason I used 6144 as the control interval size for this file, instead of 4096, has to do with the 20 percent free space requirement. With 4096-byte control intervals, a total of three average-length (1,100-byte) records would fit in each control interval. After reserving 20 percent of each control interval,

```
DEFINE CLUSTER ( NAME(MMA2.INVNTORY.MASTER)       -
                 OWNER(DLOWE2)                     -
                 INDEXED                           -
                 RECORDSIZE(1100 1600)             -
                 KEYS(11 0)                        -
                 VOLUMES(MPS800)                   -
                 UNIQUE                            -
                 TO(86365)                         -
                 SHAREOPTIONS(2 3)                 -
                 IMBED                             -
                 FREESPACE(20 10)                  -
                 SPEED )                           -
          DATA  ( NAME(MMA2.INVNTORY.MASTER.DATA)  -
                 CYLINDERS(30 3)                   -
                 CISZ(6144) )                      -
          INDEX ( NAME(MMA2.INVNTORY.MASTER.INDEX) )
```

Figure 7-9   A DEFINE CLUSTER command for an inventory master file

only two would actually be loaded. So the effective free space for the file would be 33 percent, more than the required 20 percent. To make better use of control interval space, I used 6144 as the control interval size. That allows for a total of five records, with four records loaded after allowing for the free space requirement. As a result, the amount of effective free space remaining is 20 percent.

To calculate the space allocation for the file, I considered the loss of space caused by the IMBED option and the FREESPACE specification. First, I determined from figure 6-15 that 84 control intervals would fit in each control area, after allocating the first track of each CA to the sequence set. Then, I applied the ten percent CA free space to the 84 control intervals, so only 75 control intervals are available for use. Next, I applied the twenty percent CI free space to the five records that fit per control interval, leaving four records per CI. Multiplying 75 (CI's per cylinder) by 4 (records per CI), I determined that 300 records will be loaded per cylinder. Since I need to load 9,000 records, I allocated 30 cylinders of primary space and 3 cylinders of secondary space (ten percent of the primary allocation).

DISCUSSION

Tuning a VSAM data set for optimum performance is a process that doesn't stop once the data set is defined. Throughout the life of an application, the environment in which it operates will change. As a result, you must carefully monitor the performance of your VSAM files and make adjustments when necessary. The basic tool for monitoring VSAM files is LISTCAT output, which you learned about in chapter 6. More elaborate performance monitors that give you more detailed performance statistics are available from IBM and other companies.

Terminology

physical record
seek
stolen seek
buffer
data buffer
index buffer
string
local shared resources
LSR
global shared resources
GSR
buffer subpool
keyrange data set

Objectives

1. Discuss the factors you should consider when you determine a file's control interval size, free space allocation, index options, buffer allocation, and the other performance options described in this chapter.

2. Describe how to code the DEFINE parameters that specify control interval size, free space allocation, index options, buffer allocation, and other performance options.

Chapter 8

Recovery facilities

In this chapter, I'll describe VSAM facilities that can help you recover VSAM data in the event of a failure. I want you to realize at the outset that this chapter does not cover every aspect of VSAM backup and recovery. That's well beyond the scope of this book. This chapter, then, presents just an overview of VSAM recovery facilities.

Quite frankly, VSAM's recovery facilities are disappointing. In particular, VSAM does *not* provide a comprehensive backup and recovery facility that lets you selectively back up and restore individual data sets efficiently. Instead, IBM provides separate backup and recovery utilities that are more comprehensive. And many private software houses have developed their own proprietary software for VSAM backup and recovery. So as you read this chapter, realize that your installation may have other software that supplements or replaces the standard AMS facilities I'll describe here.

The considerations for backing up and restoring VSAM data fall into three categories: (1) backing up and restoring DASD volumes that contain VSAM data, (2) backing up and restoring individual VSAM data sets, and (3) backing up and restoring catalogs.

VOLUME BACKUP AND RECOVERY

Most installations routinely backup entire DASD volumes. Strictly speaking, volume-level backup and restoration is not a VSAM consideration; it's not performed by AMS, and it doesn't directly affect VSAM files.

I do want you to realize, however, that restoring volumes that contain VSAM data can be disasterous if not done properly. Whenever a VSAM volume is backed up, all other volumes that contain files cataloged in the same user catalog must be backed up at the same time. That's because VSAM user catalogs contain extent allocation information that must be accurate. So if you restore just one of several volumes controlled by a single user catalog, the user catalog will probably be damaged, and you might not be able to access data on *any* of the volumes controlled by the catalog.

The easiest way to avoid that problem is to restrict user catalogs to a single volume. Unfortunately, that's not possible in many cases. Later in this chapter, you'll learn how VSAM catalogs can be made recoverable. Although recoverable catalogs don't eliminate the possiblity of losing data when restoring multiple volumes owned by a single user catalog, they do make it less likely.

DATA SET BACKUP AND RECOVERY

Although most shops routinely back up DASD volumes, it's still a good idea to back up critical VSAM files routinely, too. There are many ways to back up VSAM files. You can use the REPRO command to copy VSAM data sets to tape. Or, you can design backup procedures into batch processing applications so application programs create backup data as a part of their normal processing. Now, I'll show you how to use two VSAM commands, EXPORT and IMPORT, to backup and recover VSAM files. Although these commands aren't always the best choices for backup and recovery, you should know about them because they're commonly used.

The EXPORT and IMPORT commands

Two AMS commands, EXPORT and IMPORT, are used together to produce a backup copy of a data set and later restore that copy. (Another function of the EXPORT and IMPORT commands, which I don't cover in this book, is to remove a user catalog from a system.) The EXPORT command produces a backup copy of a data set, while the IMPORT command restores the data set from the exported backup.

Actually, the EXPORT and IMPORT commands were designed to make VSAM files *transportable*. That means you can use the EXPORT command to transfer a VSAM file to a removable medium (usually tape), then use the IMPORT command to transfer the exported file to another system. In practice, however, the EXPORT and IMPORT commands are used mostly for data set backup and recovery.

Of course, you could use the REPRO command to backup and restore files. All you would have to do is issue a REPRO command to copy the VSAM file to a sequential file on tape. Then, when necessary, you can issue another REPRO command to restore the file from the tape file. The basic difference between the REPRO command and the EXPORT and IMPORT commands is that a transportable file is stored in a special format that includes all of the information necessary to define the file automatically. As a result, when you use the IMPORT command to copy a previously exported file, you don't have to define the file; the IMPORT command defines the file automatically using the data stored by the EXPORT command.

Unfortunately, the EXPORT and IMPORT commands are slower than the REPRO command. As a result, it's often more efficient to use the REPRO command along with DEFINE (and possibly DELETE) commands to back up and restore files. Keep that in mind as you read this section.

The EXPORT command   Figure 8-1 gives the format of the EXPORT command as you use it to produce a backup copy of a file. Two parameters are always required: the names of the input and output files. For example, this command,

```
EXPORT MMA2.CUSTOMER.MASTER   -
       OUTFILE(TAPEDD)
```

exports the data set MMA2.CUSTOMER.MASTER to the file identified in the JCL by the TAPEDD DD or DLBL/TLBL statement.

Normally, the exported file will be deleted when the export operation is completed. To make a backup copy of a data set, you certainly want to override that by coding TEMPORARY on the EXPORT command. (If you specify PERMANENT, or allow it to default, you can also code the PURGE/NOPURGE and ERASE/NOERASE parameters, which work the same way they do for a DELETE command.)

Finally, you can specify whether the source file (the file you're exporting) and the target file (the file later restored by an IMPORT command) should be inhibited. Inhibiting a file makes it read-only. As a result, you can't run a program that opens an inhibited file for output or update processing. To inhibit the source file, code INHIBITSOURCE; to inhibit the target file, code INHIBITTARGET. Once you've inhibited a file, you can uninhibit it—that is, return it to normal—by issuing an ALTER command with the UNINIHIBIT parameter. Note that it doesn't make sense to inhibit the source file for a permanent export, since the source file is deleted anyway.

Figure 8-2 shows an OS job step that backs up a file named MMA2.CUSTOMER.MASTER to tape. The TAPEDD DD statement allocates the tape output file; you may have to adjust this DD statement according to your installation's requirements. Under DOS, you could use the same EXPORT command, but the JCL would be different. Note that I coded TEMPORARY on this command so AMS would not delete the original copy of the data set.

The EXPORT command for data set backup

```
EXPORT      entry-name[/password]

            OUTFILE(ddname)

     [ INFILE(ddname) ]

     [ TEMPORARY | PERMANENT ]

     [ PURGE | NOPURGE ]

     [ ERASE | NOERASE ]

     [ INHIBITSOURCE | NOINHIBITSOURCE ]

     [ INHIBITTARGET | NOINHIBITTARGET ]
```

Explanation

entryname	Required. Specifies the name of an existing VSAM data set or alternate index to be exported.
OUTFILE	Required. OUTFILE names a DD or DLBL/TLBL statement that defines the output file, usually on a tape device.
INFILE	Optional. Required only if the input file is on a volume that's not permanently mounted.
TEMPORARY PERMANENT	Optional. PERMANENT means that the input file should be deleted when the export operation completes; TEMPORARY means that the input file should not be deleted. PERMANENT is the default.
PURGE NOPURGE	Optional. Meaningful only when PERMANENT is in effect. PURGE means to delete the input file regardless of its expiration date; NOPURGE means to delete the input file only if it has expired. NOPURGE is the default.
ERASE NOERASE	Optional. Meaningful only when PERMANENT is in effect. ERASE means to overwrite the input file with binary zeros; NOERASE means to not overwrite with zeros. NOERASE is the default.
INHIBITSOURCE NOINHIBITSOURCE	Optional. Meaningful only when TEMPORARY is in effect. INHIBITSOURCE means to inhibit the input file when the export operation completes; NOINHIBIT-SOURCE means to not inhibit the input file. NOINHIBITSOURCE is the default.
INHIBITTARGET NOINHIBITTARGET	Optional. INHIBITTARGET means that the file, when imported later by an IMPORT command, should be inhibited. NOINHIBITTARGET means that the file should not be inhibited when it's imported. NOINHIBITTARGET is the default.

Figure 8-1   The EXPORT command for data set backup

```
//          EXEC PGM=IDCAMS
//SYSPRINT DD  SYSOUT=A
//TAPEDD   DD  DSN=MMA2.CUSTMAST.EXPORT,
//             DISP=NEW,
//             UNIT=(TAPE,,DEFER),
//             VOL=SER=01C000,
//             LABEL=(1,SL)
//SYSIN    DD  *
  EXPORT MMA2.CUSTOMER.MASTER -
         OUTFILE(TAPEDD)      -
         TEMPORARY
/*
```

Figure 8-2   An EXPORT job step

The IMPORT command   You use the IMPORT command, shown in figure 8-3, to copy a previously exported file back onto a system. In the INFILE parameter, you specify the ddname of a DD or DLBL/TLBL statement that allocates the input file (that is, the previously exported file). Normally, you'll use the OUTDATASET parameter to identify the output file by name. For example, the command,

```
IMPORT INFILE(INDD)                     -
       OUTDATASET(MMA2.CUSTOMER.MASTER)
```

imports the previously exported file defined by the INDD DD or DLBL statement to MMA2.CUSTOMER.MASTER.

If the output file already exists, the IMPORT command first deletes the existing file. If you code the PURGE parameter, IMPORT deletes the file regardless of its expiration date; if you specify NOPURGE or let it default, IMPORT terminates if the file hasn't expired. If the file is deleted, IMPORT then defines it using the information stored when the file was exported.

To change the file's characteristics, I recommend you first delete the existing cluster, then redefine it, specifying the parameters you need, before you issue the IMPORT command. When you do that, be sure to specify the INTOEMPTY parameter on the IMPORT command. Otherwise, AMS won't let you import data into the newly defined cluster.

Figure 8-4 shows a job step that imports the file that was exported in figure 8-2. I coded PURGE so that the existing data in MMA2.CUSTOMER.MASTER will be replaced even if the file's exipiration date hasn't arrived.

The IMPORT command for data set backup

```
IMPORT    INFILE(ddname)

         { OUTFILE(ddname)                    }
         { OUTDATASET(entryname[/password])   }

         [ PURGE | NOPURGE ]

         [ INTOEMPTY ]

         [ CATALOG(name[/password]) ]
```

Explanation

INFILE	Required. Identifies a DD or DLBL statement that defines the input file.
OUTFILE OUTDATASET	Required. OUTFILE names a DD or DLBL statement that defines the output file. OUTDATASET names the file directly so VSAM can dynamically allocate it.
PURGE NOPURGE	Optional. When NOPURGE is in effect, the import operation will occur only if the existing file's expiration date hasn't arrived. If PURGE is in effect, the import operation will proceed whether or not the existing file has expired. NOPURGE is the default.
INTOEMPTY	Optional. If specified, allows an import operation to an existing file that's empty. If not specified, IMPORT will terminate if the existing file has no records.
CATALOG	Optional. Identifies the catalog that contains the imported object. If omitted, the standard catalog search sequence is used.

Figure 8-3 The IMPORT command for data set backup

```
//         EXEC PGM=IDCAMS
//SYSPRINT DD   SYSOUT=A
//TAPEDD   DD   DSN=MMA2.CUSTMAST.EXPORT,
//              DISP=OLD,
//              UNIT=(TAPE,,DEFER),
//              VOL=SER=010000,
//              LABEL=(1,SL)
//SYSIN    DD   *
  IMPORT INFILE(TAPEDD)                        -
         OUTDATASET(MMA2.CUSTOMER.MASTER) -
         PURGE
  /*
```

Figure 8-4 An IMPORT job step

CATALOG RECOVERY

When a program or system failure damages a VSAM file, it's relatively easy to restore it from a previous backup copy and continue processing. However, it's a different story when a catalog is damaged. In that case, complete recovery can be difficult if not impossible. Catalog recovery is a complex subject that I can't thoroughly cover here. Instead, I'll just introduce the catalog recovery facilities VSAM provides. For more complete information, you'll have to refer to the IBM manuals.

The catalog recovery facilities I'll introduce here fall into three categories. First, I'll describe the VERIFY command, which fixes the most common type of catalog problem. Then, I'll describe the considerations for recovering VSAM catalogs. Finally, I'll describe the recovery facilities provided with ICF catalogs.

The VERIFY command

The most common type of catalog problem occurs when a program failure prevents a VSAM file from being properly closed. When that happens, VSAM doesn't get a chance to update important information in the file's catalog record, including the *high-used RBA* (or *HURBA*) field which indicates the end of the file. As a result, the information stored in the catalog record doesn't agree with the actual contents of the related file.

The VERIFY command corrects the catalog information by resetting the incorrect values in the catalog record to reflect the actual status of the data set. For example, suppose you issue this command:

```
VERIFY DATASET(MMA.CUSTOMER.MASTER)
```

Here, the VSAM file named MMA.CUSTOMER.MASTER is examined, and its catalog record is updated if necessary.

Because it's not uncommon for programs to abend and leave VSAM files unclosed, it's a standard at many VSAM installations to issue a VERIFY command for every VSAM file processed by a job. That way, the job will never terminate because of a previously unclosed file. The use of VERIFY has become so widespread that in recent releases of VSAM (VSAM under ICF and DOS/VSE), the VERIFY function is automatically performed whenever a file is opened. As a result, you don't often need to use the VERIFY command on those systems.

VSAM catalog recovery

Standard VSAM provides a facility that can help you recover catalogs that the VERIFY command can't repair: *recoverable catalogs*. Simply put, VSAM maintains two copies of critical file allocation information in a recoverable catalog. The extra information is stored in a special area called the *catalog recovery area*, or *CRA*. To define a recoverable catalog, you just specify RECOVERABLE on the DEFINE USERCATALOG command.

AMS provides several commands you can use to fix a damaged recoverable catalog, using the duplicate information stored in the CRA. The LISTCRA command compares catalog data with the corresponding CRA data and flags differences that may indicate catalog errors. The EXPORTRA and IMPORTRA commands work like the EXPORT and IMPORT commands, but get their catalog information from the CRA rather than from the catalog itself. And the RESETCAT command simply copies information from the CRA to the catalog itself. The proper use of these commands is beyond the scope of this book, so I won't describe them in detail here.

If a catalog controls more than one volume, a CRA is maintained on each. That way, the recovery data for a particular data set is stored on the same volume as the data set itself. The advantage of that is that you don't have to worry as much about recovering just one of the volumes controlled by a multi-volume user catalog. For example, suppose a user catalog owns VSAM files on four volumes, and one of the volumes needs to be restored. When you restore that volume, the user catalog will probably become inaccurate. But the CRA on the restored volume contains the correct catalog information for the files on that volume. So all you need to do is issue a RESETCAT command to copy that CRA information back to the user catalog.

ICF catalog recovery

Recovering from catalog problems under ICF is simpler than under standard VSAM. More importantly, catalog problems are less likely to occur under ICF because of the structure of its catalogs. As I described in chapter 3, an ICF catalog consists of two parts: a Basic Catalog Structure, or BCS, and a VSAM Volume Data Set, or VVDS. The BCS record for a file contains information that doesn't normally change, like the file's name, control interval size, and so on. The VVDS contains information that does change, like extent information. The VVDS is always stored on the same volume as the files it defines, so you're not likely to damage a VVDS by restoring a volume incorrectly.

It is possible, however, to damage the relationship between a BCS and a VVDS. When that happens, you can issue a DIAGNOSE command, which compares the BCS and VVDS, lists any differences, and suggests ways to correct the problems. In some cases, you'll have to delete files that exist in the BCS but not in the VVDS. In other cases, you'll have to issue a special DEFINE command with the RECATALOG parameter, which causes a BCS catalog entry to be created when there's already an existing VVDS entry for the file.

DISCUSSION

As I said at the start of this chapter, VSAM recovery is a complicated subject and the facilities provided by VSAM are sometimes inadequate. For a more complete discussion of VSAM recovery, consult the appropriate IBM manuals for your system.

I also mentioned at the start of this chapter that other software is available to make VSAM backup and recovery easier. From IBM, *Data Facility Data Set Services* (or *DFDSS*) provides a DUMP and RESTORE function that lets you selectively backup and restore VSAM data under MVS. Under DOS, the *VSE/VSAM Backup/Restore Facility* provides a similar capability. And you can get similar products from other vendors. If your installation uses one or more of these products, I suggest you review the appropriate reference manual to get an idea of how they work.

Terminology

transportable file
high-used RBA field
HURBA field
recoverable catalog
catalog recovery area
CRA
Data Facility Data Set Services
DFDSS
VSE/VSAM Backup/Restore Facility

Objectives

1. Describe the potential problems involved in backing up and restoring complete volumes that contain VSAM data.

2. List the advantages and disadvantages of using the REPRO command rather than the IMPORT and EXPORT commands for data set backup and recovery.

3. Describe the function of the VERIFY command.

4. Briefly describe the catalog recovery facilities provided by VSAM recoverable catalogs and ICF catalogs.

Chapter 9

Security facilities

An important consideration for any large VSAM installation is maintaining adequate security so data can't be accessed by unauthorized users. VSAM provides a limited security capability, which I'll describe in this chapter. Because VSAM security is limited, however, most installations use more comprehensive security packages which either supplement or replace the security facilities VSAM provides. After I describe VSAM security features, I'll briefly describe two of those products: RACF, which is used on most MVS systems, and Access Control Function, a more limited facility used on some DOS/VSE systems.

VSAM SECURITY FACILITIES

VSAM provides file security in the form of *passwords*. When you associate a password with a data set, any user who knows that password can access the data set. So the key to implementing VSAM file security is assigning appropriate passwords to data sets and distributing those passwords only to the users who need access to those data sets.

To access a password-protected data set, you must supply the correct password. There are several ways to do that, depending on how you're accessing the file. To specify a password in an AMS command, you code the password after the file name, separated by a slash, like this:

```
INDATASET(MMA.CUSTOMER.MASTER.FILE/MAD73JX7)
```

Here, the password for the customer master file is MAD73JX7.

When a batch program processes a password-protected file, it supplies the password. In an assembler-language program, you supply the password in the ACB macro for the file. In a COBOL program, you code the PASSWORD clause on the SELECT statement for the file. You'll learn how to do that in section 3. If a batch program doesn't supply the required password, VSAM prompts the system operator to enter the correct password; you can't supply a VSAM password in the JCL.

Catalogs can be password protected, too. In fact, if a VSAM data set is password protected, the catalog that defines it must also be password protected. And if a catalog is password protected, you must supply the catalog's password to define, delete, or alter an object defined in it.

If a user catalog is password protected, the master catalog must be password protected too. Usually, the password of the master catalog is a closely guarded secret, available only to the system programmers responsible for maintaining VSAM. If you know the master catalog password, you can define or delete user catalogs, or use the catalog recovery commands I described in chapter 8 (LISTCRA, IMPORTRA, EXPORTRA, and RESETCAT).

Password access levels

You can specify up to four passwords for a VSAM file: the read password, the update password, the control password, and the master password. As their names imply, each allows a higher level of access to the file.

The *read password* provides the most limited access to a file. When a program supplies a read password for a file, it can open the file only for input processing. It can't write records to the file or update existing records. The read password is sufficient to perform some AMS operations, such as PRINT or REPRO (for the input file).

The *update password* provides the next level of access; it lets a program not only read a file's records, but also write or update them. An update password is appropriate for the output file of a REPRO operation or for an application program that opens a file for output or update processing.

The *control password* lets a program process a file in control interval mode. Since control interval processing is uncommon, you probably won't need to supply a control password often.

The *master password* provides the highest level of access for a VSAM file. Besides the access granted by the read, update, or control password, the master password lets you alter or delete the file.

DEFINE parameters for password protection

Figure 9-1 shows the parameters you can code on a DEFINE command (CLUSTER, AIX, PATH, or USERCATALOG) to specify password protection for a VSAM object. The first four, READPW, UPDATEPW, CONTROLPW, and MASTERPW, specify the read, update, control, and master passwords for the object. Although you can code these parameters at the DATA or INDEX level, it's best to code them at the highest level of the DEFINE command (CLUSTER, AIX, and so on). That way, the passwords apply to the entire object, not just one of its components.

If you code any of the four password parameters, the object is password protected. You don't have to code all four passwords, though. If you omit a password at one level, VSAM uses the password you specified at a lower level. For example, if you specify just UPDATEPW, VSAM uses the value you supply as the control and master passwords as well. But no password is required for read-only processing, since the read password is at a lower level than the update password.

You use the other parameters in figure 9-1 along with the password parameters to affect how passwords are obtained for the data set. The CODE parameter has effect only when a system operator must be prompted for a password; it supplies a one- to eight-character value that's used instead of the data set name to prompt the operator. The CODE parameter is useful when you don't want the operator to know which password applies to a particular data set; it lets the operator know the password, but not the data set name.

The ATTEMPTS parameter specifies how many times an operator can try to enter a valid password; the default is two. If the operator doesn't enter the right password in the number of attempts specified, VSAM terminates the job. Under TSO, VSAM tries the user's password before it prompts the terminal operator, which counts as one attempt.

The AUTHORIZATION parameter lets an installation use a *User Security Verification Routine* (or *USVR*) to supplement VSAM's security facilities. A USVR is a user exit that's given control after a valid read, update, or control password is supplied. (The USVR is *not* invoked when a master password is supplied.) The entry-point is the name of the USVR; the string is a value that's passed to the USVR at execution time. If your shop uses USVR's, you'll be told how to code this parameter.

Parameter	Function
READPW(password)	Provides the read password for the object. Users who supply this password may read data from the object.
UPDATEPW(password)	Provides the update password for the object. Users who supply this password may read and change data in the object.
CONTROLPW(password)	Provides the control password for the object. Users who supply this password may read and change data in the object and open the object for control interval mode processing.
MASTERPW(password)	Provides the master password for the object. Users who supply this password may perform any VSAM operation against the object.
CODE(code)	Supplies a one- to eight-character code that's used instead of the object's name when the system or terminal operator is prompted for a password.
ATTEMPTS(number)	Indicates how many times an operator may try to supply a valid password. The number may be 0 through 7; the default is 2.
AUTHORIZATION(entry-point[string])	Provides the address of a User Security Verification Routine. The optional string is passed to the routine.

Note: Any of the above parameters may be coded on a DEFINE CLUSTER, DEFINE ALTERNATEINDEX, DEFINE PATH, or DEFINE USERCATALOG command.

Figure 9-1   VSAM security parameters

Other VSAM security features

Besides password protection, VSAM provides two other security features I want you to know about: erasing deleted data and data encryption.

Erasing deleted data   When you issue a DELETE command to delete a data set, VSAM updates the appropriate catalog and, if necessary, VTOC information to remove any entries associated with the file. However, the data stored on the DASD remains there until it's overwritten by another file. Although it's unlikely, someone could access that data without using a password, even though the data was password protected before the file was deleted.

As a result, VSAM lets you erase a file or alternate index when you delete it by specifying ERASE on the DELETE command. When you specify ERASE, VSAM writes binary zeros over the entire file. That way, once the file has been deleted, it can't be accessed under any circumstances.

Bear in mind, however, that deleting and erasing a file can take a lot of time, depending on its size. So use ERASE only when the file contains sensitive data that must be erased when deleted.

The cryptographic option   Under MVS, the *cryptographic option* lets you store data using the REPRO command in a form that can be read only by another REPRO command. That way, data stored for backup purposes on tape can't be read by unauthorized users. Managing the cryptographic option is a complicated subject that's well beyond the scope of this book, but I want you to have a basic understanding of how it works.

You code the ENCIPHER option on a REPRO command to *encipher* a file. An eight-byte *data encryption key* is used along with a complex mathematical algorithm to do that. To retrieve the enciphered file and *decipher* it—that is, convert it back to its original form—you specify the DECIPHER parameter on a REPRO command and supply the same key you used to encipher the file.

NON-VSAM SECURITY MANAGERS

As I pointed out at the start of this chapter, the security facilities provided by VSAM generally aren't sufficient for an installation that's serious about data security. For one thing, too many passwords are involved; it's possible to assign 12 different passwords to each VSAM KSDS (four each for the cluster, data component, and index component). As a result, a shop can easily end up managing thousands of different passwords.

Because of the inherent weaknesses of VSAM security, most installations use other security managers that provide a more comprehensive, system-wide approach to security. On MVS, the IBM product RACF is commonly used. On DOS systems, a similar but less powerful facility called Access Control Function can be used. I won't describe these facilities in detail here, but I do want to give you an overview of how they work.

RACF

RACF, which stands for *Resource Access Control Facility*, is just that: a facility to control access to MVS system resources. RACF identifies both the users and the resources of the system. Then, it can control which users have access to particular resources.

Under RACF, a *user* is anyone who can gain access to the computer system, either by submitting a job for execution or by logging on under TSO. Each user has a *user profile* which specifies, among other information, the user's name, user-id, and password. Anyone who knows a valid user-id and password can access the system under RACF, so user-id's and passwords must be tightly controlled.

Users can be combined into *groups*. Each group typically contains users who have common access requirements. For example, all of the programmers on a particular project may belong to one group, system programmers may belong to another group, and terminal operators in the accounting department may belong to a third group. Using groups simplifies RACF administration when many users require the same level of access to system resources.

A *resource* is any system facility that needs to be controlled. Resources can include data sets, tape volumes, programs, terminals, or CICS and IMS transactions. A *resource profile* identifies a resource being protected and lists the users or groups who can access the resource. So, whenever a user tries to access a resource (like a data set), RACF checks the resource profile to see if that user is permitted to access that resource. If not, access is denied.

Each user or group listed in a resource profile is assigned an *access authority*, which corresponds to one of the four VSAM password levels. *Alter authority* corresponds to the access granted by a master password, while *control authority*, *update authority*, and *read authority* correspond to the access provided by the control, update, and read passwords.

Among the most useful features of RACF is its ability to identify a *generic resource*. Simply put, a generic resource specifies only part of a resource name. Any resource whose name matches the pattern specified in the generic resource's profile is protected by that profile. To illustrate, suppose all of the data sets in an accounting application begin with a high-level qualifier of ACCT. You could create a profile for a generic resource that consists of all data sets whose names begin with ACCT. Then, all of the accounting data sets would be protected in the same way.

One final point about RACF: it completely replaces the password protection available under VSAM. As a result, if a data set is RACF protected, any VSAM password specifications you make are ignored.

Access Control Function

Access Control Function is a standard component of DOS/VSE which may be activated to provide limited system-wide security checking. Like RACF, Access Control Function defines users and resources. Each user is assigned one or more of 32 *access control classes*. For example, user AAAA might be assigned access control classes 1, 3, and 5. Similarly, each resource is assigned one or more of the 32 access classes. When a user tries to access a resource, Access Control Function allows the access only if both the user and the resource have at least one access control class in common.

In the user profile, you can also indicate for each specified access control class whether read-only or update access is allowed. However, read-only protection works only for VSAM data sets; non-VSAM DASD data sets can't be read protected.

Access Control Function does not replace VSAM security checking as RACF does. Instead, Access Control Function supplements the security provided by VSAM. So, to access a password-protected VSAM data set, the user must have a proper access control class and supply a valid VSAM password.

Terminology

password
read password
update password
control password
master password
User Security Verification Routine
USVR
cryptographic option
encipher
data encryption key
decipher
RACF
Resource Access Control Facility
user
user profile
group
resource
resource profile
access authority
alter authority
control authority
update authority
read authority
generic resource
Access Control Function
access control class

Objectives

1. Describe the four levels of access provided by VSAM passwords and the DEFINE parameters used to assign them.

2. Distinguish among RACF users, user groups, resources, and generic resources.

3. Describe how access control classes let users access resources when Access Control Function is used under DOS/VSE.

Section 3

Application programming

The three chapters in this section show you how to code application programs that process VSAM files using three languages: COBOL, command-level COBOL under CICS, and assembler language. These chapters are independent, so you can read them in any order you want.

Chapter 10

Application programming in COBOL

In this chapter, you'll learn the COBOL language elements that let you process VSAM data sets. Since COBOL is the most widely used programming language in industry today, I'm going to assume you're already familiar with it. In particular, I assume you understand the basics of writing file processing programs in COBOL, so I won't explain how to code simple report preparation or file maintenance programs. Instead, I'll concentrate on the COBOL language elements that apply to VSAM.

The OS/MVS and DOS/VSE versions of the VS COBOL compiler, based on the ANS COBOL standards adopted in 1974, are the most commonly used COBOL compilers today. A new compiler, called the VS COBOL II compiler, was released in the mid-1980s and will probably become widely used soon. VS COBOL II is based on the ANS 1985 COBOL standards, which include several new features that make COBOL more useful. Most of those features, however, don't directly affect VSAM file processing.

This chapter first describes the COBOL elements you code in the Environment and Data

Divisions to identify a VSAM file and specify its characteristics. Then, it explains the Procedure Division statements you can code to process VSAM files. Finally, it explains how to process VSAM error conditions in a COBOL program.

ENVIRONMENT AND DATA DIVISION ENTRIES FOR VSAM FILES

To identify a VSAM file in a COBOL program, you code entries in the Environment and Data Divisions just as you do for a non-VSAM file. In the Input-Output Section of the Environment Division, you code a SELECT statement. And in the File Section of the Data Division, you code an FD entry and your file's record description.

The SELECT statement

Figure 10-1 gives the format of the SELECT statement for VSAM files. The SELECT statement has two functions for VSAM files. First, it relates the internal file name your COBOL program uses to an external name the system uses to identify the file at execution time. Second, it specifies how the file is organized and how the program will access it.

The ASSIGN clause   The ASSIGN clause specifies an assignment name for the file. This name is used in the JCL on a DD statement (OS/MVS) or a DLBL statement (DOS/VSE) to allocate the file. The format of the assignment name depends on your operating system and the file's organization. Figure 10-2 shows the various formats along with an example of each.

The ORGANIZATION clause   You code the ORGANIZATION clause on a SELECT statement to indicate a VSAM file's organization. For an entry-sequenced data set, specify SEQUENTIAL; for a key-sequenced data set, specify INDEXED; and for a relative-record data set, specify RELATIVE. The value you code must agree with the organization you specified for the file when you defined it.

The ACCESS MODE clause   You use the ACCESS MODE clause to specify how your program will process the file. For an entry-sequenced data set, you must specify SEQUENTIAL as the access mode. However, for a key-sequenced or relative-record data set, you can specify SEQUENTIAL if you want to process records sequentially or RANDOM if you want to process records randomly by key or relative record number. And if you specify DYNAMIC as the access mode for a KSDS or RRDS, your program can alternate between sequential and random access.

The KEY clauses   The next three SELECT statement clauses, RELATIVE KEY, RECORD KEY, and ALTERNATE RECORD KEY,

```
SELECT file-name     ASSIGN TO assignment-name

                                           ⎧SEQUENTIAL⎫
                     ORGANIZATION IS        ⎨INDEXED   ⎬
                                           ⎩RELATIVE  ⎭

                                           ⎧SEQUENTIAL⎫
                     [ ACCESS MODE IS       ⎨RANDOM    ⎬ ]
                                           ⎩DYNAMIC   ⎭

                     [ RELATIVE KEY IS data-name ]

                     [ RECORD KEY IS data-name ]

                     [ PASSWORD IS data-name ]

                     [ ALTERNATE RECORD KEY IS data-name
                         [ PASSWORD IS data-name ]
                         [ WITH DUPLICATES ] ] . . .

                     [ FILE STATUS IS data-name ]
```

Figure 10-1	The SELECT statment for VSAM files

Operating system	File organization	Syntax	Example
OS/MVS	KSDS RRDS	[comment-]name	CUSTMAST
OS/MVS	ESDS	[comment-]AS-name	AS-INVTRAN
DOS/VSE	KSDS RRDS	SYSnnn-[class-][device-]name	SYS100-CUSTMAS
DOS/VSE	ESDS	SYSnnn-[class-][device-]AS-name	SYS100-AS-INVTRAN

Figure 10-2	Assignment names under OS/MVS and DOS/VSE

specify the key fields used to access records in the file. You can code RELATIVE KEY only for relative-record data sets, and you can code RECORD KEY and ALTERNATE RECORD KEY only for key-sequenced data sets. None of these clauses is valid for entry-sequenced data sets.

For a relative record data set, you must code the RELATIVE KEY clause for random or dynamic access; it's optional for sequential access. In it, you name a working-storage field that will contain a relative record number. For efficiency, I recommend you define the relative key field as an unsigned binary fullword, like this:

```
05  RELATIVE-KEY           PIC 9(8)        COMP.
```

You can also define the relative key field as a zoned- or packed-decimal field.

For a key-sequenced data set, you must code the RECORD KEY clause to name the file's primary key field, regardless of the file's access mode. This field must be defined within one of the record descriptions coded in the File Section entry for the file.

If you need to access a key-sequenced data set via alternate indexes, you identify the alternate keys by coding one or more ALTERNATE RECORD KEY clauses. The field you name in each ALTERNATE RECORD KEY clause must be within one of the file's record descriptions, and an alternate index that uses that field as an alternate key must exist. If the alternate index allows non-unique keys, specify WITH DUPLICATES; for unique keys, omit WITH DUPLICATES.

If you code the ALTERNATE RECORD KEY clause, you must include a DD or DLBL statement in the JCL for the path associated with each alternate index you specify. To form the ddname (OS) or file-name (DOS) for each path, use the assignment name for the file followed by a number: 1 for the first alternate index you specify in the SELECT statement, 2 for the second, and so on. If the resulting name is longer than seven (DOS) or eight (OS) characters, drop characters from the end of the file's assignment name. For example, if the assignment name for a KSDS under OS is CUSTMAST, the ddnames for any two alternate index paths would be CUSTMAS1 and CUSTMAS2. I dropped the letter T from the end of the file's ddname to make the path ddnames eight characters.

The PASSWORD clauses   If your file is protected by VSAM passwords, you can supply the passwords by coding one or more PASSWORD clauses in the file's SELECT statement. Usually, you'll just have to code one PASSWORD clause; you need two or more only when you specify alternate keys for a key-sequenced data set.

For a relative-record or entry-sequenced data set, you can code the PASSWORD clause anywhere in the SELECT statement. For a key-sequenced data set, however, the PASSWORD clause must come right after the RECORD KEY or ALTERNATE RECORD KEY clause. To supply a password for a KSDS base cluster, you code the PASSWORD clause right after the RECORD KEY clause. And to supply a password for an alternate index path, you code the PASSWORD clause right after the ALTERNATE RECORD KEY clause, but before the WITH DUPLICATES clause, if it's included.

In the PASSWORD clause, you name a field that contains the eight-byte password value. This value is checked when you issue an OPEN statement for the file, so you should move the correct password value to the password field before you issue the OPEN statement. The password value must match a password specified for the file on the DEFINE (or ALTER) command, and must be at a high enough level (read, update, control, or master) to permit the COBOL operations that will be performed against the file.

The FILE STATUS clause   The FILE STATUS clause specifies a field that's updated by VSAM after each I/O statement for the file is executed. The FILE STATUS field must be defined in working storage, and its PICTURE should be XX. When an I/O statement executes successfully, VSAM puts 00 in the FILE STATUS field. But when an error condition occurs, VSAM puts a non-zero two-digit error code in the FILE STATUS field. Therefore, your programs should examine the FILE STATUS field after each I/O statement to determine whether an error occurred and, if so, what action to take.

FILE STATUS codes can indicate two types of errors. The first are errors your program should anticipate, like end-of-file or record-not-found. Your program can detect these errors by testing the FILE STATUS field or by using the AT END clause on sequential READ statements or the INVALID KEY clause on other I/O statements. Errors of the second type, like hardware failures or internal VSAM errors, are more serious. For these types of errors, your program should probably be terminated. I'll have more to say about the FILE STATUS field and error handling later in this chapter.

If you're using the VS COBOL II compiler, you can code a second data name on the FILE STATUS clause. Then, whenever an error occurs, VSAM puts more detailed feedback information in that field. Quite frankly, the amount of information provided in the standard FILE STATUS field is enough for most COBOL programs. So I won't describe the second FILE STATUS field here.

Examples of the SELECT statement for VSAM files   Figure 10-3 shows five typical SELECT statements for VSAM files. All of them are for OS/MVS systems; for DOS/VSE, you must code the assignment name differently.

The first example shows a SELECT statement for an entry-sequenced data set (ORGANIZATION IS SEQUENTIAL). It will be processed sequentially (ACCESS MODE IS SEQUENTIAL); that's the only valid processing mode for an ESDS in COBOL. The FILE STATUS field is INVTRAN-STATUS.

The second example shows a SELECT statement for a relative-record data set (ORGANIZATION IS RELATIVE) that will be accessed randomly (ACCESS MODE IS RANDOM). The relative-record number is in a field named ITEM-NUMBER.

Examples 3 and 4 are for key-sequenced data sets (ORGANIZATION IS INDEXED). In example 3, the KSDS will be accessed sequentially. The primary key field for this file is CM-CUSTOMER-NUMBER. In example 4, the KSDS will be accessed dynamically. In addition to the primary key, EM-EMPLOYEE-NUMBER, two alternate keys are specified for this file. The first, EM-LAST-NAME, allows duplicates; the second, EM-SOCIAL-SECURITY-NUMBER, doesn't. (The ddnames for the two alternate indexes are EMPMAST1 and EMPMAST2.)

Example 1

```
SELECT INVTRAN   ASSIGN TO AS-INVTRAN
                 ORGANIZATION IS SEQUENTIAL
                 ACCESS MODE IS SEQUENTIAL
                 FILE STATUS IS INVTRAN-STATUS.
```

Example 2

```
SELECT INVMAST   ASSIGN TO INVMAST
                 ORGANIZATION IS RELATIVE
                 ACCESS MODE IS RANDOM
                 RELATIVE KEY IS ITEM-NUMBER
                 FILE STATUS IS INVMAST-STATUS.
```

Example 3

```
SELECT CUSTMAST  ASSIGN TO CUSTMAST
                 ORGANIZATION IS INDEXED
                 ACCESS MODE IS SEQUENTIAL
                 RECORD KEY IS CM-CUSTOMER-NUMBER
                 FILE STATUS IS CUSTMAST-STATUS.
```

Example 4

```
SELECT EMPMAST   ASSIGN TO EMPMAST
                 ORGANIZATION IS INDEXED
                 ACCESS MODE IS DYNAMIC
                 RECORD KEY IS EM-EMPLOYEE-NUMBER
                 ALTERNATE RECORD KEY IS EM-LAST-NAME
                     WITH DUPLICATES
                 ALTERNATE RECORD KEY IS EM-SOCIAL-SECURITY-NUMBER
                 FILE STATUS IS EMPMAST-STATUS.
```

Example 5

```
SELECT EMPMAST   ASSIGN TO EMPMAST
                 ORGANIZATION IS INDEXED
                 ACCESS MODE IS DYNAMIC
                 RECORD KEY IS EM-EMPLOYEE-NUMBER
                 PASSWORD IS EMPMAST-PASSWORD
                 ALTERNATE RECORD KEY IS EM-LAST-NAME
                     PASSWORD IS EMPMAST-NAME-PASSWORD
                     WITH DUPLICATES
                 ALTERNATE RECORD KEY IS EM-SOCIAL-SECURITY-NUMBER
                     PASSWORD IS EMPMAST-SSN-PASSWORD
                 FILE STATUS IS EMPMAST-STATUS.
```

Figure 10-3   Examples of the SELECT statement for VSAM files

```
 FD   EMPMAST
      LABEL RECORDS ARE STANDARD.
 *
 01   EMPLOYEE-MASTER-RECORD.
 *
      05   EM-EMPLOYEE-NUMBER              PIC 9(5).
      05   EM-LAST-NAME                    PIC X(15).
      05   EM-SOCIAL-SECURITY-NUMBER       PIC 9(9).
      .
      .
      .
```

Figure 10-4   The File Section entry for the VSAM file whose SELECT statement was shown in example 4 of figure 10-3

Example 5 is similar to example 4, except that I coded a PASSWORD clause for the base cluster and each alternate index. The three password fields, EMPMAST-PASSWORD, EMPMAST-NAME-PASSWORD, and EMPMAST-SSN-PASSWORD, are defined as eight-byte alphanumeric fields in the Working-Storage Section. Valid passwords must be moved to these fields before the file is opened.

File Section entries for VSAM files

As for any other file, you must code an FD entry in the File Section for a VSAM file. There's only one required entry: LABEL RECORDS ARE STANDARD. Following the FD entry, you must code at least one record description for the file. If the file is a key-sequenced data set, that record description must include the record key field and all alternate key fields you specified in the file's SELECT statement. Figure 10-4 shows the FD entry for the file whose SELECT statement was shown in example 4 of figure 10-3.

PROCEDURE DIVISION STATEMENTS FOR VSAM FILES

Now that you know the Environment and Data Division requirements for VSAM files, you're ready to learn about the Procedure Division statements you can code to process VSAM files. Figure 10-5 presents those statements. You use the OPEN statement to connect your program to a VSAM file. Then, you can use the READ, WRITE, REWRITE, DELETE, and START statements to process the file's records. Notice that the READ statement has two forms: one for sequential processing, the other for random processing. Finally, you use the CLOSE statement to disconnect your program from the VSAM file.

Before I describe the statements individually, I want you to realize that each of them returns a status code in the FILE STATUS field. As a result, you should follow each of these statements with statements that test the status code field to make sure there's no error. Although some of the VSAM I/O statements have clauses that let you test certain conditions (like the AT END clause of a sequential READ statement), I recommend you don't use them. Instead, test the completion of each VSAM I/O statement by examining the FILE STATUS field. I'll explain how to do that after I describe the I/O statements themselves.

The OPEN and CLOSE statements

Before your program can issue any other I/O statements against a VSAM file, it must issue an OPEN statement. That connects your program to the VSAM file and indicates what I/O operations will be permitted for the file. If you specify INPUT, you can only retrieve records from the file. If you specify OUTPUT or EXTEND, you can only add records to the file. And if you specify I-O, you can retrieve or update records.

I want to be sure you understand the difference between OUTPUT and EXTEND. You can specify OUTPUT only for unloaded files (files that have been defined but never used). Once you write records to a file, you can't open it for output. You can specify EXTEND for an unloaded file or for a file that contains records. Specifying EXTEND for an unloaded file is the same as specifying OUTPUT. But when you specify EXTEND for a file that contains records, VSAM positions the file after the last record, so that WRITE statements add records to the end of the file.

For a reusable file, you can specify OUTPUT even if the file already contains records. If you specify OUTPUT for a reusable file, the file is considered to be unloaded whether or not it actually contains records. If you specify EXTEND, records that exist in the file are retained.

Just as VSAM files must be opened at the beginning of a program, they must be closed at the end. If you don't issue a CLOSE statement for a VSAM file, the catalog information for the file might be incorrect. The format of the CLOSE statement for VSAM files is the same as for non-VSAM files.

Procedure Division statements for sequential access

If you specify ACCESS MODE IS SEQUENTIAL for a VSAM file, you can use any of the I/O statements in figure 10-5 except the random READ statement. However, you must also consider the processing mode you specify on the OPEN statement. If you open the file for INPUT, you can use only READ and START statements for the file; if you open the file for OUTPUT or EXTEND, you can use only WRITE statements; and if you open the file for I-O, you can use READ, START, REWRITE, and DELETE statements.

Sequential processing in INPUT mode In INPUT mode, you issue READ statements to retrieve records in sequence. For an entry-sequenced data set, records are retrieved in the order in which they were written; for a key-

| The OPEN statement | OPEN | $\begin{cases} \text{INPUT} & \text{file-name} \ldots \\ \text{OUTPUT} & \text{file-name} \ldots \\ \text{EXTEND} & \text{file-name} \ldots \\ \text{I-0} & \text{file-name} \ldots \end{cases}$ | $\ldots$ |

The CLOSE statement

```
CLOSE file-name ...
```

The READ statement (sequential)

```
READ file-name
  [ NEXT ]
  [ INTO data-name ]
  [ AT END imperative-statement ]
```

The READ statement (random)

```
READ file-name
  [ INTO data-name ]
  [ KEY IS data-name ]
  [ INVALID KEY imperative-statement]
```

The WRITE statement

```
WRITE record-name
  [ FROM data-name ]
  [ INVALID KEY imperative-statement ]
```

The REWRITE statement

```
REWRITE record-name
  [ FROM data-name ]
  [ INVALID KEY imperative-statement ]
```

The DELETE statement

```
DELETE file-name
  [ INVALID KEY imperative-statement ]
```

The START statement

$$\text{START file-name [KEY IS } \begin{cases} \text{EQUAL TO} \\ = \\ \text{GREATER THAN} \\ > \\ \text{NOT LESS THAN} \\ \text{NOT} < \end{cases} \text{data-name]}$$

```
  [ INVALID KEY imperative-statement]
```

Figure 10-5   Procedure Division statements for VSAM processing

sequenced data set, records are retrieved in the order of their primary keys (unless you're using an alternate index, as I'll explain later); for a relative-record data set, records are retrieved in relative-record-number sequence, and empty slots are automatically skipped.

The word NEXT is optional on a sequential READ statement; it's required only when you specify dynamic access for the file. The AT END clause, which detects the end-of-file condition, is optional too. I recommend you omit it, and instead, test the FILE STATUS field after each READ statement to see if the end of the file has been reached or if any other error has occurred. I'll show you how to do that later.

When you open a file in INPUT mode, the file is automatically positioned at the first record. For a KSDS or RRDS, however, you can issue a START statement at any point in your program to change the current position. First, you place the key or number of the record at which you wish to start processing in the RECORD or RELATIVE KEY field for the file. Then, you code the KEY clause on the START statement, specifying the RECORD or RELATIVE KEY field and a relationship. For example, suppose you code this statement:

```
START INVMAST
      KEY NOT LESS THAN IM-ITEM-NUMBER.
```

Here, I issue a START statement for a KSDS, specifying that the key should be not less than the value in IM-ITEM-NUMBER, the file's RECORD KEY field. As a result, the file will be positioned to the first record whose key value is equal to or greater than the value in IM-ITEM-NUMBER.

If you omit the KEY clause altogether on a START statement, the file is positioned to the record indicated by the RECORD KEY field (KSDS) or RELATIVE KEY field (RRDS). If the record doesn't exist, an error occurs. For this reason, I usually include the KEY clause and use the NOT LESS THAN relation so that processing begins at the first record equal to or greater than the value in the key field.

For a relative-record data set, the data-name you supply in a START statement must always be the file's RELATIVE KEY field. For a key-sequenced data set, however, the data-name can be the file's RECORD KEY field or any one of its ALTERNATE RECORD KEY fields. I'll describe how you use the START statement for alternate indexes later.

Sequential processing in I/O mode   If you specify ACCESS MODE IS SEQUENTIAL in a file's SELECT statement and I-O mode in the file's OPEN statement, you can use the READ and START statements just as I described for INPUT mode. In addition, you can use the REWRITE statement to update records in the file and you can use the DELETE statement to remove records from the file. In each case, the statement refers to the record that was read by an immediately preceding READ statement. In other words, you must read a record before you can rewrite or delete it using sequential access. For an ESDS or RRDS, the REWRITE statement can *not* change the length of the record. You can, however, change the length of a KSDS record with a REWRITE statement, as long as you don't exceed the maximum record length specified when the file was defined.

Sequential processing in OUTPUT or EXTEND mode   If you open a sequentially accessed file in OUTPUT or EXTEND mode, you can issue only WRITE statements for the file. The records are always written to the end of the file. For key-sequenced data sets, that means you must write the records in ascending key sequence.

Procedure Division statements for random access

If you specify ACCESS MODE IS RANDOM for a VSAM key-sequenced or relative-record data set, the I/O statements you can use depend on whether you open the file for INPUT, I-O, or OUTPUT. (You can't specify EXTEND on the OPEN statement for a file with random access.) If you open the file for INPUT, you can issue only READ statements. Likewise, you can use only WRITE statements if you open the file for OUTPUT. If you open the file for I-O, you can issue READ, WRITE, REWRITE, and DELETE statements for the file.

The READ, WRITE, REWRITE, and DELETE statements for random processing all depend on the value in the file's RECORD KEY or RELATIVE KEY field. Before a READ statement is executed, for example, you must place the key of the desired record in the key field. Then, the READ statement attempts to read the record with that key. Likewise, the DELETE statement knows which record to delete by the value in the key field, so you don't have to issue a READ statement before the DELETE statement. And the WRITE and REWRITE statements use the key field value to write records.

As you know, when an I/O error occurs, the FILE STATUS field is updated by VSAM. Although you can use the INVALID KEY clause to test for I/O errors, the statements in the clause are executed only for three error conditions: record not found, duplicate key, and insufficient space. Since it's an optional clause and it doesn't provide for all error conditions, I recommend you omit it and instead test the FILE STATUS field after each I/O operation.

Procedure Division statements for dynamic access

Many programs require that you process a key-sequenced or relative-record file using a mixture of sequential and random access. Using the sequential processing features I've already described, you can do that to a limited extent; the START statement lets you position a file to any point (random processing), then sequentially retrieve records (sequential processing). Although that's helpful in many situations, there are cases when you need the full capabilities of both random and sequential processing. That's where dynamic access comes in.

When you use dynamic access, you can use any of the I/O statements in figure 10-5. The WRITE, REWRITE, and DELETE statements work just as they do for random access. In other words, they depend on the value in the RECORD KEY or RELATIVE KEY field. The START statement, naturally, works as it does for sequential access; it establishes position for sequential retrieval. The READ statement retrieves records sequentially or randomly, depending on how you code it. If you specify NEXT on the READ statement, records are retrieved sequentially. If you omit NEXT, records are retrieved randomly based on the value in the RECORD KEY or RELATIVE KEY field.

The key to understanding dynamic access is knowing how to switch from sequential to random access. The current position for sequential retrieval is changed only by a START or READ statement. As a result, you can issue a random READ statement to retrieve a specific record, then issue sequential READ statements (with the NEXT option) to retrieve records sequentially from that point. But if you issue a WRITE, REWRITE, or DELETE statement, positioning for sequential retrieval is *not* changed.

Quite frankly, most of the programs you develop will *not* require dynamic access. However, I usually specify dynamic access for key-sequenced and relative-record files, even if I don't need it. That way, I'm able to use both sequential and random processing, and I don't have to worry about the restrictions of sequential or random access mode.

Procedure Division statements for alternate indexes

As you already know, you can specify alternate indexes in the SELECT statement for a key-sequenced data set. The Procedure Division elements for working with alternate indexes are simple. You need to know just two things: (1) how to switch from the primary key to an alternate key to retrieve records and (2) how the sequential and random versions of the READ statement differ when an alternate key is used. (The WRITE, REWRITE, and DELETE statements aren't affected by alternate indexes, with the exception that if you issue a WRITE or REWRITE for a file with alternate indexes that do *not* allow duplicates, the values of those alternate key fields in the new record must be unique.)

Changing the key of reference   When you issue a READ statement for a file with alternate keys, you must know which key is the *key of reference*. When you open a file, the RECORD KEY field is established as the key of reference, so that subsequent READ statements use the primary key for retrieval. You can change the key of reference in two ways: (1) by issuing a START statement (sequential or dynamic access only) or (2) by coding the KEY clause on a random READ statement (random or dynamic access only).

For example, suppose you issue this statement:

```
START EMPMAST
     KEY IS EQUAL TO EMP-SOCIAL-SECURITY-NUMBER.
```

Here, the file is positioned to the record indicated by the social security number alternate key. Then, subsequent sequential READ statements will retrieve records in social security number sequence. To switch back to the primary key, issue another START statement, this time specifying the RECORD KEY field or omitting the KEY clause altogether.

When you use random or dynamic access, the random READ statement uses the RECORD KEY field unless you code the KEY clause, like this:

```
READ EMPMAST
     KEY IS EMP-SOCIAL-SECURITY-NUMBER.
```

Here, an employee-master record is read based on the contents of its social security number. The social security number alternate key becomes the key of reference for subsequent sequential READ statements (that is, READ statements with the NEXT option). However, the key of reference applies only to *sequential* READ statements; a subsequent random READ statement uses the primary key field unless you code the KEY clause again.

Processing duplicate keys   When you process records via an alternate key that allows duplicates, you may get FILE STATUS code 02 rather than 00 even though the I/O statement you issued executed successfully. In many cases, that won't significantly affect the way you code your program; all you have to do is check for 02 as well as 00 to see if the statement was successful. In other cases, your program may need to take some special action when the 02 FILE STATUS is encountered. As a result, you need to know when the 02 FILE STATUS code is generated.

When you issue a WRITE or REWRITE statement, you'll get the 02 FILE STATUS code if a duplicate key is created for any of the alternate keys you named, and for which you coded WITH DUPLICATES, in the file's SELECT statement. This is a normal condition, and your program probably doesn't need to take special action because of it. Note that if a WRITE or REWRITE statement creates a duplicate key value for an alternate key that does *not* allow duplicates, file status 22 rather than 02 is returned; that *is* an error condition.

When you issue a random READ statement that names an alternate key in the KEY clause, the record retrieved is the first record written to the file with the key value you specify. If there are additional records with the same alternate key value, you'll get the 02 FILE STATUS code. The only way to retrieve those additional records is by issuing sequential READ statements.

When you issue a sequential READ statement, and the key of reference is an alternate key that allows duplicates, the 02 status code is returned if there is at least one more record in the file that has the same alternate key value, not counting the record being read. When you read the last, or only, record that has a particular alternate key value, status code 00 is returned. For example, suppose a file has three records with alternate key 10001. When the first is read (either by a random or sequential READ statement), status code 02 is returned because there are more records with the same alternate key. When the second is read (only by a sequential READ statement), status code 02 is returned again. But when the third record is read, status code 00 is returned because there are no more records in the file with the same alternate key value.

Depending on the application, you may need to test for status code 02 during sequential retrieval via an alternate index. For example, if you need to retrieve all of the records that have a particular alternate key value, you can issue a START statement to establish the key of reference and position the file to the first record that has the desired key. Then, you can issue sequential READ statements repeatedly until status code 00 is returned. As long as status code 02 is returned, you know there's at least one more record in the file with the desired alternate key value.

VSAM ERROR PROCESSING

Because of the way VSAM handles error conditions, many I/O errors that would cause programs to abend under non-VSAM access methods do *not* cause an abend under VSAM. Instead, the FILE STATUS field is set to indicate the nature of the problem and control returns to the COBOL program. Depending on the problem, an error message may or may not be printed in the JCL listing for the job. But whether or not a message is printed, it's easy for serious errors to go undetected.

The only way to avoid the problems caused by undetected errors is to test the FILE STATUS field after every I/O statement to ensure that no error has occurred. If there's no error, or if the error is one that should be anticipated by the program (like end-of-file), processing can continue. If there is a serious error, you should display an appropriate error message, close all open files, and issue a STOP RUN statement. Or, you may want to abend the program in order to get a dump, either by invoking an assembler-language subprogram that issues an ABEND macro (OS) or a CANCEL macro (DOS), or by doing a simple COBOL operation that will cause an abend, like dividing a number by zero.

FILE STATUS error codes

Figure 10-6 lists all of the possible FILE STATUS codes, the meaning of the codes for each I/O statement, and a recommendation for handling the error. The codes between 00 and 23 represent errors that your program might anticipate. Code 00 means that the statement executed correctly. Code 02 means that the statement executed correctly, but a duplicate alternate key value was detected. Code 10 means that a sequential READ statement encountered the end of the file. Code 21 means that a record was written out of sequence during sequential output processing. Code 22 means that you tried to write a record with a duplicate primary key, or a duplicate alternate key when you didn't specify WITH DUPLICATES in the ALTERNATE RECORD KEY clause. And code 23 means you tried to access a record that doesn't exist.

FILE STATUS code	OPEN	CLOSE	READ	WRITE	REWRITE	DELETE	START	Recommended program action
00	File successfully opened	File successfully closed	Record successfully read	Record successfully written	Record successfully rewritten	Record successfully deleted	Successful completion	Continue processing
02			Valid duplicate alternate key follows	Valid duplicate alternate key created	Valid duplicate alternate key created			Continue processing
10			End of file reached					Normal AT END processing
21				Record out of sequence (sequential access only)				Print error message and continue
22				Duplicate key				Print error message and continue
23			Record not found			Record not found	Specified key not found	Print error message and continue
24				No more space allocated to file				Terminate job
30	Uncorrectable I/O error	Uncorrectable I/O error	Uncorrectable I/O error	Uncorrectable I/O error	Uncorrectable I/O error	Uncorrectable I/O error	Uncorrectable I/O error	Terminate job
90	Unusable file-possibly an empty file opened as INPUT or I-O	VSAM logic error	VSAM logic error	VSAM logic error	VSAM logic error	VSAM logic error	VSAM logic error	Terminate job

Figure 10-6   File status codes (part 1 of 2)

FILE STATUS code	OPEN	CLOSE	READ	WRITE	REWRITE	DELETE	START	Recommended program action
91	Password failure							Terminate job
92	File already opened	File not open	File is not open or end of file already reached	File is not open; incorrect key for EXTEND file	File is not open; no previous READ	File is not open;no previous READ (sequential access)	Invalid request; probably file not open	Terminate job
93	Not enough virtual storage for VSAM task	Not enough virtual storage for VSAM task	Not enough virtual storage for VSAM task	Not enough virtual storage for VSAM task	Not enough virtual storage for VSAM task	Not enough virtual storage for VSAM task	Not enough virtual storage for VSAM task	Terminate job
95	Conflicting file attributes							Terminate job
96	No DD statement							Terminate job
97	File not closed by previous job							Terminate job

Figure 10-6   File status codes (part 2 of 2)

All of the codes that are 24 or higher represent serious error conditions that generally can't be corrected by your COBOL program. As a result, the recommended action for these codes is program termination. Of course, specific program requirements or your shop's standards may dictate some other action. But in most cases, I think it's best to terminate the program when one of these errors occurs.

FILE STATUS codes 30, 90, and 93 represent system errors that don't often occur, so you probably won't encounter those codes. Code 30 usually indicates a hardware problem. Code 90 indicates some type of VSAM logic error. It might be caused by a bug in the COBOL compiler or in VSAM. Or, this code could occur if VSAM system data has been destroyed. Code 93 means that VSAM didn't have enough virtual storage to perform an I/O operation. As I said, these error codes aren't common, so you won't see them often.

FILE STATUS code 92 means you tried to do something that's not allowed. For example, you may be trying to read records from or write records to a file that isn't open or rewrite a record (using sequential access) before a record has been successfully read. In any event, the error is caused by a logic problem in your COBOL program, so it's best to terminate the program, then fix it.

Some of the FILE STATUS codes (91, 95, 96, and 97) are caused only by OPEN errors. Code 91 means your COBOL program is denied access to the file because it didn't supply a proper password. If your installation uses VSAM password protection for its files, you may encounter this error from time to time. Code 95 means the file has conflicting attributes. For example, a COBOL program may have specified that the file's record key is in positions 2 through 9 but the file was defined with its key in positions 4 through 11. And code 96 means there is no DD or DLBL statement for the file.

Code 97 means that the file wasn't properly closed by the last program that processed it. Before your program processes the file then, you should invoke AMS and issue a VERIFY command to reset incorrect catalog information. Under DOS/VSE, MVS/XA, and ICF, a VERIFY command is automatically issued. Even so, you should probably terminate your program if you encounter code 97. If a previous program abended while it was processing the file, it's best to wait until you find out what caused the failure and correct any damage that was done before you process the file again.

Terminology

key of reference

Objective

Given specifications for a COBOL program that processes VSAM files, code an acceptable solution.

Chapter 11

Application programming under CICS/VS

In this chapter, you'll learn how CICS/VS supports VSAM file processing. If you're already familiar with CICS, this chapter will help you understand more about how your CICS programs relate to VSAM. And you'll learn about some advanced VSAM features CICS supports that you may not have used before. If you're new to CICS, this chapter won't show you all you need to know to write a CICS program, although it will introduce you to the CICS environment.

In the first section of this chapter, I'll describe CICS and introduce the basic concepts and terms you need to know. Then, in the second section, I'll describe the basic CICS commands you use to process VSAM files. If you're an experienced CICS programmer, these two sections will be mostly review, so you may just want to skim them quickly. The third section of this chapter presents four advanced VSAM file-processing features available under CICS: locate-mode I/O, generic keys, mass sequential insertion, and multiple browse operations.

CICS CONCEPTS AND TERMINOLOGY

This section briefly describes how CICS works. Then, it presents some basic CICS programming considerations.

How CICS/VS works

CICS was designed to support multiple users running a variety of interactive (terminal-oriented) programs at the same time. One way to think of CICS is as an interface between the application programs in an interactive system and the host operating system, as figure 11-1 shows. Application programs communicate with CICS, which in turn communicates with access methods through the host operating system. As far as the operating system is concerned, CICS is an application program. That means CICS runs in one of the system's partitions or address spaces.

Another way to think of CICS is as an operating system itself. Although CICS runs under the control of MVS or DOS/VSE, it performs many of the functions normally associated with an operating system. For example, CICS is responsible for managing its own processor storage. As a part of that function, CICS decides how much storage to allocate to each of its active programs. In addition, CICS manages the execution of the programs under its control. That process is called *task control*, and understanding it is a key to understanding CICS.

Task control   In CICS, a *task* is the execution of an application program (or perhaps several application programs) for a specific user. The task control component of CICS is responsible for coordinating the execution of many tasks simultaneously. This is called *multitasking*. For example, figure 11-2 shows CICS running in an address space under MVS. As you can see, six tasks are running within CICS.

Multitasking is similar to multiprogramming. Basically, *multiprogramming* means that an operating system lets several jobs execute at the same time. (A job is the execution of one or more programs for a particular user.) Multitasking under CICS is similar, except that several tasks execute together within CICS, which is itself a job running within a partition (DOS/VSE) or address space (MVS).

Notice in figure 11-2 that three of the CICS terminal users (1, 3, and 6) are running the same application program: order entry. If the same program were loaded into storage at three different locations, valuable virtual storage would be wasted. CICS uses a concept called *multithreading* so only one copy of a program is loaded into storage no matter how many users are running it. Fortunately, that's transparent to you as an application programmer.

To start a task, a terminal user invokes a *transaction*, which is a predefined unit of work a terminal user can invoke. When a transaction is invoked, a specified application program is loaded into storage (if it's not already there)

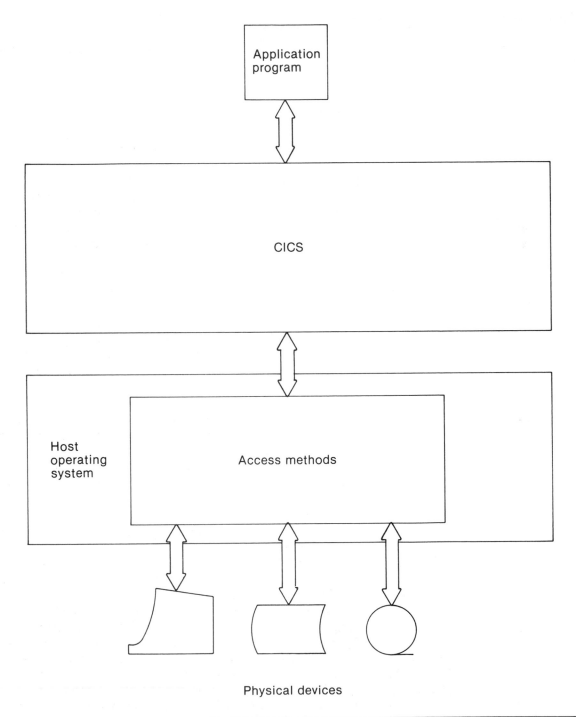

Figure 11-1   How CICS acts as an interface between the operating system and application programs

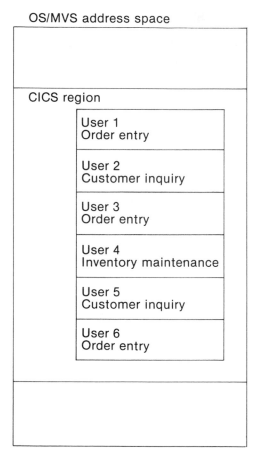

OS/MVS address space

CICS region

| User 1
Order entry |
| User 2
Customer inquiry |
| User 3
Order entry |
| User 4
Inventory maintenance |
| User 5
Customer inquiry |
| User 6
Order entry |

Figure 11-2   Multitasking within an address space under OS/MVS

and a task is started. The difference between a transaction and a task is that while many users can invoke the same transaction, each is given a separate task.

Each transaction is identified by a unique four-character code called a *transaction identifier* (or just *trans-id*). An operator initiates a transaction (and, as a result, starts a task) by entering its trans-id into the terminal. For example, to run an order entry program, the operator might enter a trans-id like ORD1.

File control   Another major component of CICS, called the *file-control program*, handles all file I/O for CICS application programs. So whenever a CICS application program needs to perform an I/O operation against a file, it invokes the file-control program. The file-control program, in turn, communicates with the access method (which is usually VSAM) to actually perform the I/O operation.

Because the file-control program manages all file I/O for CICS programs, you don't use standard COBOL elements for file processing under CICS. That means you don't code SELECT statements or FD entries, OPEN or CLOSE statements, or READ, WRITE, REWRITE, or DELETE statements. Instead, you code CICS commands that invoke the file-control program to perform the I/O functions you need.

Because CICS itself (via the file-control program) manages VSAM files, all of the VSAM data sets available under CICS are allocated to the CICS region or partition. When CICS is initiated, the file-control program opens each of the VSAM files. And when CICS is terminated, the file-control program closes the VSAM files. As a result, application programs don't have to issue any CICS commands to open or close VSAM files; they're always open. (A CICS terminal operator can temporarily close a file, but that's unusual.)

The file-control program uses a special table called the *File Control Table* (or *FCT*) to keep track of each file CICS uses. The FCT lists each file's organization and other characteristics like its buffer space allocation and number of strings. In addition, the FCT lists the file control operations that are valid for each file: deleting records, adding new records, updating records, and so on. In general, the FCT is maintained by the system programmer responsible for maintaining CICS, so you don't have to worry about keeping the FCT up to date.

As I mentioned earlier, multitasking lets several application programs execute at the same time under CICS. The file-control program handles all of the details necessary to allow those programs to access VSAM data sets concurrently. In particular, the file-control program insures that two programs don't try to update data in the same control interval of a data set at the same time. As a programmer, you don't have to do anything special to make sure that happens; it's automatic.

Another important file control function is recovering from errors that cause tasks to terminate abnormally. In most cases, file control automatically reverses changes made to VSAM data sets when a task abends. So if the abending task updated a record, the record is restored to its state before the update. This facility is called *dynamic transaction backout*, and it's normally transparent to you as an application programmer.

Basic CICS programming considerations

An application program that executes under CICS is somewhat different from a batch application program. Although most CICS programs are developed using COBOL, many of the features of standard COBOL are replaced by special *CICS commands* that invoke CICS services like task control and file control. A program that uses those commands is called a *command-level program*.

Before I show you how to code the CICS commands that process VSAM files, I want you to know about four basic CICS programming considerations. First, I want you to understand how CICS commands are processed and how

Original source code

```
EXEC CICS
     RECEIVE MAP('MORMAP1')
             MAPSET('MORSET1')
             INTO(MORTGAGE-CALCULATION-MAP)
END-EXEC.
```

Translated source code

```
*EXEC CICS
*    RECEIVE MAP('MORMAP1')
*            MAPSET('MORSET1')
*            INTO(MORTGAGE-CALCULATION-MAP)
*END-EXEC.
     MOVE '                   00079   ' TO DFHEIVO
     MOVE 'MORMAP1' TO DFHC0070
     MOVE 'MORSET1' TO DFHC0071
   CALL 'DFHEI1' USING DFHEIVO  DFHC0070
     MORTGAGE-CALCULATION-MAP DFHDUMMY DFHC0071.
```

Figure 11-3   Sample source and translated code

they relate to the other COBOL statements in your program. Second, I want you to understand how a CICS feature called Basic Mapping Support manages terminal I/O for most CICS programs. Third, I want you to understand a common CICS programming technique called pseudo-conversational programming. And fourth, I want you to understand how error conditions are handled in a command-level program.

CICS commands   The top section of figure 11-3 shows a typical CICS command. This command (RECEIVE) causes data from the user's terminal to be moved to a working storage area in the program. There are dozens of CICS commands, and, as you'd expect, their formats vary. However, a CICS command always begins with EXEC CICS and ends with END-EXEC.

Because CICS commands aren't standard COBOL, they don't make sense to the COBOL compiler. As a result, to compile a CICS COBOL program, you first must process your source code with the *CICS command-level translator* to convert CICS commands to a form meaningful to the COBOL compiler. Figure 11-4 shows that process.

The translator converts each CICS command into a series of COBOL MOVE statements followed by a CALL statement, as you can see in the bottom section of figure 11-3. The MOVE statements assign values to the fields that are the arguments of the CALL statement. (The translator also inserts those fields in your program.) The CALL statement activates the CICS command-level interface to invoke the required CICS services. As you can see,

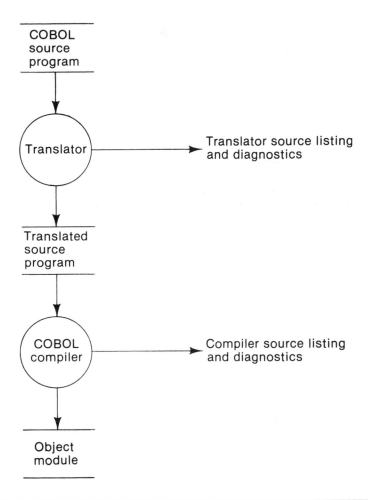

Figure 11-4   The translation and compilation process

the source code for the original command is included as comments in the translated version of the program; it's there only to help you read the translated program.

Basic Mapping Support   A part of CICS you'll probably use is *Basic Mapping Support*, or *BMS*. BMS is an interface within CICS between application programs and terminals. Simply put, BMS lets you concentrate on how data appears on the terminal screen, rather than the detailed requirements of various terminal devices like the 3270. To receive data from or send data to a terminal, the application program issues a CICS command that invokes BMS.

To format terminal data, BMS uses map definitions you code in a special kind of assembler-language program called a *mapset*. When you use BMS, you have a high degree of control over the format of data displayed on and retrieved from a terminal. Although I don't show how to code and use BMS mapsets in this chapter, I do want you to realize that they're used in most CICS programs.

Pseudo-conversational program design   Most CICS application programs have to be written so they don't tie up valuable virtual storage resources. Although a single CICS system can support hundreds of terminals, it can't operate efficiently if all of those terminals have tasks running that are sitting idle, waiting for operators to enter data. As a result, most CICS programs are written using the *pseudo-conversational programming* technique.

With pseudo-conversational programming, a program (and its task) ends after it sends data to a terminal. Then, it's restarted when the operator completes an entry. This is called "pseudo-conversational" because although the program appears to be carrying on a conversation with the terminal user, it's actually not present in storage. However, the terminal user doesn't realize that the program ends each time it sends output to the terminal.

This programming technique can be confusing and complicated because your program has to be able to figure out where it is when it is restarted. Much of the difficulty in developing CICS programs then, is in implementing pseudo-conversational design.

Exceptional conditions   Whenever CICS encounters an unusual or error situation, an *exceptional condition* (or just *condition*) is raised. Each condition has a name. For example, if you try to read a record from a file that doesn't exist, the DSIDERR (data-set identification error) condition is raised. Almost all of the exceptional conditions abnormally terminate your task, although a few of them are ignored. (If you're familiar with COBOL or assembler-language coding for VSAM, you'll see right away how this is different; in both COBOL and assembler-language, you must explicitly test status codes to make sure VSAM operations complete without error.)

Since most exceptional conditions indicate serious errors, abnormal termination is appropriate. However, some of the exceptional conditions don't represent errors, but rather conditions you'd expect during routine processing. For example, if your program tries to read a KSDS record that doesn't exist, the NOTFND condition is raised and the task is terminated. Normally, however, you don't want a task to terminate just because a record wasn't found. Instead, you want your program to inform the operator of the error so he or she can correct it.

You use the HANDLE CONDITION command to specify what actions your program should take when certain exceptional conditions are raised. On it, you specify a paragraph or section name that's given control when a particular condition occurs. For example, this command:

```
EXEC CICS
    HANDLE CONDITION NOTFND(210-NOTFND)
END-EXEC
```

Condition	Cause
DSIDERR	The data set isn't defined in the FCT.
DUPKEY	Another record with the same alternate key exists.
DUPREC	The record already exists.
ENDFILE	The end (READNEXT) or beginning (READPREV) of the file has been reached.
ILLOGIC	A VSAM error has occurred.
INVREQ	The I/O request is invalid.
IOERR	An I/O error has occurred.
LENGERR	A length error has occurred.
NOSPACE	The data set cannot be extended.
NOTFND	The record doesn't exist.
NOTOPEN	The data set isn't open.

Figure 11-5   File control exceptional conditions

causes control to pass immediately to 210-NOTFND if the NOTFND condition is raised. Note that 210-NOTFND is *not* given control when the HANDLE CONDITION command is executed, but only when the NOTFND condition is raised. In effect, a GO TO is done to 210-NOTFND from the part of the program that's executing when the NOTFND condition is raised.

Figure 11-5 shows the exceptional conditions that can be raised by the file control commands this chapter presents. Of those listed, only DUPKEY, DUPREC, ENDFILE, and NOTFND represent conditions your programs should anticipate. The others are program, CICS, or VSAM errors.

FILE CONTROL COMMANDS

Now that you have a basic understanding of how CICS works, you're ready to learn about the file control commands you use in a command-level program to process VSAM files. Those commands fall into two groups. The first group lets you read, write, rewrite, and delete records randomly. The second group lets you retrieve records sequentially from a data set. After I describe these two groups of commands, I'll present some variations you should be aware of when you use them for alternate indexes.

The READ command

```
EXEC CICS
    READ DATASET(data-name|literal)
        INTO(data-name)
      [ LENGTH(data-name) ]
        RIDFLD(data-name)
      [ RRN|RBA ]
      [ UPDATE ]
END-EXEC
```

The WRITE command

```
EXEC CICS
    WRITE DATASET(data-name|literal)
          FROM(data-name)
        [ LENGTH(data-name|literal) ]
          RIDFLD(data-name)
        [ RRN|RBA ]
END-EXEC
```

The REWRITE command

```
EXEC CICS
    REWRITE DATASET(data-name|literal)
            FROM(data-name)
          [ LENGTH(data-name|literal) ]
END-EXEC
```

The DELETE command

```
EXEC CICS
    DELETE DATASET(data-name|literal)
         [ RIDFLD(data-name) ]
         [ RRN|RBA ]
END-EXEC
```

Figure 11-6   File control commands for random processing

File control commands for random processing

Figure 11-6 summarizes the file-control commands you can use for random processing. You can use all of these commands for any type of VSAM data set: KSDS, RRDS, or ESDS. Their functions correspond to the equivalent COBOL statements, so you shouldn't have much trouble understanding how they work.

The READ command   You use the READ command to retrieve a record from a file. In its simplest form, you code the READ command like this:

```
EXEC CICS
    READ DATASET('CUSTMAST')
         INTO(CUSTOMER-MASTER-RECORD)
         RIDFLD(CM-CUSTOMER-NUMBER)
END-EXEC
```

Here, a record is read from a KSDS named CUSTMAST and placed in a working-storage field named CUSTOMER-MASTER-RECORD. The

RIDFLD option names the field that contains the value of the key used for retrieval. So, if CM-CUSTOMER-NUMBER has a value of 10567, the record with key 10567 is retrieved.

If the requested record isn't in the file, the NOTFND condition is raised. As a result, you should code a HANDLE CONDITION command for the NOTFND condition before you issue a READ command. If you don't, the NOTFND condition will cause your program to terminate.

To read a record from a file whose records vary in length, you must code the LENGTH option on the READ command. Before you issue the first READ command for the file, you should place the length of the longest record your program will process in the length field. CICS will place the actual length of the record retrieved in the length field when it processes the READ command.

To read a record from a relative-record data set, you specify the RRN option. Then, the RIDFLD value represents a relative-record number rather than a key. In the Working-Storage Section, you define the record number field as a binary fullword, like this:

```
01   INVMAST-RRN              PIC S9(8)  COMP.
```

If the value of INVMAST-RRN is 1, the first record is processed; if it's 2, the second record is processed, and so on.

To read a record from an entry-sequenced data set, you code the RBA option. Then, the RIDFLD field represents the relative byte address, or RBA, of the record being processed. Like a relative-record number, a relative byte address should be a fullword binary item.

If you intend to update the record read by a READ command, you must specify the UPDATE option. The UPDATE option causes the entire control interval that contains the requested record to be reserved by your task so that you can issue a REWRITE or DELETE command to update or delete the record. As a result, other tasks can't update the record while your task is holding it.

The WRITE command   The WRITE command adds a record to a file. As you can see, the WRITE command is similar in format to the READ command. The DATASET option indicates the name of the data set, the FROM option names the output record to be written, and the LENGTH option identifies the record's length (required only if records vary in length).

For a KSDS or RRDS, the RIDFLD field provides the key or relative record number of the record you're inserting. If a record with that key or relative record number already exists, the DUPREC condition is raised. So be sure to provide for DUPREC by issuing a HANDLE CONDITION command before you issue a WRITE command for a KSDS or RRDS.

For an ESDS, records are always written to the end of the file. So the initial contents of the RIDFLD field are ignored. When the WRITE command finishes, CICS sets the RIDFLD field to indicate the relative byte address of the record just written.

The REWRITE command   The REWRITE command updates a record in a file. Before you issue a REWRITE command, you must first issue a READ command with the UPDATE option. To change the length of a KSDS or ESDS record, you specify the length of the new record in the length field.

The DELETE command   The DELETE command deletes a record from a VSAM file. You can use the DELETE command in two ways. The first is to issue a READ command with the UPDATE option and then issue a DELETE command like this:

```
EXEC CICS
    DELETE DATASET('CUSTMAST')
END-EXEC
```

Since the READ command identified the record, the RIDFLD option isn't needed on this DELETE command.

The second way to use the DELETE command is to code the RIDFLD option on the DELETE command like this:

```
EXEC CICS
    DELETE DATASET('CUSTMAST')
            RIDFLD(CM-CUSTOMER-NUMBER)
END-EXEC
```

In this case, you don't have to issue a READ command first since the DELETE command identifies the record to be deleted. If the record doesn't exist, the NOTFND condition is raised. So you should issue a HANDLE CONDITION command first to provide for the NOTFND condition.

File Control commands for browse processing

Most on-line applications process files using the random file processing elements I've just described. Still, some on-line applications need to access files sequentially. Under CICS, accessing a file sequentially is called *browsing*. Figure 11-7 shows the commands you use to access a file sequentially, called *browse commands*.

You can issue browse commands for all three types of VSAM data sets: KSDS, RRDS, and ESDS. Sequential processing of a KSDS is based on the file's key values. For an RRDS, browse operations use relative-record numbers. And for an ESDS, browse operations are based on relative byte addresses.

The STARTBR command   You use the STARTBR command to initiate a browse operation and identify the location within the data set where the browse begins. The STARTBR command doesn't retrieve a record from the file; it just establishes a position in the file so that subsequent READNEXT or READPREV commands can retrieve records.

| **The STARTBR command** | ```
EXEC CICS
      STARTBR DATASET(data-name|literal)
              RIDFLD(data-name)
            [ RRN|RBA ]
            [ GTEQ|EQUAL ]
END-EXEC
``` |
| **The READNEXT command** | ```
EXEC CICS
      READNEXT DATASET(data-name|literal)
               INTO(data-name)
             [ LENGTH(data-name) ]
               RIDFLD(data-name)
             [ RRN|RBA ]
END-EXEC
``` |
| **The READPREV command** | ```
EXEC CICS
      READPREV DATASET(data-name|literal)
               INTO(data-name)
             [ LENGTH(data-name) ]
               RIDFLD(data-name)
             [ RRN|RBA ]
END-EXEC
``` |
| **The ENDBR command** | ```
EXEC CICS
      ENDBR DATASET(data-name|literal)
END-EXEC
``` |
| **The RESETBR command** | ```
EXEC CICS
      RESETBR DATASET(data-name|literal)
              RIDFLD(data-name)
            [ RRN|RBA ]
            [ GTEQ|EQUAL ]
END-EXEC
``` |

Figure 11-7   File control commands for browse processing

You can think of a STARTBR command like a standard COBOL START statement; its function is similar. The main difference is that a STARTBR command is *always* required when you want to browse a data set, even if you want to begin with the first record in the file. In contrast, standard batch COBOL requires a START statement only when you want to begin sequential retrieval at a point other than the first record in the file.

You code the GTEQ or EQUAL options to indicate what happens if the record identified by the RIDFLD field doesn't exist. If you specify GTEQ, or let it default, the browse is started at the next record in sequence. If you specify EQUAL, the NOTFND condition is raised if the record doesn't exist. Usually, you'll specify GTEQ or let it default. (Note that the NOTFND condition will always be raised if the value specified in the RIDFLD field is beyond the end of the file, even if you specified GTEQ.)
```

The READNEXT and READPREV commands   You use the READNEXT and READPREV commands to retrieve records during a browse. Each time you issue a READNEXT command, the next record in the file identified by the DATASET option is retrieved and stored in the INTO field. For a READPREV command, records are retrieved in reverse order. In short, the READPREV command lets you browse a file backwards, from the current position toward the beginning of the file.

When there are no more records in the file, the ENDFILE condition is raised. For a READNEXT command, the ENDFILE condition means you've reached the end of the file. For a READPREV command, however, it means you've reached the beginning of the file. In either case, be sure to issue a HANDLE CONDITION command to provide for the ENDFILE condition before you issue a READNEXT or READPREV command.

The data-name you specify in the RIDFLD option on a READNEXT or READPREV command must be the same as the one you've already specified in the STARTBR command. Your program shouldn't alter the contents of this field during the browse. Instead, the READNEXT command updates it to indicate the key, RRN, or RBA value of the record it retrieved. That way, subsequent READNEXT and READPREV commands continue to retrieve records in sequence.

The ENDBR command   The ENDBR command terminates a browse operation. Usually, you don't need to issue an ENDBR command, since your browse is terminated automatically when your task ends. However, if your program does extensive processing after it completes a browse operation, you should issue an ENDBR command for efficiency's sake. As long as your browse is active, VSAM resources are allocated to your task. Releasing those resources by terminating your browse frees them for other users.

The RESETBR command   You use the RESETBR command, whose format is similar to the STARTBR command, to restart a browse operation at a new position. It has the same effect as issuing an ENDBR command followed by a STARTBR command, but it's more efficient. That's because when you issue an ENDBR command, the VSAM resources allocated to your task are released and a subsequent STARTBR command must reallocate them. In contrast, when you issue a RESETBR command, VSAM resources aren't released, so they don't have to be reallocated.

Alternate index processing

To process a KSDS or ESDS via an alternate index, you use the file-control commands for random processing and browsing I've just described, with three variations. First, you supply the name of the alternate index path in the DATASET option, rather than the name of the base cluster itself. That tells CICS to access the base cluster via the alternate index. Second, the key field you specify in the RIDFLD option is the alternate key, not the base cluster's primary key.

The third variation for alternate index processing is a little more complex. Whenever you retrieve a record using a READ, READNEXT, or READPREV command, the DUPKEY condition is raised if at least one *more* record—*not* counting the one currently being read—exists with the same alternate key.

To illustrate, suppose a program is reading invoice records via a customer number alternate key, retrieving all of the invoices for customer 10000. If there's just one invoice record for customer 10000, the DUPKEY condition isn't raised, because when the program reads the first invoice record, there aren't any additional invoice records with the same alternate key. If there are two invoices for customer 10000, DUPKEY is raised when the program reads the first record. But when the program reads the second and last record, DUPKEY isn't raised. If there are three invoices for the customer, DUPKEY is raised for the first two but not the third, and so on. In short, DUPKEY is raised for each record except the last with a given alternate key value.

Although it may seem a bit odd, you must provide for the DUPKEY condition. If you don't, your program will abend even though DUPKEY doesn't really represent an error condition.

ADVANCED FILE CONTROL FEATURES

Now that you've learned the basics of CICS file control, I'll describe four advanced file control features: locate-mode I/O, generic keys, mass sequential insertion, and multiple string processing. Although it's not essential that you know how to use these processing features, there are occasions when they're appropriate.

Locate-mode I/O

When you specify the INTO or FROM option on a file-control command, you use *move-mode I/O*. Simply put, move-mode I/O means that CICS moves data to and from areas in your program's Working-Storage Section. Although move-mode I/O is more common, another technique called *locate-mode I/O* is used at some installations.

When you use locate-mode I/O, CICS doesn't move data to and from areas in your program's Working-Storage Section. Instead, your program processes data while it's still in a CICS buffer area. Figure 11-8 shows sections of a program that adds a record to a VSAM file using locate-mode I/O.

When you use locate-mode I/O, you define your file's record areas in the Linkage Section rather than in the Working-Storage Section. Then, you use a technique called *base-locator for linkage*, or *BLL*, to provide addressability to those areas. I'm not going to describe how BLL works here. For now, just

```
        .
        .
        .
    LINKAGE SECTION.
    *
     01  BLL-CELLS.
    *
         05  FILLER                  PIC S9(8) COMP.
         05  CM-BLL                  PIC S9(8) COMP.
    *
     01  CUSTOMER-MASTER-RECORD.
    *
         05  CM-CUSTOMER-NUMBER      PIC X(5).
         05  CM-NAME                 PIC X(30).
         05  CM-ADDRESS              PIC X(30).
         05  CM-CITY                 PIC X(21).
         05  CM-STATE                PIC XX.
         05  CM-ZIP-CODE             PIC X(5).
    *
     PROCEDURE DIVISION.
    *
         .
         .
         .
         EXEC CICS
             GETMAIN SET(CM-BLL)
                     LENGTH(93)
         END-EXEC.
         MOVE WS-CUSTOMER-NUMBER TO CM-CUSTOMER-NUMBER.
         MOVE WS-NAME               TO CM-NAME.
         MOVE WS-ADDRESSS           TO CM-ADDRESS.
         MOVE WS-CITY               TO CM-CITY.
         MOVE WS-STATE              TO CM-STATE.
         MOVE WS-ZIP-CODE           TO CM-ZIP-CODE.
         EXEC CICS
             WRITE DATASET('CUSTMAST')
                   SET(CM-BLL)
                   LENGTH(93)
                   RIDFLD(CM-CUSTOMER-NUMBER)
         END-EXEC.
```

Figure 11-8	Writing a record using locate-mode I/O

realize that when you use BLL, you define a Linkage Section field called a *BLL cell* for each record area described in the Linkage Section. That BLL cell contains the address of the record area. In figure 11-8, CM-BLL is the BLL cell for CUSTOMER-MASTER-RECORD.

When you issue a file-control command using locate-mode I/O, you don't specify the INTO or FROM option. Instead, you specify the name of the record area's BLL cell in the SET option:

```
     EXEC CICS
         WRITE DATASET('CUSTMAST')
               SET(CM-BLL)
               LENGTH(93)
               RIDFLD(CM-CUSTOMER-NUMBER)
     END-EXEC
```

Rather than move the record from your program's Working-Storage Section, this WRITE command specifies the address of the record area in CM-BLL, the BLL cell for the Linkage Section description of the record area. The length field (93) indicates the size of that area.

For a READ command, CICS acquires the storage used to hold the record. For a WRITE command, however, you must acquire that storage yourself. You do that by using a GETMAIN command, like this:

```
EXEC CICS
    GETMAIN SET(CM-BLL)
            LENGTH(93)
END-EXEC
```

Here, a 93-byte area of storage is acquired. The storage area's address is placed in CM-BLL, the BLL cell for the record area. After you issue the GETMAIN command, you can format data in the area and use it in a WRITE command.

I hope you see why locate-mode I/O isn't used as often as move-mode I/O. Managing storage allocation yourself isn't easy. With move-mode I/O, you don't have to worry about storage management because it's done automatically for you. Still, locate-mode I/O is inherently more efficient than move-mode I/O. And, at many installations, it's the norm. So you may have to use locate-mode I/O on occasion.

Generic keys

When you retrieve records from a KSDS using a READ command without the UPDATE option or issue a STARTBR command for a KSDS, you can specify a key value that's shorter than the full key defined for the file. When you do that, you specify a *generic key*. The first record for which the generic key matches the left-most characters of the full key satisfies the READ or STARTBR command.

Typically, you use generic keys when a file's key field consists of several subfields. For example, a customer file might have a key field that consists of a two-digit district number followed by a four-digit salesman number and a four-digit customer number. Using generic keys, you could retrieve the first customer record for a particular district by supplying only the district-number portion of the full key.

To use a generic key, you code two options on the READ or STARTBR command: GENERIC and KEYLENGTH. The GENERIC option simply specifies that you're using a generic key. In the KEYLENGTH option, you code a data-name or numeric literal that indicates the length of the generic key.

For example, suppose you issue this command:

```
EXEC CICS
    READ DATASET('CUSTMAST')
         INTO(CUSTOMER-MASTER-RECORD)
         RIDFLD(CM-DISTRICT-NUMBER)
         GENERIC
         KEYLENGTH(2)
END-EXEC
```

Here, the first record whose key matches the two-digit district number specified is retrieved. If there is no record with that district number, the NOTFND condition is raised.

Mass sequential insertion

Some CICS applications require that more than one record be inserted at the same point in a file. For example, suppose a customer file is set up with three record types: customers, invoices, and line items. For each customer record, there may be one or more invoice records. For each invoice record, there may be one or more line item records. The file's primary key is arranged so that line item records follow their related invoice record, and invoice records follow their related customer record. A CICS data-entry program creates the invoice and line item records for an existing customer by inserting them after the customer record. On average, each new invoice requires a total of six records: one invoice record and five line item records.

As you know, when a record is written to a control interval that's already full, a control interval split occurs. The *mass sequential insertion* option improves performance when more than one record is inserted at the same point by changing the way control interval splits are done. Rather than split the control interval at the middle, which is the normal technique, mass sequential insertion causes VSAM to split the control interval at the point of insertion, whether it's at the beginning, middle, or end of the control interval. That leaves free space after the inserted record, so subsequent records can be inserted without unnecessary control interval splits.

I want to be sure you understand that mass sequential insertion is appropriate only when you're inserting several records in sequence at a single location. So, in the customer/invoice/line item file, mass sequential insertion would be appropriate when writing invoice and line item records, because that involves inserting an average of six records at a single point. It would *not* be appropriate if the file was arranged so that the records did not follow each other in sequence.

To use mass sequential insertion, you issue WRITE commands specifying the MASSINSERT option, like this:

```
EXEC CICS
    WRITE DATASET('CUSTMAST')
          FROM(LINE-ITEM-RECORD)
          LENGTH(90)
          RIDFLD(CM-RECORD-KEY)
          MASSINSERT
END-EXEC
```

Here, the 90-byte line item record is inserted using the mass sequential insertion technique.

Multiple browse operations

In some unusual applications, you need to perform two browse operations simultaneously for a single file, maintaining two distinct positions within the file. For example, suppose a file has two types of records: type-A and type-B. Each type-A record has a corresponding type-B record, but the primary key field is set up so that all of the type-A records come before all of the type-B records. Using multiple browse operations, you can browse the type-A and type-B records simultaneously, maintaining two positions in the file.

To begin a browse operation which you want to remain distinct from other browse operations, you code the REQID option on the STARTBR command, like this:

```
EXEC CICS
    STARTBR DATASET('CUSTMAST')
            RIDFLD(CM-CUSTOMER-KEY)
            GTEQ
            REQID(1)
END-EXEC
```

Here, the request-id is 1. Any other browse commands (READNEXT, READPREV, RESETBR, or ENDBR) that specify the same request-id are a part of the same browse operation. Browse commands that specify a different request-id are a part of a different browse operation. If you omit the REQID option, zero is assumed.

Browsing is one of the most resource-consuming CICS functions. Each browse operation requires one VSAM string. (A string is a set of control blocks required to maintain a position for subsequent access.) Typically, only four or five strings are assigned to each on-line VSAM file. As you can imagine, those strings would be quickly tied up if multiple browse operations were frequently used. Fortunately, there are few applications for multiple browse operations.

DISCUSSION

Quite frankly, CICS programming is a complicated subject; the file-control commands I've presented in this chapter are among the easiest CICS commands to understand. If you're new to CICS, then, you're not ready to start writing CICS programs. However, you are in a good position to learn CICS programming. If you're an experienced CICS programmer, much of this chapter was probably review. But you should now have a better understanding of the VSAM file-processing facilities available to you as a CICS programmer.

Terminology

task control	Basic Mapping Support
task	BMS
multitasking	mapset
multiprogramming	pseudo-conversational programming
multithreading	exceptional condition
transaction	condition
transaction identifier	browse
trans-id	browse command
file-control program	move-mode I/O
File Control Table	locate-mode I/O
FCT	base locator for linkage
dynamic transaction backout	BLL
CICS command	BLL cell
command-level program	generic key
CICS command-level translator	mass sequential insertion

Objectives

1. Explain how a task is started under CICS.

2. Describe the operation of each of the following CICS file-control commands:

   READ
   WRITE
   REWRITE
   DELETE
   STARTBR
   READNEXT
   READPREV
   ENDBR
   RESETBR

3. Explain the following advanced CICS file-control facilities:

   locate-mode I/O
   generic keys
   mass sequential insertion
   multiple browse operations

4. If you're an experienced CICS programmer, develop a CICS program that processes VSAM files using any of the facilities described in this chapter.

Chapter 12

Application programming
in assembler language

In this chapter, you'll learn about a variety of assembler-language facilities you can use to process VSAM files. Quite frankly, it's not easy to program for VSAM files in assembler language. As a result, simple report-preparation or update programs are seldom written in assembler language. Instead, assembler language is used mostly for applications that require a VSAM feature that's not available from a high-level programming language like COBOL.

The assembler-language interface to VSAM consists of a series of macro instructions, much like the interface to other access methods like ISAM and QSAM. Unlike other access methods, however, the VSAM macros are essentially the same whether you're a DOS user or an OS user. So this chapter applies to both operating systems.

In this chapter, I'll first show you how to code macros to create VSAM control blocks. Then, I'll show you how to code macros to access a VSAM file. Next, I'll show you how to manipulate control blocks. After that, I'll show you how to detect errors. And finally, I'll present a sample assembler-language program that uses some of the macros this chapter presents.

HOW TO CREATE VSAM CONTROL BLOCKS

Before you can access a file using assembler language, you must code one or more macros to create the necessary control blocks. For non-VSAM access methods, you create just one type of control block, using a DCB macro under OS or a DTF macro under DOS. For VSAM, however, you can create three types of control blocks. An *ACB* (*Access method Control Block*) contains descriptive information about a VSAM file; an *RPL* (*Request Parameter List*) contains specific information about a particular request to access a record in a file; and an *EXLST* (*Exit List*) identifies error-handling routines. An ACB macro and RPL macro are always required; an EXLST macro is optional.

There are two ways to create these control blocks in your program. The first, and simplest, is to code one ACB, RPL, or EXLST macro for each control block you wish to generate. These macros define the storage areas required by the control block at assembly time. Because these macros don't generate executable code, it's important that you place them apart from the executable portion of your program. I usually code them immediately after the executable code.

The second way to create a VSAM control block is to use the GENCB macro. When your program is assembled, the GENCB macro doesn't define the storage needed by the control block. Instead, it generates code that invokes a VSAM routine that allocates storage for the control block when your program is executed. Because the GENCB macro *does* generate executable code, you should place it within the executable part of your program, before any other VSAM I/O macros.

Whether you use ACB, RPL, and EXLST macros or the GENCB macro depends on your particular requirements and your shop's standards. The advantage of using GENCB is that it dynamically allocates control blocks each time your program executes, so you don't have to reassemble your programs if the control block format changes. (Although it's unlikely, it's possible that IBM might announce a release or version of VSAM that changes the format of a control block.) The disadvantage of using GENCB is that it's less efficient than the ACB, RPL, or EXLST macros. That's because additional CPU overhead is required to allocate the control blocks at execution time.

Now, I'll show you how to create the control blocks using the ACB, RPL, and EXLST macros. After that, I'll show you how to use the GENCB macro to create the control blocks dynamically.

The ACB macro

Figure 12-1 gives the format of the ACB macro instruction. Although you can code other parameters, I've omitted them because they're used for advanced applications. Because the parameters in figure 12-1 aren't positional, you can code them in any order you wish. And, although the syntax in figure 12-1 shows commas following the parameters, you need to follow a parameter with a comma only if you code another parameter after it. In other words, you don't code a comma after the last parameter on the macro.

The ACB macro

```
label    ACB  [ AM=VSAM, ]
              [ DDNAME=ddname, ]
              [ EXLST=address, ]
              [ MACRF=(subparameter [,subparameter]...), ]
              [ BUFND=number, ]
              [ BUFNI=number, ]
              [ BUFSP=number, ]
              [ PASSWD=address ]
```

Explanation

AM   Specifies that the ACB should be generated for a VSAM file.

DDNAME   Specifies the external name used to identify the file via a DD statement (OS) or DLBL statement (DOS). If omitted, the ACB macro label is used.

EXLST   Specifies the name of an EXLST macro associated with this ACB.

MACRF   Specifies the processing allowed for the file. See figure 12-2 for the valid subparameters.

BUFND   Specifies the number of data buffers used for the file.

BUFNI   Specifies the number of index buffers used for the file.

BUFSP   Specifies the number of bytes used for buffers.

PASSWD   Specifies the address of an eight-byte area that contains a valid password for the file.

Figure 12-1   The ACB macro

The AM parameter   Because the telecommunications access method VTAM uses control blocks and macro instructions that are similar to VSAM control blocks and macros instructions, you can code AM=VSAM to indicate you're creating a VSAM control block rather than a VTAM control block. You don't have to code AM=VSAM, because VSAM is the default. However, I suggest that you do for clarity.

The DDNAME parameter   The DDNAME parameter relates your VSAM file to the DD or DLBL statement that allocates the file in the JCL. Under OS, you code a one- to eight-character ddname that's the same as the ddname on the DD statement for the file. Under DOS, you code a one- to seven-character name that's used as the file name on the file's DLBL statement. If you omit the DDNAME parameter, the label you code on the ACB macro is used instead.

The EXLST parameter   You use the EXLST parameter along with the EXLST macro to set up one or more exit routines that will process error conditions or keep a log of updates made to your file. On the EXLST

Subparameter	Explanation
KEY ADR CNV	Specifies whether the records will be processed by key or RRN (KEY), relative byte address (ADR), or control interval (CNV). You may code more than one of these subparameter values to let your program switch from one mode to another. KEY is the default.
DIR SEQ SKP	Specifies the processing mode. DIR allows random processing of records, SEQ allows sequential processing, and SKP allows skip-sequential processing. You may code more than one of these subparameter values to let your program switch from one mode to another. SEQ is the default.
IN OUT	Specifies whether the file will be opened for retrieval or update. IN lets you read records; OUT lets you read, write, replace, or delete records. IN is the default.
NIS SIS	Specifies insertion strategy. NIS (normal insertion strategy) splits control intervals roughly in half; SIS (sequential insertion strategy) splits them at the point of insertion. SIS is more efficient in some cases. NIS is the default.
NRS RST	Specifies how a reusable data set will be processed. NRS means that the file should be processed like a non-reusable file; RST means that the file should be reset when it's opened.

Figure 12-2   MACRF subparameters for the ACB macro

parameter, you specify the address of the EXLST for the file. Usually, you just supply the label of the EXLST macro, which I'll describe later on.

The MACRF parameter   You code the MACRF parameter to specify what processing options will be allowed for the file. In the MACRF parameter, you code one or more subparameters. Figure 12-2 shows the subparameters you can code. As you can see, there are five groups of subparameters, each with a default value. For some of the groups, you must select just one subparameter. For others, you can select more than one subparameter.

The first subparameter group for the MACRF parameter indicates how data will be accessed. If you code KEY, individual records will be accessed based on their key values or relative record numbers. Obviously, that's valid only for key-sequenced or relative-record data sets. If you code ADR, records are accessed based on their relative byte addresses. That's valid only for key-sequenced or entry-sequenced data sets. If you code CNV, records are not processed individually. Instead, your program processes entire control intervals. When you use control-interval access, you refer to control intervals by RBA. If you code more than one subparameter from this group, your program can switch from one mode to another.

The next subparameter group in figure 12-2 indicates whether you'll access data sequentially, directly, or skip-sequentially. DIR allows direct access to data; you must supply a key, relative record number, or RBA to access records. SEQ allows sequential processing; VSAM maintains a position in the file, and lets you access records in a forward or backward direction. SKP allows skip-sequential processing; records are retrieved sequentially in a forward direction, but you can skip ahead to a record directly. If you code more than one subparameter from this group, your program can switch from one mode to another.

The next subparameter group indicates whether you can update records or just retrieve them. If you specify IN, the file is read-only; you can't write new records or update or delete existing records. If the file is password protected, you must supply a read or higher level password. If you specify OUT, you can retrieve records as well as add new records or update or delete existing records. To do that, you must specify an update or higher level password if the file is password protected.

The next subparameter group affects how control interval splits are done when records are inserted. If you specify *NIS*, *Normal Insert Strategy* is used; the full control interval is split in half, and the new record is inserted at the appropriate point. If you specify *SIS*, *Sequential Insert Strategy* is used; the control interval is split at the location of the inserted record, so only the records that follow the new record are moved to a free control interval. (Specifying SIS is the same as specifying MASSINSERT on a CICS WRITE command.) You can't specify both NIS and SIS, so your program can't alternate between normal and sequential insert strategy.

SIS is more efficient than NIS when your program inserts several records at the same location. That's because subsequent insertions at the same location won't cause additional control interval splits until enough records have been inserted to cause the free control interval to be filled. In contrast, normal insert strategy may result in a control interval split for each insertion, even though records are all inserted at the same location. Normal insert strategy, though, is better when insertions are distributed throughout the data set rather than clustered around one location.

The last subparameter group in figure 12-2 indicates how reusable data sets should be processed. If you specify NRS, a reusable data set is processed like a non-reusable data set. But if you specify RST, a reusable data set is reset when it's opened. In other words, the high-used RBA field for the file is reset to zero, and any existing records in the file are ignored. NRS and RST have no effect for files that aren't reusable.

The BUFNI, BUFND, and BUFSP parameters   The values you code for these parameters specify the amount of buffer space allocated to your file. You can specify how many data and index buffers to allocate with the BUFNI and BUFND parameters, or you can specify a total amount of buffer space with the BUFSP parameter. Although buffer allocation is among the most important VSAM file performance considerations, you're unlikely to specify it in the ACB macro. Instead, you'll probably specify BUFFERSPACE in the file's DEFINE command, or use the BUFND and BUFNI parameters in the file's DD statement under OS.

The PASSWD parameter   If your file is protected by VSAM passwords, you supply a password by coding the PASSWD parameter. In it, you specify

Example 1

```
CUSTMAST ACB    AM=VSAM,DDNAME=CUSTMAST,MACRF=(KEY,DIR,OUT)
```

Example 2

```
TRANFILE ACB    AM=VSAM,DDNAME=TRANFILE,MACRF=(ADR,SEQ,OUT,RST),
                PASSWD=PASSWORD
PASSWORD DS     CL8
```

Figure 12-3	Two examples of the ACB macro

the name of an eight-byte field that contains a valid password for the file. The password you supply must be at a high enough level to permit the operations you specify in the MACRF parameter.

Examples of the ACB macro   Figure 12-3 shows two examples of the ACB macro. Example 1 shows an ACB macro for a key-sequenced or relative-record file identified by the CUSTMAST DD statement. The MACRF parameter indicates that the file's records will be accessed directly by key or RRN and that records can be added, updated, or deleted as well as retrieved. Example 2 shows an ACB for a reusable file identified by the TRANFILE DD statement. The file will be processed sequentially by RBA, records can be retrieved, added, updated, or deleted, and the reusable file will be reset when it's opened. A password is contained in the PASSWORD field.

The RPL macro

The RPL macro generates the information needed to access a record in a VSAM file. When you issue as access request macro (GET, PUT, ERASE, or POINT) to access a record in a VSAM file, you specify just one parameter: the address of an RPL. It's the RPL that specifies the details of each VSAM file processing request.

Figure 12-4 shows the format of the RPL macro. Before I explain its parameters in detail, there's one important point I want you to realize about the RPL macro. The parameters you code on the RPL macro indicate only initial values for the RPL control block. Depending on your program's requirements, you may need to change one or more RPL parameter settings during program execution by issuing a MODCB macro. (I will present the MODCB macro later in this chapter.) For example, to switch from direct to sequential processing, you issue a MODCB macro to change the appropriate RPL parameter to indicate the desired processing mode. If possible, though, you should try to set up your RPL so that you don't have to modify it later on.

The AM parameter   Like the ACB macro, the RPL macro can be used for VSAM or VTAM. So you can specify AM=VSAM to document this macro as a VSAM RPL.

The RPL macro

```
label     RPL [ AM=VSAM, ]
              [ ACB=address, ]
              [ AREA=address, ]
              [ AREALEN=number, ]
              [ RECLEN=number, ]
              [ ARG=address, ]
              [ OPTCD=(subparameter [,subparameter] ) ]
```

Explanation

AM	Specifies that the RPL should be generated for a VSAM file.
ACB	Specifies the ACB macro to which this RPL applies.
AREA	Specifies the work area for the record to be processed.
AREALEN	Specifies the length of the work area.
RECLEN	Specifies the length of a record written to the file.
ARG	Specifies the field that contains the key, RRN, or RBA used to locate the record being processed.
OPTCD	Specifies the processing options for the request. See figure 12-5 for valid subparameters.

Figure 12-4   The RPL macro

The ACB parameter   Each RPL must be associated with an ACB that defines the file being accessed. As a result, you must code the ACB parameter on the RPL macro. The easiest way to code the ACB parameter is to specify the label of the corresponding ACB macro.

The AREA, AREALEN, and RECLEN parameters   The AREA parameter specifies the work area used to process records. What this area contains depends on whether the file is processed using *move-mode* or *locate-mode*. When you use move-mode, as you usually will, the work area contains the record being processed. When you use the less common locate-mode, the work area contains the address of another area that contains the record; the record is actually processed in a VSAM buffer area. You specify whether you're using move-mode or locate-mode in the OPTCD parameter of the RPL macro, which I'll describe in a moment.

To specify the length of the work area, you code the AREALEN parameter. If you use move-mode, you need to specify a work area big enough to hold the largest record the file contains. If you use locate-mode, the work area must be four bytes long to hold the address of the VSAM buffer area where the record is being processed.

To write a record to a file, you must also code the RECLEN parameter to indicate the length of the record you're writing. When you use move-mode, you'll often code the same value for AREALEN and RECLEN. For a file whose records vary in length, however, the AREALEN value represents the size of the largest record in the file, and the RECLEN value is the size of the record currently being processed. As your program executes, you can change the RECLEN value with the MODCB macro. That way, you can specify varying record lengths as you write records.

The ARG parameter   You use the ARG parameter to identify the search key field used to retrieve records directly. (ARG is also required to write a record directly to an RRDS.) For a key-sequenced data set, you indicate the field that contains the file's key value. Then, that key value is used as the search argument when you read a record. For a relative-record or entry-sequenced data set, the ARG field should be a binary fullword that represents a relative record number or relative byte address.

The OPTCD parameter   You code the OPTCD parameter to indicate the options used for a particular processing request. In it, you code one or more subparameters. Figure 12-5 shows the subparameters you can code. Like the MACRF parameter of the ACB macro, the subparameters of the OPTCD parameter are in groups, with a default value for each group. However, unlike the MACRF parameter of the ACB macro, you can select just one option from each group for the OPTCD parameter. And the options you select must be consistent not only with one another, but also with the subparameters you selected for the ACB macro's MACRF parameter.

The first two groups of subparameters in figure 12-5 correspond to the subparameters of the ACB MACRF parameter. As a result, if you coded more than one processing mode for a file, you can select which mode to use for a particular RPL. But you can't select a subparameter from one of these groups if you didn't code the corresponding subparameter in the ACB macro.

The third subparameter group in figure 12-5 indicates whether the file is to be processed in a forward or backward direction. This option is only significant when you're retrieving records sequentially. The next subparameter group is related; it specifies whether positioning for subsequent sequential retrieval is to be established based on the ARG field (ARD) or at the last record in the file for backward sequential retrieval (LRD). Specify LRD only when you want to process a file sequentially starting with the last record in the file.

The fifth subparameter group specifies whether a record is to be updated and, if not, whether the file should be positioned for sequential processing. If you're retrieving a record you intend to update or delete, you should specify UPD on the RPL macro. Otherwise, specify NUP or NSP. NUP and NSP are the same, except that NSP positions the file at a particular record so that you can process records sequentially from that point.

The last subparameter group in figure 12-5 indicates whether you're using move-mode or locate-mode. As I already mentioned, that affects how you use the field specified in the AREA parameter.

Subparameter	Explanation
KEY ADR CNV	Specifies whether records will be processed by key or RRN (KEY), relative byte address (ADR), or control interval (CNV). The option you code here must also have been coded on the ACB macro for the file. KEY is the default.
DIR SEQ SKP	Specifies the processing mode. DIR allows random processing of records, SEQ allows sequential processing, and SKP allows skip-sequential processing. The option you code here must also have been coded on the ACB macro for the file. SEQ is the default.
FWD BWD	Specifies whether sequential processing proceeds forward (FWD) or backward (BWD). FWD is the default.
ARD LRD	Specifies positioning for subsequent sequential retrieval. ARD means that sequential processing starts with the record identified by the ARG field. LRD means, for backward processing only, that processing is to start with the last record in the file. ARD is the default.
UPD NUP NSP	Specifies whether the record is to be updated and, if not, whether the file should be positioned for sequential retrieval. UPD means that the record can be updated. NUP means the record can not be updated. NSP is the same as NUP, except that positioning is established for subsequent sequential retrieval. NUP is the default.
MOV LOC	Specifies whether move- or locate-mode is to be used. MOV means that move-mode I/O is used; LOC means that locate-mode I/O is used. MOV is the default.

Figure 12-5   OPTCD subparameters for the RPL macro

Example 1

```
LOADRPL RPL  AM=VSAM,ACB=CUSTMAST,AREA=CUSTREC,AREALEN=200,RECLEN=200,
             ARG=CUSTNO,OPTCD=(KEY,SEQ,FWD)
```

Example 2

```
UPDRPL  RPL  AM=VSAM,ACB=CUSTMAST,AREA=CUSTREC,AREALEN=200,RECLEN=200,
             ARG=CUSTNO,OPTCD=(KEY,DIR,UPD)
```

Figure 12-6   Examples of the RPL macro

Examples of the RPL macro   Figure 12-6 shows two examples of the RPL macro. The first example shows an RPL used to write records to a VSAM file. The AREA and AREALEN parameters identify a 200-byte work area; the RECLEN parameter indicates that the record currently being processed is also 200 bytes long. The OPTCD parameter specifies keyed sequential access in a forward direction. Note that all of the OPTCD sub-parameters listed in example 1 are default values, so I could have omitted the OPTCD parameter altogether.

The second example in figure 12-6 is for a program that will read and update records in a VSAM file. In the OPTCD parameter, I specified keyed direct access and UPD so retrieved records can be updated.

The EXLST macro

The EXLST macro, which is optional, produces a list of addresses for routines that VSAM may branch to when a particular condition occurs. Figure 12-7 shows the format of the EXLST macro. Like the ACB and RPL macros, the EXLST macro can be used for VSAM or VTAM. As a result, you should code AM=VSAM to identify the EXLST macro as a VSAM macro. The other parameters supply the addresses of routines that will be invoked when specific conditions occur. Normally, the addresses are given as the label of the exit routine.

Following the address of an exit routine, you can indicate whether the exit is active or inactive. If you specify A, or let it default, the exit is active. If you specify N, the exit is inactive and won't be invoked. To change an inactive exit to active, or an active exit to inactive, you use the MODCB macro, which I'll describe later in this chapter.

Rather than provide the address of an exit routine, you can provide the address of an area that contains the name of a module (MVS) or phase (DOS/VSE) that can be loaded at execution time if the exit is invoked. To do that, you must specify the L subparameter in the EXLST entry for the routine. In addition, the library that contains the module or phase must be made available to your program when it executes. Under MVS, you allocate the library with a JOBLIB or STEPLIB DD statement; under DOS/VSE, you identify the library with a LIBDEF statement.

I want you to realize that it's not necessary to supply an EXLST macro at all. Rather than establish exits to detect error conditions, you can test the results of each I/O macro you issue in other ways. I'll explain how you do that later in this chapter.

The GENCB macro

As I've already mentioned, the GENCB macro lets you generate an ACB, RPL, or EXLST control block at execution time rather than at assembly time. That way, if the format of a VSAM control block changes, you don't have to reassemble your programs. The disadvantage, of course, is that it takes additional processing time to generate the control blocks each time the application program is executed.

Figure 12-8 gives the format of the GENCB macro. To indicate what type of control block you're generating, you code the BLK parameter. If you want to create more than one control block of a particular type, you can code the COPIES parameter. Each control block will be identical, however, so you'll probably want to make changes using the MODCB macro.

The EXLST macro

```
label    EXLST    AM=VSAM,
                [ EODAD=(address[,A|N][,L]) ]
                [ JRNAD=(address[,A|N][,L]) ]
                [ LERAD=(address[,A|N][,L]) ]
                [ SYNAD=(address[,A|N][,L]) ]
                [ UPAD=(address[,A|N][,L]) ]
                [ EXCPAD=(address[,A|N][,L]) ]
```

Explanation

AM
Specifies that the EXLST should be generated for a VSAM file.

EODAD
Specifies the address of a routine that receives control when the end of a data set is encountered during sequential processing.

JRNAD
Specifies the address of a routine that receives control whenever a change is made to a data set by a GET, PUT, or ERASE macro.

LERAD
Specifies the address of a routine that receives control whenever a logical error occurs. If LERAD is specified and EODAD is not, the end-of-file condition is handled by the LERAD routine.

SYNAD
Specifies the address of a routine that receives control whenever a physical I/O error occurs.

UPAD
(MVS only) Specifies the address of a routine that receives control just after any I/O operation has been initiated.

EXCPAD
(DOS/VSE only) Specifies the address of a routine that receives control just after any I/O operation has been initiated.

Note: both UPAD and EXCPAD can be used to overlap I/O with user-program processing.

A
N
Specifies whether the exit is active or inactive.

L
Specifies that the routine is a module in a load or core-image library.

Figure 12-7   The EXLST macro

If you want, you can have GENCB format the control block in a storage area you provide. To do that, you specify the address of the area in the WAREA parameter and the area's length in the LENGTH parameter. Usually, you'll let GENCB acquire the storage area for the control block automatically. Then, VSAM returns the address of the control block in register 1 and its length in register 0.

In addition to the parameters I've describe so far, you can code any parameter that's valid for an ACB, RPL, or EXLST macro, depending on which type of control block you're generating. For example, if you specify

The GENCB macro

```
label     GENCB [ AM=VSAM,
                  BLK= { ACB|RPL|EXLST } ,
                [ COPIES=number, ]
                [ WAREA=address, ]
                [ LENGTH=number, ]
                [ keyword=value ] [ ,keyword=value ]...
```

Explanation

AM	Specifies that the control block should be generated for a VSAM file.
BLK	Specifies the type of control block being generated: ACB, RPL, or EXLST.
COPIES	Specifies how many copies of the control block are to be generated. The default is 1.
WAREA	Specifies the address of the area in which the control blocks are to be generated. If omitted, VSAM allocates storage for the control blocks and returns the address in register 1.
LENGTH	Specifies the length of the WAREA work area. If omitted, VSAM returns the length of the acquired area in register 0.
keyword	Any valid keyword for the type of control block being generated.

Figure 12-8   The GENCB macro

BLK=ACB, you can also code DDNAME, EXLST, MACRF, BUFND, BUFNI, BUFSP, and PASSWD on the GENCB macro; those parameters have the same functions as they do for an ACB macro.

Figure 12-9 gives two examples of the GENCB macro. The first generates an ACB, letting VSAM acquire the storage needed by the control block. The second generates an RPL, using storage already acquired by the program. (To acquire that storage, the program used other facilities which I don't cover here.)

HOW TO ACCESS A VSAM FILE

To process the records of a VSAM file, you issue two types of macros. The OPEN and CLOSE macros connect and disconnect your program and one or more VSAM files. The record management request macros (GET, PUT, ERASE, POINT) perform I/O operations for the file.

Example 1

```
GENCB    AM=VSAM,BLK=ACB,DDNAME=TRANFILE,
         MACRF=(ADR,SEQ,OUT,RST)
```

Example 2

```
GENCB    AM=VSAM,BLK=RPL,WAREA=RPLAREA,LENGTH=(0)
```

Figure 12-9   Two examples of the GENCB macro

The OPEN macro

   MVS

```
label    OPEN (address [,,address]...)
```

   DOS/VSE

```
label    OPEN (address [,address]...)
```

The CLOSE macro

   MVS

```
label    CLOSE (address [,,address]...)
```

   DOS/VSE

```
label    CLOSE (address [,address]...)
```

Explanation

address   The address of an ACB to be opened. If you code more than one ACB under MVS, separate them with two commas.

Figure 12-10   The OPEN and CLOSE macros

The OPEN and CLOSE macros

Before you can process records in a VSAM file, you must connect your program to the file by issuing an OPEN macro instruction. Similarly, before you terminate your program, you should disconnect it from the VSAM file by issuing a CLOSE macro instruction. Figure 12-10 shows the format of both the OPEN and CLOSE macros.

The GET macro

```
label    GET      RPL=address
```

The PUT macro

```
label    PUT      RPL=address
```

The ERASE macro

```
label    ERASE    RPL=address
```

The POINT macro

```
label    POINT    RPL=address
```

Explanation

RPL   Specifies the address of the RPL that contains the detailed information for the
                           GET, PUT, ERASE, or POINT operation.

Figure 12-11   The record management macros

You can open or close more than one file at once by coding more than one
ACB name on the macros. Under MVS, you must separate the ACB names
with two commas, like this:

```
OPEN (ACB1,,ACB2)
```

The extra comma provides for an entry required for non-VSAM files; under
DOS/VSE, the extra comma isn't required.

You can mix VSAM and non-VSAM files on the OPEN and CLOSE
macros, too. As you'll learn later in this chapter, the OPEN and CLOSE
macros issue a return code that indicates whether the files were opened successfully. If you mix VSAM and non-VSAM files on an OPEN macro, though,
the return code won't apply to any VSAM files listed before a non-VSAM file.
As a result, I suggest you list all of the non-VSAM files first.

Record management macros

To request record management functions like retrieving or storing records,
you issue GET, PUT, ERASE, and POINT macros. These macros work
together with an RPL macro, which specifies the details of each record
management request. Figure 12-11 gives the format of the record management
macros. As you can see, each has just one parameter: RPL. In it, you provide
the name of the related RPL.

To write a record to a VSAM file, you issue a PUT macro. For a KSDS or RRDS, the value in the ARG field determines the new record's position in the file. For a ESDS, the new record is added to the end of the file.

You can also use the PUT macro to update an existing record in the file. First, you must issue a GET macro, specifying UPD in the RPL's OPTCD parameter. Then, you issue a PUT macro. The record in the work area for the PUT replaces the record read by the previous GET.

Deleting a record from a VSAM file is like updating a record. First, you must issue a GET macro, specifying UPD in the RPL. Instead of replacing the record by issuing a PUT macro, however, you then delete the record by issuing an ERASE macro. That physically deletes the record from the file and makes the space it occupied available for other records.

The last record management macro, POINT, establishes a position at a specific record so that you can retrieve records sequentially from that position. The POINT macro doesn't actually retrieve a record. It's like the COBOL START statement or the CICS STARTBR command; it just establishes position for subsequent sequential retrieval.

Quite frankly, the way the record management macros work together with the RPL macro is a little confusing. In a moment, I'll show you a simple program that writes a record to a file. When you see that program, I think you'll better understand how these macros work. But first, I'll introduce three more macros that let you manipulate VSAM control blocks.

HOW TO MANIPULATE VSAM CONTROL BLOCKS

In an assembler language program that processes VSAM files, you can examine, test, and modify the information that's stored in the VSAM control blocks. You do that by using the SHOWCB, TESTCB, and MODCB macros.

The SHOWCB macro

Figure 12-12 gives the format of the SHOWCB macro. This macro lets you examine information in a VSAM control block by moving data from one or more fields in a control block to an area you supply. To identify the control block being processed, you code the ACB, RPL, or EXLST parameter, which specifies the address of the control block. The AREA parameter provides the address of the area into which the SHOWCB macro moves data. And the LENGTH parameter provides the length of that area. Most of the fields that you can retrieve with the SHOWCB macro are binary fullwords, which require a four-byte work area.

The OBJECT parameter, which is only valid for a key-sequenced data set, specifies whether information retrieved from the control block relates to the data or index component. By default, the information is from the data component.

The SHOWCB macro

```
label      SHOWCB    {ACB=address,  }
                     {RPL=address,  }
                     {EXLST=address,}

                     AREA=address,

                     LENGTH=number,

              [ OBJECT= {DATA|INDEX} , ]

                     FIELDS=(keyword [,keyword]...)
```

Explanation

ACB RPL EXLST	Specifies the address of the control block from which data is to be extracted. May be either a label or a general register.
AREA	Specifies the address of the area into which data from the control block will be moved.
LENGTH	Specifies the length of the area identified in the AREA parameter.
OBJECT	For a KSDS only, specifies whether to extract information related to the data or index component.
FIELDS	Specifies one or more fields to be extracted. See figure 12-13 for details.

Figure 12-12   The SHOWCB macro

In the FIELDS parameter, you name one or more fields that you want to retrieve. Figure 12-13 shows some of the fields you can retrieve for each type of control block and indicates the length of each field. Of those listed, the most useful are the ones that return attributes of an open file from an ACB, such as AVSPAC (the amount of free space in the file) or CINV (the size of the file's control intervals). In the program example I'll present in a moment, you'll see how to use the SHOWCB macro to retrieve the maximum record length of a file.

The TESTCB macro

The TESTCB macro, shown in figure 12-14, is similar to the SHOWCB macro. But instead of moving data from one or more fields of a control block, the TESTCB macro tests the value of a single control block field. The results of the test are indicated by the computer's condition code, so you can test it using one of the branch-on-condition instructions, like BE or BNE.

Control block	Keyword	Length in bytes	Description
ACB	ACBLEN	4	Length of the ACB.
	AVSPAC	4	Bytes of free space in the component.
	BUFND	4	Number of data buffers.
	BUFNI	4	Number of index buffers.
	BUFSP	4	Amount of buffer space.
	CINV	4	Control interval size.
	DDNAME	8	External name associated with the file.
	ENDRBA	4	High used RBA (HURBA).
	ERROR	4	Reason code returned by OPEN or CLOSE.
	EXLST	4	Address of an associated exit list.
	FS	4	Free control intervals per control area.
	HALCRBA	4	High allocated RBA (HARBA).
	KEYLEN	4	Length of the key field.
	LRECL	4	Maximum record length.
	NCIS	4	Number of control interval splits.
	NDELR	4	Number of records deleted.
	NEXCP	4	Number of I/O operations.
	NEXT	4	Number of allocated extents.
	NINSR	4	Number of records inserted.
	NIXL	4	Number of levels in the index.
	NLOGR	4	Number of records in the component.
	NRETR	4	Number of records retrieved.
	NSSS	4	Number of control area splits.
	NUPDR	4	Number of records updated.
	PASSWD	4	Address of the password field.
	RKP	4	Relative position of key field.
	STRMAX	4	Maximum number of strings for the ACB.
	STRNO	4	Number of strings currently active.
	STMST	8	Time stamp, updated when file is closed.
RPL	ACB	4	Address of the associated ACB.
	AREA	4	Address of the work area.
	AREALEN	4	Length of the work area.
	ARG	4	Address of the search argument.
	FDBK	4	Reason code from record management macros.
	FTNCD	4	Function code from record management macros.
	KEYLEN	4	Length of the ARG field.
	RBA	4	RBA of the record just processed.
	RECLEN	4	Length of the current record.
	RPLLEN	4	Length of the RPL.
EXLST	EODAD	4	Address of the end of data exit.
	EXLLEN	4	Length of the EXLST.
	JRNAD	4	Address of the journal exit.
	LERAD	4	Address of the logical error exit.
	SYNAD	4	Address of the physical error exit.

Figure 12-13   Selected keywords for the FIELDS parameter of the SHOWCB macro

The TESTCB macro

```
label     TESTCB  { ACB=address,   }
                  { RPL=address,   }
                  { EXLST=address, }

          [ ERET=address, ]

          [ OBJECT= {DATA|INDEX} , ]

            keyword=value
```

Explanation

ACB   Specifies the address of the control block that contains the field to be tested.
RPL   May be either a label or a general register.
EXLST

ERET   Specifies the address of a routine to receive control if an error occurs.

OBJECT   Specifies, for a KSDS only, whether the field to be tested applies to the data com-
                    ponent or to the index component.

keyword = value   Specifies the control block field to be tested. May be any field that can be
                    displayed with SHOWCB, or one of the special keywords listed below.

Special keywords for ACB

ATRB   Tests the attributes of the file. You can test the file's organization by specifying
                    ESDS, KSDS, or RRDS. Specify REPL to see if the index is replicated, SSWD to
                    see if the index is imbedded, SPAN to see if the records are spanned, and WCK to
                    see if write verification is active. Test for UNQ to see if an alternate index
                    requires unique keys.

OFLAGS   Specify OFLAGS = OPEN to see if the data set is open.

OPENOBJ   Specify OPENOBJ = BASE, OPENOBJ = AIX, or OPENOBJ = PATH to see
                    whether a base cluster, alternate index, or path is open.

Figure 12-14   The TESTCB macro

On the TESTCB macro, you can specify any of the SHOWCB keywords
listed in figure 12-13. In addition, for an ACB, you can use the three special
keywords shown at the bottom of figure 12-14: ATRB, OFLAGS, and
OPENOBJ. To illustrate, suppose you want to open a file if it's not already
open. To do that, you could issue this instruction:

```
TESTCB ACB=INVMSTR,OFLAGS=OPEN
```

The condition code will indicate an equal condition if the file is open. Then,
you can follow this macro with a BNE instruction to branch to a routine that
opens the file.

The MODCB macro

```
label     MODCB  ⎧ ACB=address,   ⎫
                 ⎨ RPL=address,   ⎬
                 ⎩ EXLST=address, ⎭

              [ keyword=value ] [,keyword=value ]...
```

Explanation

ACB
RPL
EXLST

Specifies the address of the control block to be modified. May be either a label or a general register.

keyword = value

Specifies a new value for a control block field. You can code any keyword and value that's valid for the corresponding GENCB (ACB, RPL, or EXLST).

Figure 12-15   The MODCB macro

The MODCB macro

You use the MODCB macro, shown in figure 12-15, to modify one or more fields in a control block. You can change any of the parameters you can specify on an ACB, RPL, or EXLST macro, and only the parameters you code are modified; there are no default parameter values. As you can see in figure 12-15, the format of the MODCB macro is similar to the SHOWCB and TESTCB macros.

There are two common situations in which you'll need to use the MODCB macro. The first is when you're writing variable-length records. Since the PUT macro requires that the RPL RECLEN field indicate the length of the record being written, you must issue a MODCB macro to specify the correct length in the RPL *before* you issue the PUT macro. For example, consider this macro:

```
MODCB RPL=INVRPL,RECLEN=200
```

Here, I change the record length field in the RPL named INVRPL to 200. Note that you don't have to use the MODCB macro if all of the file's records are of the same length. In that case, just specify the correct record length when you create the RPL.

The second common use of MODCB is to change the processing mode of an RPL from sequential to direct and back again. For example, this macro,

```
MODCB RPL=INVRPL,OPTCD=(DIR)
```

changes the processing mode to direct. To switch back to sequential processing, code the macro this way:

```
MODCB RPL=INVRPL,OPTCD=(SEQ)
```

Besides these parameters, you can specify any other parameter you can specify on an ACB, RPL, or EXLST macro.

HOW TO HANDLE VSAM ERRORS

When you issue a VSAM macro instruction, control returns to the instruction following the macro whether or not an error occurs (unless you've established error exits with the EXLST macro). As a result, it's important that you check to see whether the operation you requested was successful or not. If you don't, major errors will go undetected. In some cases, you might want to use exit routines for comprehensive error handling. Usually, though, you won't use exit routines. Instead, you'll code instructions following each VSAM macro to see if an error occurred.

VSAM provides two codes you can use to detect errors. The first is called the *return code*. It's placed in register 15 after each VSAM macro instruction is executed and indicates whether or not an error was encountered. If an error was encountered, the return code also indicates its severity. As a result, you should follow every VSAM request macro with code that tests the contents of register 15; if it's not zero, some type of error occurred.

A simple way to test the return code in register 15 is to issue a load-and-test-register (LTR) instruction. Simply put, the LTR instruction loads a value into a register, then tests the value and sets the condition code to indicate whether the value is less than, equal to, or greater than zero. If you use the LTR instruction to load register 15 into itself, the effect is to test the value of register 15 and set the condition code accordingly. Then, you can use a branch-on-condition instruction to branch to an appropriate error-handling routine if register 15 isn't zero. For example, consider these instructions:

```
LTR    15,15
BNZ    ERROR
```

Here, the LTR instruction tests the value in register 15 and sets the condition code accordingly. If the condition code indicates that the value in register 15 isn't zero, control is transferred to a routine named ERROR.

I suggest you code instructions like these to detect errors following each VSAM macro you issue. How you handle the errors you detect, however, depends on whether they occur during OPEN/CLOSE processing, during a record management request, or during control block manipulation.

The second code VSAM provides is called the *reason code*. It provides additional information that may explain why a particular return code was issued. For errors that occur when you open or close a data set, the reason code is placed in a field in the file's ACB. For a record management request macro (GET, PUT, ERASE, or POINT), the reason code is placed in the RPL. In

Return code	Meaning
0	All files were opened or closed successfully.
4	For OPEN, the files were successfully opened but a minor error was encountered. For CLOSE, a major error was encountered and one or more of the files could not be closed.
8	OPEN only. A major error was encountered, and one or more of the files could not be opened.
12	OPEN only. A major error was encountered for a non-VSAM file and the file could not be opened.

Figure 12-16   OPEN/CLOSE return codes

both cases, you can extract the reason code using the SHOWCB macro or you can test it using the TESTCB macro. I'll show you how to do that in a minute. For a control block manipulation macro (GENCB, SHOWCB, TESTCB, or MODCB), the reason code is placed in register 0. That's because VSAM can't guarantee that a valid control block exists when an error occurs while one of these macros is being processed.

How to handle OPEN/CLOSE errors

Figure 12-16 shows the return codes that might be found in register 15 following an OPEN or CLOSE macro. For an OPEN macro, return code 4 means that although errors were encountered, VSAM was able to open all of the data sets. Although VSAM is able to continue processing when return code 4 is issued for an OPEN macro, the errors may be serious, so you should probably terminate your program for any non-zero return code. For a CLOSE macro, return code 4 means that one or more files could not be closed. Return codes 8 or 12 both mean that at least one data set could not be opened.

There are about 50 reason codes that can be associated with OPEN and CLOSE errors. If you wish, you can issue a SHOWCB or TESTCB macro to test the reason code in each file's ACB to see exactly what caused the error. But that's not usually necessary since VSAM writes a message for these errors to the system console and the programmer log that's printed as part of the JCL listing. That message usually contains enough information to figure out what went wrong.

How to handle record management errors

A non-zero return code from a record management request macro (GET, PUT, ERASE, and POINT) indicates that an error occurred and the request could not be completed. As a result, you should follow each of these macros

Return code	Reason code	Meaning
0	0	Successful.
	4	Successful; another volume was mounted or extent allocated.
	8	A duplicate key exists or was created for an alternate index with nonunique keys.
8	4	The end of the file was encountered during sequential processing.
	8	You tried to write a record that already exists.
	12	You tried to write a record out of order during sequential output processing.
	16	You tried to retrieve a record that doesn't exist.

Figure 12-17   Common reason codes for I/O macros

with an LTR instruction to test register 15, and a branch instruction that transfers control to an error routine if the return code is non-zero.

As I mentioned earlier, you can use the SHOWCB or TESTCB macros to extract the reason code from the RPL after an I/O request. To do that, you code FDBK as the keyword. Figure 12-17 lists the reason codes you're likely to encounter. For a complete list, consult the IBM VSAM macro reference manual for your system. Notice in figure 12-17 that a reason code is provided even when the return code is zero. That lets you test for certain conditions that don't represent errors but might affect your program's logic.

The RPL reason codes shown in figure 12-17 don't represent serious errors. Instead, they represent conditions your program should anticipate, like encountering the end of the file during sequential retrieval, or trying to read a record that doesn't exist. As a result, your error handling routine should check to see if one of these conditions occurred and handle it accordingly. If a more serious error occurs, you'll probably want to close any files that are open and terminate the program.

How to handle control-block manipulation errors

As I've already mentioned, when an error occurs while processing a SHOWCB, TESTCB, MODCB, or GENCB macro, a non-zero value is placed in register 15 and a reason code is placed in register 0 rather than in a control block. There's little point in having your program examine the reason code when an error occurs, though, because all of the reason codes indicate serious errors. Instead, I suggest you close any open files, terminate your program, and check the contents of register 0 in the storage dump to see what went wrong.

```
          PRINT NOGEN
VSAMINIT  START 0
BEGIN     SAVE  (14,12)
          BALR  3,0
          USING *,3
          ST    13,SAVE+4
          LA    13,SAVE
          OPEN  VSAMFILE
          LTR   15,15
          BNZ   OPENERR
          SHOWCB ACB=VSAMFILE,AREA=RECLEN,LENGTH=4,FIELDS=(LRECL)
          LTR   15,15
          BNZ   SHOWERR
          GETMAIN EU,LV=RECLEN,A=WORKADDR
          L     4,WORKADDR
          L     5,RECLEN
          MODCB RPL=RPL1,AREA=(4),AREALEN=(5),RECLEN=(5)
          LTR   15,15
          BNZ   MODERR
          L     6,BCONO
          L     7,BCONO
          MVCL  4,6
          PUT   RPL=RPL1
          LTR   15,15
          BNZ   PUTERR
          CLOSE VSAMFILE
          LTR   15,15
          BNZ   CLOSEERR
          L     13,SAVE+4
          RETURN (14,12)
OPENERR   ABEND 100,DUMP
SHOWERR   ABEND 101,DUMP
MODERR    ABEND 102,DUMP
PUTERR    ABEND 103,DUMP
CLOSEERR  ABEND 104,DUMP
VSAMFILE  ACB   AM=VSAM,DDNAME=VSAMFILE,MACRF=(DIR,OUT)
RPL1      RPL   AM=VSAM,ACB=VSAMFILE
WORKADDR  DS    F
RECLEN    DS    F
BCONO     DC    F'0'
SAVE      DS    18F
          END   BEGIN
```

Figure 12-18   An assembler-language program that writes a null record to a VSAM file

A SAMPLE PROGRAM

Now that you've learned the basic assembler-language programming elements for VSAM files, I'll present a simple program that illustrates how those elements are used together. The program, shown in figure 12-18, writes a single record to a VSAM key-sequenced data set so the file can be processed by CICS or in I-O mode by a COBOL program. (In both cases, the file must contain at least one record.) The record that's written contains all hexadecimal zeros, so it will always have the lowest key value in the file. Although the program in figure 12-18 is for an MVS system, it would run under DOS/VSE with only minor modification.

Writing a single record to a VSAM file is simple enough. Near the end of the program, you can see the ACB macro that identifies the file and the RPL macro that specifies the options used to write the record. Further up in the program, you can see the OPEN, PUT, and CLOSE macros that open the file, write the record, and close the file. Following each of those three macros is error testing code that checks to see whether or not errors occurred.

The only real complication of the program is that it must work for any file, regardless of its record length. As a result, the program doesn't know how long the output record should be until it opens the file. Then, the record length, specified when the data set was defined, is available in the ACB. To make the record length available, I issue a SHOWCB macro to extract the logical record length field (LRECL) from the ACB. The SHOWCB macro places the record length in a field named RECLEN. Following the SHOWCB macro, I issue LTR and BNZ instructions to see if an error occurred.

Next, I issue a GETMAIN macro instruction to acquire an area of virtual storage large enough for the record. Don't worry about the format of the GETMAIN macro; just realize that the length of the acquired storage is indicated by the RECLEN field, and the address of the storage is placed in the WORKADDR field.

After I acquire virtual storage for the output record, I load the address of that storage into register 4 and its length into register 5. Then, I issue a MODCB instruction to change three RPL fields: the work area field (AREA) is set to the address indicated by register 4, and the work area and record length fields (AREALEN and RECLEN) are set to the length value in register 5. Following the MODCB macro, LTR and BNZ instructions test for errors.

The next three instructions (L, L, and MVCL) set the record area to hexadecimal zeros. The operation of the move characters long instruction (MVCL) is tricky, so I won't explain it here. Just realize that this instruction uses the address in register 4 and the length in register 5 to move hexadecimal zeros to the work area. Then, the PUT macro actually writes the record to the file.

After the RETURN macro, I code the error routines that handle the errors that may be detected by the OPEN, SHOWCB, MODCB, PUT, or CLOSE macros. Each error routine issues an ABEND macro, specifying a different code so that I can easily identify the error. Although I could have done more elaborate error checking here, it's not really necessary in a program this simple.

DISCUSSION

Quite frankly, learning the assembler-language requirements for processing VSAM files isn't easy. Although this chapter is just an introduction to assembler-language programming for VSAM files, it's a good start. If you understand the concepts this chapter presents, you shouldn't have much trouble learning the more advanced VSAM features available to you through assembler language.

In a way, it's those advanced features that justify the use of assembler language programming for VSAM. Programs that use just the basic VSAM file processing facilities should probably *not* be coded in assembler language. Instead, you should use a high-level language like COBOL, which provides basic VSAM support in a way that's simpler to use and less error prone.

Even so, there are applications for which assembler language is more appropriate than COBOL. If you're involved in one of those applications, this chapter will help you get started. If you're not, understanding how VSAM works at the assembler-language level will help you better understand how VSAM is supported by both COBOL and CICS.

Terminology

ACB	Normal Insert Strategy
Access method Control Block	SIS
RPL	Sequential Insert Strategy
Request Parameter List	move-mode
EXLST	locate-mode
Exit List	return code
NIS	reason code

Objectives

1. Describe the purpose of the three VSAM control blocks, and identify the VSAM macro instructions used to create them both at assembly time and at execution time.

2. List six VSAM macros used to access a file and describe the function of each.

3. Describe the function of the SHOWCB, TESTCB, and MODCB macros.

4. Describe the techniques used to evaluate both the return code and the reason code following an OPEN/CLOSE macro, an I/O macro, and a control block manipulation macro.

5. Given specifications for an assembler-language program that requires any of the elements presented in this chapter, code an acceptable solution.

Index

Comment form

Your opinions count

If you have comments, criticisms, or suggestions, I'm eager to get them. Your opinions today will affect our products of tomorrow. If you have questions, you can expect an answer within one week of the time we receive them. And if you discover any errors in this book, typographical or otherwise, please point them out so we can make corrections when the book is reprinted.

Thanks for your help.

Mike Murach
Fresno, California

Book title: VSAM: AMS and Application Programming

Dear Mike: _____

_____

_____

_____

_____

_____

_____

_____

_____

_____

_____

_____

_____

_____

_____

_____

_____

_____

_____

_____

Name & Title _____
Company (if company address) _____
Address _____
City, State, Zip _____

Fold where indicated and tape closed.
No postage necessary if mailed in the U.S.

BUSINESS REPLY MAIL
FIRST-CLASS MAIL   PERMIT NO. 3063   FRESNO, CA

POSTAGE WILL BE PAID BY ADDRESSEE

Mike Murach & Associates, Inc.

4697 West Jacquelyn Avenue
Fresno, CA 93722-9960

fold

fold

fold

fold

Order Form

Our Unlimited Guarantee

To our customers who order directly from us: You must be satisfied. Our books must work for you, or you can send them back for a full refund . . . no matter how many you buy, no matter how long you've had them.

Name & Title _____

Company (if company address) _____

Address _____

City, State, Zip _____

Phone number (including area code) _____

Qty	Product code and title	*Price

VSAM

	VSMX	VSAM: Access Method Services and Application Programming	$25.00
	VSMR	VSAM for the COBOL Programmer (Second Edition)	17.50

Job Control Language

	VJLR	DOS/VSE JCL (Second Edition)	$32.50
	MJCL	MVS JCL	32.50

COBOL Language Elements

	SC1R	Structured ANS COBOL: Part 1	$27.50
	SC2R	Structured ANS COBOL: Part 2	27.50
	VSC2	VS COBOL II	25.00

COBOL Program Development

	DDCP	How to Design and Develop COBOL Programs	$30.00
	CPHB	The COBOL Programmer's Handbook	20.00

☐ Bill me the appropriate price plus UPS shipping and handling (and sales tax in California) for each book ordered.

☐ Bill the appropriate book prices plus UPS shipping and handling (and sales tax in California) to my _____VISA _____MasterCard:

Card number _____

Valid thru (month/year)_____

Cardowner's signature _____
(not valid without signature)

☐ I want to **save** UPS shipping and handling charges. Here's my check or money order for $_____. California residents, please add 6% sales tax to your total. (Offer valid in the U.S. only.)

* Prices are subject to change. Please call for current prices.

Qty	Product code and title	*Price

CICS

	CIC1	CICS for the COBOL Programmer: Part 1	$27.50
	CIC2	CICS for the COBOL Programmer: Part 2	27.50
	CREF	The CICS Programmer's Desk Reference	35.00

Assembler Language

	VBAL	DOS/VSE Assembler Language	$32.50
	MBAL	MVS Assembler Language	32.50

Data Base Processing

	IMS1	IMS for the COBOL Programmer Part 1: DL/I Data Base Processing	$30.00
	IMS2	IMS for the COBOL Programmer Part 2: Data Communications and MFS	32.50

Operating System Subjects

	VMCC	VM/CMS: Commands and Concepts	$25.00
	VMXE	VM/CMS: XEDIT	25.00
	ICCF	DOS/VSE ICCF	27.50
	TSO	MVS TSO	27.50
	OSUT	OS Utilities	15.00

To order more quickly,

Call **toll-free** 1-800-221-5528

(Weekdays, 9 to 4 Pacific Std. Time)

In California, call 1-800-221-5527

Mike Murach & Associates, Inc.

4697 West Jacquelyn Avenue
Fresno, California 93722
(209) 275-3335
Fax: (209) 275-9035

fold

fold

fold

fold